THE CATHOLIC QUESTION
IN ENGLISH POLITICS
1820 TO 1830

Oxford University Press, Amen House, London E.C.4

GLASGOW NEW YORK TORONTO MELBOURNE WELLINGTON
BOMBAY CALCUTTA MADRAS KARACHI LAHORE DACCA
CAPE TOWN SALISBURY NAIROBI IBADAN ACCRA
KUALA LUMPUR HONG KONG

THE CATHOLIC QUESTION IN ENGLISH POLITICS
1820 TO 1830

By

G. I. T. MACHIN

Lecturer in History
University of Singapore

CLARENDON PRESS · OXFORD
1964

TO
MY MOTHER

PREFACE

No one who reads the diaries, correspondence and parliamentary debates of the 1820s can fail to be impressed with the large (but hitherto curiously neglected) part played by the Catholic emancipation question in English politics during that period. This study seeks to give a comprehensive account of the issue during its most important decade, hoping at the same time to illustrate the nature of English politics immediately before the first Reform Act.

This book is a condensation of my D.Phil. thesis entitled 'Catholic Emancipation as an Issue in English Politics, 1820–30'. My greatest debt is to my supervisor, Mr. M. G. Brock, for unstinting encouragement and advice and for generously lending me transcripts from the Althorp and Londonderry Papers. I also benefited from the stimulating guidance of Mr. C. H. Stuart. Others to whom I owe special thanks are Dr. G. F. A. Best, for introducing me to the question of the Brunswick clubs and encouraging me to explore the resources of local history; the Marquess of Anglesey, for very kindly lending me the typescript of his Life of the First Marquess before it went to press; and Messrs. W. B. Elvins and Llewelyn Jones, for allowing me to read their theses, whose titles will be found in the Bibliography. I must further acknowledge the kind assistance I received from Mr. J. M. Golby, Dr. U. R. Q. Henriques, Professor R. T. Jenkins, Mr. F. R. D. Needham, the Rev. W. H. Pritchard, Dr. J. D. Walsh, and Professor A. C. Wood.

A considerable amount of political correspondence in the 1820s has already been published; particularly useful are the volumes edited by Professor Aspinall. Most of my research, however, was done amongst unpublished papers in the British Museum, in university libraries and local record offices, and in private hands. I am particularly grateful for the hospitable assistance of the Earl of Harrowby and Lord Kenyon in allowing me to examine and make use of the manuscripts in their possession. I must also thank Lord Hatherton for permission to quote from the Hatherton Papers. My debt to archivists, university librarians, and public librarians is a large one. Mention must be made of Mr. J. E. Fagg and Dr. Doig of Durham University; Mr. J. H. Hodson of Nottingham University; Mr. E. Gwynne Jones of the University College of North Wales, Bangor; Miss Skerl of University College, London; Mr. S. O. Stewart of the University of Keele; Mrs. English of the National Register of Archives (West Riding division); and the following county archivists: Mr. P. L. Hull (Cornwall), Mr. P. King (Northamptonshire), and Mr. F. B. Stitt (Staffordshire). Further, I am grateful to the staffs of libraries too numerous to list.

Parts of this study have been contributed in the form of articles to the *English Historical Review*, the *Historical Journal*, the *Journal of Ecclesiastical History*, and the *Transactions of the Honourable Society of Cymmrodorion*. I wish to acknowledge the kind permission of the editors to reproduce some of this material.

Singapore   G. I. T. MACHIN
1963

CONTENTS

ABBREVIATIONS

Add. Mss.	Additional Manuscripts in the British Museum
EHR	English Historical Review
Hansard	Hansard's Parliamentary Debates; Second Series (unless otherwise stated)
HMC	Publications of the Historical Manuscripts Commission
PP	Peel Papers
WND	Second Duke of Wellington (ed.): *Despatches, Correspondence and Memoranda of the Duke of Wellington ... in continuation of the former series* (8 vols., London, 1867–80).

NOTE

THE politicians for and against Catholic emancipation have usually been described as 'Catholics' and 'Protestants' respectively. In this book such terms might invite confusion with those who were actually Catholic or Protestant in religion, and it would be unsatisfactory to distinguish them continually by means of inverted commas. I have therefore rejected the conventional terms in favour of 'pro-catholics' and 'anti-catholics'—terms which were, in fact, often used in contemporary correspondence.

The term 'ultra' is conventionally used to describe tories whose politics were reactionary, in opposition to the more liberal views of the Canningites and others. Yet many of the tories who were otherwise reactionary supported Catholic emancipation in 1829. I have therefore used 'ultra' only to describe those die-hards who were always the most stubborn opponents of Catholic relief and resisted it to the end. The term 'anti-catholic' is sometimes used collectively to describe all those who opposed Catholic emancipation. But the ultras were a distinct group within this larger body, as will be made clear in the text.

CHAPTER I

INTRODUCTORY

THE problem of Ireland was the most protracted of all those which beset English politicians in the nineteenth century. The Catholic emancipation question was essentially a part of the Irish problem, and it set the stage for later developments of the larger issue by appropriating a great deal of English political attention in the century's first three decades. For much of the 1820s it was the most pressing question of all. The Catholic question, wrote a correspondent of Peel's in 1827, was 'mixed up with every thing we eat or drink or say or think'.[1] Parliamentary reform was completely overshadowed by it. Lord John Russell, the champion of parliamentary reform, was advised in 1826 that it would be more profitable to devote himself to the Catholic question instead.[2] In previous decades the question had had its political impact. Pitt resigned over the issue in 1801, the Talents were overthrown in 1807 because they favoured a partial measure of Catholic relief, and the question played a considerable part in the ministerial crisis of 1812. But in the 1820s the crises became more frequent and more intense. In 1825 the progress of Catholic emancipation nearly drove Liverpool to resign. The question was largely responsible for the ministerial divisions of 1827, and wholly responsible for the tory split of 1829.

Such crises could not have occurred in the era of monolithic political parties. In the early nineteenth century party divisions were so blurred that the names whig and tory were practically meaningless as significant political terms. Important political issues existed, but they transcended party boundaries. 'Whig and Tory, Foxite and Pittite, Minister and Opposition have ceased to be distinctions,' wrote Lord Holland to Earl Grey, 'but the divisions of classes and great interests are arrayed against each other —grower and consumer, lands and funds, Irish and English,

1. Charles Lloyd, Bishop of Oxford, to Peel, 14 August 1827; PP, Add. Mss. 40343, f. 63.
2. Lord William Russell to Lord John Russell, 5 November 1826. Spencer Walpole, *Life of Lord John Russell* (2 vols., London, 1891), i. 138.

Catholick and Protestant.'[3] In such issues politicians voted not according to 'party' but according to individual interest or conviction. A few whigs, for example, opposed freer trade; a few 'ultra' tories were in favour of parliamentary reform and some whigs were against it.

All the great contemporary issues were non-party, but Catholic emancipation was the non-party issue *par excellence*. The composition of the opposing sides on the question amply exemplifies the party fragmentation of the time. On the pro-catholic side the basis was the great majority of the whig party, whose numbers approached 200 after the election of 1826.[4] But a handful of whigs were confirmed anti-catholics. A sizeable section of 'liberal' tories—numbering sixty-six M.P.s in 1821—was also pro-catholic. But there were also some tory pro-catholics who cannot be called liberal. Such was the Marquess of Londonderry, brother of Lord Castlereagh, whose pro-catholic votes seem to have been grudgingly inherited from his brother, and were embarrassingly anomalous when compared with his general views. Conversely there were some anti-catholics, notably Peel, who were otherwise liberal. A further complication on the pro-catholic side was provided by the Irish members. Owing to the peculiar importance of the question for Ireland, both whig and tory pro-catholics who represented Irish constituencies were more wholehearted than their British colleagues in their enthusiasm for emancipation.

The basis of anti-catholic strength was the majority of tories. But they differed significantly in their degree of hostility to Catholic emancipation. Some of them—such as Liverpool, Wellington, and Peel—were prepared to compromise in relaxing the penal laws which remained in the 1820s. Only a minority of tories refused to yield to the final Relief Bill in 1829. Whether one were a rigid or a flexible anti-catholic came to depend very largely on whether one were a member of the Government or not. The true ultras, who opposed Catholic emancipation to the last ditch and beyond, were almost invariably outside the Government. We have not to wait until 1829 before noticing a pressure-

3. 21 December 1826; quoted in K. Feiling, *The Second Tory Party* (London, 1938), p. 401.
4. Sir James Macdonald to the Marquess of Lansdowne, 14 April 1827. A. Aspinall (ed.), *The Formation of Canning's Ministry*, Camden Soc., third series, lix (London, 1937), p. 78.

among its votaries.[6] The ultras did not play an important part in the political struggle until its final stage, but long before this they were active in the anti-catholic cause. For many years Lord Colchester in particular had made it his business to keep a jealous watch on the growth of Catholic institutions in Britain and Ireland. The foundation of monasteries and schools such as Stonyhurst produced from Colchester constant demands that such institutions should be checked by legislation. The ultras were in constant touch with their counterparts, the upholders of Protestant Ascendancy in Ireland. They patronized a movement known as the 'New Reformation', in which Protestant Bible societies sought converts among the Irish Catholics. Colchester frequently corresponded with leaders of the established Church in Ireland, and their letters contained exaggerated accounts of the menace from Catholic associations and from Jesuits in alliance with continental Catholics.

Sure support for the anti-catholic resistance was provided by the established clergy. The Church of England was still firmly Protestant at this time. Hints of the future Oxford Movement were as yet confined to a small minority, and it was perhaps fortunate for the cause of emancipation that it was so, since a move towards Rome would have stiffened popular no-popery. The anti-catholic views of most anglican clergy were naturally marked by a sensitive concern to preserve their privileges against Catholic encroachment. Until 1829 nearly all the bishops were anti-catholics. The lesser clergy could always be relied on to encourage anti-catholic petitions in their localities, and to support the anti-catholic side whenever they could—as, for example, at the Oxford University by-election of 1829, when the country parsons came up in force to turn out the apostate Peel. So pervasive was anti-catholicism among the clergy that if a pro-catholic family sent a son into the Church he was liable to be lost to their cause.[7] There were, however, important exceptions to the rule.

6. Poets who in their youth had enthusiastically welcomed the French Revolution, now in their middle age had become sober upholders of Church and King. Southey in his *Book of the Church* and Wordsworth in his letters both showed strong anti-catholic opinions. Sir Walter Scott, on the other hand, supported Wellington and Peel in 1829.

7. It was said of the Rev. George Spencer, brother of the whig Viscount Althorp: 'He is already so emancipated from the emancipation doctrines in which he has been bred up, as to be quite persecuted by his family.' G. W. Marriott to Thomas Burgess, Bishop of Salisbury, 27 September 1827; Bishop Burgess MSS.

group amongst tory peers without office—such as the Duke of Newcastle, the Marquess of Winchilsea, and Lord Kenyon—who were discontented with the lack of anti-catholic determination in the Government's policy. There are traces of such a group from 1824 onwards. The English ultras were considerably influenced by the views of the Protestant Ascendancy men in Ireland, who feared the weakening in their position which Catholic emancipation would entail. Finally, amongst the anti-catholics there were some anomalous whigs, amounting to twelve in 1821. These misfits seem to have acted on individual motives, for there is no hint of any conjunction between them. Some were flexible anti-catholics, in the sense that they accepted emancipation in 1829 or before, but some were ultras who opposed emancipation to the end.

Most of the pro-catholic tories belonged either to the Canningite or Grenville groups. The Grenville tories were an example of the family and parliamentary connexion which had been characteristic of the eighteenth century and lasted until the first Reform Act. Separated from the main body of the whigs after 1815 because they disagreed with the whigs' war policy and opposed parliamentary reform, the Grenvilles remained unattached until 1822, when they were given places in the tory Government. They supported Catholic emancipation, and when they joined the Government they made a condition that they should be free to express their attachment to this cause. It is conspicuous, however, that one of their members, the Marquess of Chandos, was a firm anti-catholic. This, with other examples, shows that membership of a particular family or connexion was not always a reliable guide to an individual's political views. A much larger floating body than the Grenvilles was the Canningite connexion. Their numbers and talent, together with the fact that the moderate whigs were trying to form a coalition with them, made the Government particularly anxious to give Canning Cabinet office in 1822 and thereby secure the support of his following.

Once in the Government, the Canningites and Grenvilles found that the free pursuit of their pro-catholic principles was restricted by a system of government neutrality on the Catholic question. This system had arisen because neither the pro- nor anti-catholic ministerialists were strong enough to decide the question as they wished. The anti-catholics could count on a majority in the Lords and (at least until George III died) on the support of the Crown. But in the Commons they were either in a minority or had a majority so narrow as to be indecisive. Further, they had not sufficient ministerial quality in their ranks to fill a front bench with confidence and success. The pro-catholic tories, on the other hand, though they were talented, were too small in number to form a lasting ministry. They could count on whig support for Catholic emancipation, but with this support they could only push a relief measure through the Commons: they were still faced with the anti-catholic barrier of Crown and Lords. Because of these difficulties a compromise had been arranged in 1812. In this solution Catholic emancipation was shelved so far as it concerned the Government as a whole. Pro- and anti-catholic ministers could express their individual opinions on the matter, but they were to respect the principle that the Government, as a body, would neither encourage nor suppress the constitutional demand for Catholic emancipation.

This was known as the 'open' system, but the hint of freedom in its title was belied by its effects. For seventeen years it made impossible the major achievement of Catholic emancipation; the benefits it gave the Catholics were but minor ones. All parties to the 'open' system became its prisoners. The convictions of both pro- and anti-catholic ministers were perforce weakened by the exigencies of statesmanship, the necessity of working together with colleagues who held contrary views on the question, and by the fact that ministers who disagreed on the Catholic issue were in agreement on other issues. Canning pointed out that Catholic emancipation was the only question on which he disagreed with Peel.[5] It is not surprising if Canning came to regard that question as a troublesome one which hindered the co-operation of ministers and should be kept quiet so long as there was no prospect of carrying it. This was the response of pro-catholic tories after they had had a taste of government office under the 'open' system. Anti-catholics also showed the effects of compromise. Some anti-catholic ministers relaxed their principles and agreed to minor concessions; some began to think that a settlement of the Catholic claims might eventually have to be reached; and one—the Duke of Wellington—began to for-

5. Canning to Peel, 26 November 1825; PP, 40311, ff. 156–7.

mulate possible schemes for a settlement as early as 1825. The pro- and anti-catholic ministers became alienated from the pro- and anti-catholics outside the Government. At first the whigs on one side and the ultras on the other looked down with exasperated contempt on those who compromised with neutrality. But the eventual reactions of the two groups were divergent. Most whigs were themselves to compromise with neutrality in 1827, leaving only a small minority high and dry; but the ultras increasingly drew together in resistance to the system.

The destruction of the 'open' system in 1829 undermined the prestige of the two institutions whose attitude had made that system necessary—the House of Lords and the Crown. Nearly all the anti-catholic ministers were in the Lords. Between 1823 and 1827 Peel was the only anti-catholic Cabinet minister in the Commons. Whereas in the Commons there was usually a narrow pro-catholic majority in the 1820s, in the Lords there were decided anti-catholic majorities. In the final crisis of 1829 the Lords yielded to the Commons. Thus through their success over Catholic emancipation the Commons advanced their prestige at the expense of the Lords. They also triumphed at the expense of the Crown. George III had championed Protestant Ascendancy so successfully that its preservation had come to symbolize the integrity of royal power. George IV wished to resist Catholic emancipation for this reason, although he had nothing of his father's pious conviction in the matter. But during his reign the demand from Ireland for emancipation became irresistible; and in 1829 the circumstances were such that it would have been extremely dangerous for George IV to make a demonstration such as his father had made in the opening years of the century. He yielded to necessity, and with this the Crown suffered an important symbolic decline.

The Commons enjoyed yet a third relative triumph in 1829, and this was at the expense of the majority of Britons. There can be no doubt that most of the inhabitants of Great Britain were opposed to civil equality for Catholics, as they had been for over 200 years. Popular anti-catholicism was a continuous undercurrent to political crises. It was stimulated by ultra politicians, by the great body of the established clergy, and by many evangelicals and methodists, and included the Romantic poets

One was Henry Bathurst, Bishop of Norwich, for many years the only pro-catholic bishop in the Lords and an active fighter for emancipation. Another was the Rev. Sydney Smith, whose pithy pro-catholic arguments were exhibited in election addresses, at meetings of provincial clergy, and in the columns of the *Edinburgh Review*.

Enthusiasm often generates intolerance, and the products of the eighteenth-century religious revival were largely anti-catholic. This was especially true of the methodists, who formed a solid corps in the anti-catholic resistance. Among the low-church evangelicals there was more diversity. Most evangelicals in Parliament were pro-catholics, and William Wilberforce himself was one, but the latter could still say that 'all the religious people are on the other side'.[8] The older nonconformist denominations were distinct from the methodists in their attitude to emancipation, at least so far as their leaders were concerned. Many of their ministers petitioned for emancipation, largely as a *quid pro quo* for help given by pro-catholics towards the relief of dissenters. But the pro-catholic inclinations of dissenting ministers certainly did not extend to their flocks.[9]

In comparison with the large bodies which opposed Catholic emancipation, the support for it was meagre and fragmentary. The pro-catholic dissenting ministers could not compare numerically with the anti-catholic anglican clergy, and since they did not carry their congregations with them their support did not have much weight. Many lawyers were said to support emancipation, and the legal profession was sometimes represented as counterbalancing the established clergy. But there is not much evidence, beyond the wishful thinking of pro-catholics, to show that the lawyers as a body were enthusiastic for Catholic relief. It was the same with the politicians. No group of English (as distinguished from Irish) politicians championed Catholic emancipation as intensely as the ultras opposed it. The whigs on the whole were more whole-hearted pro-catholics than the liberal tories, but this distinction could scarcely be maintained (except

8. J. H. Hexter, 'The Protestant Revival and the Catholic Question in England, 1778–1829', *Journal of Modern History*, viii (1936), p. 306.

9. Sympathy for unitarianism was perhaps a deciding factor in the matter: 'The more sophisticated leaders of Dissent petitioned for Catholic Emancipation, while their trinitarian troops marched in the opposite direction.' Ursula Henriques, *Religious Toleration in England, 1787–1833* (London, 1961), p. 147.

on the theoretical level) when most whigs yielded to the 'open' system in 1827. The radicals upheld religious liberty on principle, but their support for Catholic emancipation was hardly more than lukewarm. Unbelieving utilitarians were naturally antipathetic to the Catholic creed, as is evident from Bentham's writings. Moreover, the radicals were interested in religious liberty only as an aid to their obsessive demand for political reform; and they were alienated when the Irish Catholics sometimes gave up supporting parliamentary reform in an effort to conciliate the tories. Bentham clearly stated that he was 'against Catholic Emancipation by any other instrument than radicalism';[1] and Cobbett, despite extravagant praise of the mediaeval Church in his *History of the Reformation*, promptly reversed his attitude in 1825 when the Catholic leaders accepted a policy which was opposed to the strict principles of parliamentary reform.

Anti-catholic opinion thus had a great advantage in the extent of its leadership. But in spite of this the anti-catholic masses were not sufficiently stimulated to make effective resistance to emancipation. The numerous anti-catholic societies—Orange associations, Pitt clubs, and later Brunswick clubs—were patronized mainly by the upper classes. The deep-rooted anti-catholic sentiments of the English masses remained, in contrast, unorganized and inert. The Gordon Riots of 1780 were the last great violent outburst of anti-popish sentiment, and the general election of 1806 was the last in which this sentiment had much influence. The 1826 election, in contrast, seemed only to show that it was possible for a great many pro-catholic candidates to succeed in spite of the prevailing opinion. Even in the final crisis of 1828–9 the ultras did no more than stir the surface of anti-catholic feeling. Mass opinion was still decidedly anti-catholic and remained so for many years. But it had changed gradually and imperceptibly from an aggressive movement into one of dormant impassivity. The ultra failure to revive the flame allowed the Government to carry emancipation without significant active resistance in the country.

1. Bentham to John Cam Hobhouse, 31 January 1821. J. Bowring (ed.), *Works of Jeremy Bentham* (11 vols., Edinburgh, 1843), x. 524. See also Bentham to O'Connell, 15 July 1828 (ibid., 594–5); and O'Connell to Bentham, 3 August 1828 (ibid., 597).

Any attempt to understand the Catholic emancipation struggle takes us back to the first years of Catholic exclusion. The object of the Tudor Supremacy Acts was not to deprive Catholics as such, but only those who countenanced the ambitions of foreign potentates and were therefore traitors to the realm. Catholics whose loyalty could be ascertained were sometimes advanced by Elizabeth I to the highest positions of state. Penalties became more stringent as a result of the great Spanish and Catholic menace of the 1580s, but this was only because religion was inextricably interwoven with politics. Under the early Stuarts, when the foreign threat had lifted, the pressure on Catholics eased and they enjoyed the favour of the court. But an attempt by Charles II to renew this favour in a form more dangerous to the anglican establishment proved disastrous to the Catholics. His desire to re-establish Catholicism, professed in the Secret Treaty of Dover (whether sincerely or not need not concern us here), was defeated by a staunchly anglican parliament which passed the Test Act of 1673. On account of the anti-catholic panic caused by Titus Oates's rumours of a Popish plot, the provisions of the earlier measure were extended in a second Test Act in 1678. Charles II had to accept these enactments in his last years, and the clumsy extremist efforts of James II to reverse this policy only produced the emphatically anti-catholic Revolution Settlement and the Penal Code.

The enactment of anti-catholic legislation continued for fifty years after the Revolution, but the main lines of Catholic exclusion were laid down in the last quarter of the seventeenth century. Basically its motives were the same as those which had produced the Elizabethan legislation—resistance to the menace of Catholic and foreign domination. The threat had been more dangerous under James II and consequently the ensuing settlement was more rigid. Even so, the law did not extend to the active suppression of Catholics until James II had made his attempt to rouse Ireland with French help. This was the last straw. After it came the Penal Code with its implicit assumption that every Catholic was a potential traitor. Its successive enactments, challenging religious faith, material security, professional advancement, and the unity of family life, deliberately sought to depress the Catholics to the lowest level of society. But for all its severity the Penal Code was only a temporary institution.

Relief measures began to vitiate its provisions in the early 1770s, and by the early nineteenth century most of the Code had vanished. There remained, however, the original measures excluding Catholics from parliament and government office. The Test Act of 1673 called on all office-holders and members of the House of Commons to take an oath against transubstantiation; the Act of 1678 extended this oath to peers, thus for the first time excluding Catholics from the upper House. It was against these Acts that the campaign for Catholic emancipation was directed.

In England a movement for Catholic emancipation first became active in the 1780s. The English lay Catholics formed committees to negotiate compromise solutions with the Government. The first of these, comprising five laymen, was founded in 1782, with Charles Butler as secretary;[2] and a larger committee was established in 1787-8.[3] This organization was inspired by a movement for the relief of dissenters which arose in the 1770s and gathered force in the following decade. Compared with the powerful dissenting movement, the English Catholics were a small and isolated body. They sought to compensate for their weakness by allying as closely as possible with the dissenters. It was apparently their object to give the impression that they were just another English nonconformist sect, rather than members of a universal Church which transcended national boundaries. Thus the second Catholic committee took the significant name of 'Protesting Catholic Dissenters'. Similarly in 1788 the committee drew up a 'Protestation', which denied temporal authority to the Pope and rejected papal infallibility. It was partly reproduced in an oath which was embodied in the Relief Act of 1791. These views survived in the Cisalpine Club, established in 1792, which boldly announced that it would resist any ecclesiastical interference which might obstruct the freedom of the English Catholics.

But in spite of their adaptability it is most unlikely that the English Catholics could have obtained emancipation by their own efforts. The main concessions, including the final one of 1829, were only made because Catholic emancipation was mainly

2. After a Relief Act of 1791 Butler became the first English Catholic barrister for over a century.
3. For further details, see Charles Butler, *Historical Memoirs respecting the English, Irish and Scottish Catholics* (4 vols., London, 1819-21), ii. 110-11.

an Irish question. Ireland provides the connecting link for the whole story of Catholic persecution and concession: the Irish situation explains both the repression of the later seventeenth century and the concession of the early nineteenth. On both occasions the reason was the same: Catholic Ireland was a standing threat to the unity and security of the British Isles. Catholic emancipation was a constant aim of Irish agitators in the eighteenth century, but the character of their demands was very different from that of the English Catholics. The latter were a small, largely aristocratic minority, but the Irish Catholics were a large majority, mainly peasant in composition. The English Catholics wanted only the removal of their civil and political disabilities. But the Irish Catholics had a whole range of grievances of which religious exclusion was only one; these grievances were basically social and economic, and ultimately nationalist. Catholic emancipation, a final objective to the English Catholics, was likely to be only one step towards satisfying the Irish. Moreover, whereas in England the Catholic laymen adopted extreme cisalpinism to forward their political aspirations, in Ireland religious orthodoxy was in the ascendant.[4] It may seem unlikely that the Irish attitude would win concessions. But the Irish had an all-important advantage: unlike the English, they could bring political pressure to bear on the Government, and this fact eventually proved to be decisive.

The conflict with revolutionary France in the 1790s again brought up the political dangers of the Irish situation. A French invasion of Ireland was threatened and was encouraged by the Society of United Irishmen. This body was largely composed of the presbyterians of the north. The Catholics at first avoided it, hoping that this show of loyalty would win them concessions from the British Government. A considerable concession was indeed obtained. By the Franchise Act of 1793 parliamentary suffrage was given to Irish Catholics who qualified as forty-shilling county freeholders—the same terms as were enjoyed by the Protestants in both Ireland and Britain. In Ireland a higher

---

4. The distinction was not quite clear-cut. There was a small group of aristocratic Irish Catholics, led by Lord Fingall, who sympathized with the views of English Catholics against those of the Irish Catholics. Conversely, the more militant of the English vicars-apostolic (the leading Catholic ecclesiastics) took the side of the Irish Catholic clerics and the majority of Irish Catholic laymen.

proportion of the population attained this qualification than in England.[5] This concession, however, was not enough for the Irish Catholics. They hoped that it would lead to the final repeal of their disabilities, but Pitt's Government clearly showed that it was not prepared to go any further. Moreover, when a pro-catholic Lord Lieutenant, Earl Fitzwilliam, indiscreetly attacked Protestant Ascendancy, he was quickly recalled from his post. Consequently the Catholics veered towards the United Irishmen, and joined in planning a rebellion with French aid in 1798. The famous uprising was put down. After its suppression Pitt resolved that similar threats must be guarded against in the future by eliminating the separate Irish parliament and thereby binding Ireland more closely to Britain. This was done in the Union Act of 1800, and with it the political struggles over Catholic emancipation began in earnest.

The Irish Catholics did not oppose the Union, since they thought that emancipation was more likely to be granted by the new united Parliament than the old Irish one. Indeed Pitt had given the impression that Catholic relief would follow the Union and the Catholics regarded this as a pledge. But George III stepped in. He was persuaded that consent to an emancipation measure would violate the Coronation Oath whereby he had sworn to uphold Protestant Ascendancy, and therefore refused to countenance any such measure. Pitt thereupon resigned in 1801 and the Irish Catholics were convinced that they had been duped. George III's action had emphasized the Crown's constitutional power; and in subsequent ministerial changes this power was again vindicated. Pitt returned to power in 1804 on condition that he would not raise the obnoxious question of Catholic relief. On his death in January 1806 he was succeeded by 'All the Talents'. The pro-catholic members of this ministry, such as Fox, did not want to raise the issue of emancipation at the cost of upsetting the King and destroying their Government. But the Irish Catholics were insistent: at the beginning of 1807 they presented a further petition for emancipation. In order to put off this awkward demand and secure their own position the whig ministers looked for a partial reform which would, they hoped,

5. This later became an argument against Catholic emancipation: it was said that if emancipation passed, irresponsible Catholic members would be returned by an irresponsible mob.

group amongst tory peers without office—such as the Duke of Newcastle, the Marquess of Winchilsea, and Lord Kenyon—who were discontented with the lack of anti-catholic determination in the Government's policy. There are traces of such a group from 1824 onwards. The English ultras were considerably influenced by the views of the Protestant Ascendancy men in Ireland, who feared the weakening in their position which Catholic emancipation would entail. Finally, amongst the anti-catholics there were some anomalous whigs, amounting to twelve in 1821. These misfits seem to have acted on individual motives, for there is no hint of any conjunction between them. Some were flexible anti-catholics, in the sense that they accepted emancipation in 1829 or before, but some were ultras who opposed emancipation to the end.

Most of the pro-catholic tories belonged either to the Canningite or Grenville groups. The Grenville tories were an example of the family and parliamentary connexion which had been characteristic of the eighteenth century and lasted until the first Reform Act. Separated from the main body of the whigs after 1815 because they disagreed with the whigs' war policy and opposed parliamentary reform, the Grenvilles remained unattached until 1822, when they were given places in the tory Government. They supported Catholic emancipation, and when they joined the Government they made a condition that they should be free to express their attachment to this cause. It is conspicuous, however, that one of their members, the Marquess of Chandos, was a firm anti-catholic. This, with other examples, shows that membership of a particular family or connexion was not always a reliable guide to an individual's political views. A much larger floating body than the Grenvilles was the Canningite connexion. Their numbers and talent, together with the fact that the moderate whigs were trying to form a coalition with them, made the Government particularly anxious to give Canning Cabinet office in 1822 and thereby secure the support of his following.

Once in the Government, the Canningites and Grenvilles found that the free pursuit of their pro-catholic principles was restricted by a system of government neutrality on the Catholic question. This system had arisen because neither the pro- nor anti-catholic ministerialists were strong enough to decide the question as they wished. The anti-catholics could count on a majority in the Lords and (at least until George III died) on the support of the Crown. But in the Commons they were either in a minority or had a majority so narrow as to be indecisive. Further, they had not sufficient ministerial quality in their ranks to fill a front bench with confidence and success. The pro-catholic tories, on the other hand, though they were talented, were too small in number to form a lasting ministry. They could count on whig support for Catholic emancipation, but with this support they could only push a relief measure through the Commons: they were still faced with the anti-catholic barrier of Crown and Lords. Because of these difficulties a compromise had been arranged in 1812. In this solution Catholic emancipation was shelved so far as it concerned the Government as a whole. Pro- and anti-catholic ministers could express their individual opinions on the matter, but they were to respect the principle that the Government, as a body, would neither encourage nor suppress the constitutional demand for Catholic emancipation.

This was known as the 'open' system, but the hint of freedom in its title was belied by its effects. For seventeen years it made impossible the major achievement of Catholic emancipation; the benefits it gave the Catholics were but minor ones. All parties to the 'open' system became its prisoners. The convictions of both pro- and anti-catholic ministers were perforce weakened by the exigencies of statesmanship, the necessity of working together with colleagues who held contrary views on the question, and by the fact that ministers who disagreed on the Catholic issue were in agreement on other issues. Canning pointed out that Catholic emancipation was the only question on which he disagreed with Peel.[5] It is not surprising if Canning came to regard that question as a troublesome one which hindered the co-operation of ministers and should be kept quiet so long as there was no prospect of carrying it. This was the response of pro-catholic tories after they had had a taste of government office under the 'open' system. Anti-catholics also showed the effects of compromise. Some anti-catholic ministers relaxed their principles and agreed to minor concessions; some began to think that a settlement of the Catholic claims might eventually have to be reached; and one—the Duke of Wellington—began to for-

5. Canning to Peel, 26 November 1825; PP, 40311, ff. 156–7.

mulate possible schemes for a settlement as early as 1825. The pro- and anti-catholic ministers became alienated from the pro- and anti-catholics outside the Government. At first the whigs on one side and the ultras on the other looked down with exasperated contempt on those who compromised with neutrality. But the eventual reactions of the two groups were divergent. Most whigs were themselves to compromise with neutrality in 1827, leaving only a small minority high and dry; but the ultras increasingly drew together in resistance to the system.

The destruction of the 'open' system in 1829 undermined the prestige of the two institutions whose attitude had made that system necessary—the House of Lords and the Crown. Nearly all the anti-catholic ministers were in the Lords. Between 1823 and 1827 Peel was the only anti-catholic Cabinet minister in the Commons. Whereas in the Commons there was usually a narrow pro-catholic majority in the 1820s, in the Lords there were decided anti-catholic majorities. In the final crisis of 1829 the Lords yielded to the Commons. Thus through their success over Catholic emancipation the Commons advanced their prestige at the expense of the Lords. They also triumphed at the expense of the Crown. George III had championed Protestant Ascendancy so successfully that its preservation had come to symbolize the integrity of royal power. George IV wished to resist Catholic emancipation for this reason, although he had nothing of his father's pious conviction in the matter. But during his reign the demand from Ireland for emancipation became irresistible; and in 1829 the circumstances were such that it would have been extremely dangerous for George IV to make a demonstration such as his father had made in the opening years of the century. He yielded to necessity, and with this the Crown suffered an important symbolic decline.

The Commons enjoyed yet a third relative triumph in 1829, and this was at the expense of the majority of Britons. There can be no doubt that most of the inhabitants of Great Britain were opposed to civil equality for Catholics, as they had been for over 200 years. Popular anti-catholicism was a continuous undercurrent to political crises. It was stimulated by ultra politicians, by the great body of the established clergy, and by many evangelicals and methodists, and included the Romantic poets

among its votaries.[6] The ultras did not play an important part
in the political struggle until its final stage, but long before this
they were active in the anti-catholic cause. For many years Lord
Colchester in particular had made it his business to keep a
jealous watch on the growth of Catholic institutions in Britain
and Ireland. The foundation of monasteries and schools such as
Stonyhurst produced from Colchester constant demands that
such institutions should be checked by legislation. The ultras
were in constant touch with their counterparts, the upholders of
Protestant Ascendancy in Ireland. They patronized a movement
known as the 'New Reformation', in which Protestant Bible
societies sought converts among the Irish Catholics. Colchester
frequently corresponded with leaders of the established Church
in Ireland, and their letters contained exaggerated accounts of
the menace from Catholic associations and from Jesuits in alliance with continental Catholics.

Sure support for the anti-catholic resistance was provided by
the established clergy. The Church of England was still firmly
Protestant at this time. Hints of the future Oxford Movement
were as yet confined to a small minority, and it was perhaps
fortunate for the cause of emancipation that it was so, since a
move towards Rome would have stiffened popular no-popery.
The anti-catholic views of most anglican clergy were naturally
marked by a sensitive concern to preserve their privileges against
Catholic encroachment. Until 1829 nearly all the bishops were
anti-catholics. The lesser clergy could always be relied on to
encourage anti-catholic petitions in their localities, and to support the anti-catholic side whenever they could—as, for example,
at the Oxford University by-election of 1829, when the country
parsons came up in force to turn out the apostate Peel. So pervasive was anti-catholicism among the clergy that if a pro-catholic
family sent a son into the Church he was liable to be lost to their
cause.[7] There were, however, important exceptions to the rule.

6. Poets who in their youth had enthusiastically welcomed the French
Revolution, now in their middle age had become sober upholders of Church and
King. Southey in his *Book of the Church* and Wordsworth in his letters both
showed strong anti-catholic opinions. Sir Walter Scott, on the other hand,
supported Wellington and Peel in 1829.
7. It was said of the Rev. George Spencer, brother of the whig Viscount
Althorp: 'He is already so emancipated from the emancipation doctrines in
which he has been bred up, as to be quite persecuted by his family.' G. W.
Marriott to Thomas Burgess, Bishop of Salisbury, 27 September 1827; Bishop
Burgess MSS.

One was Henry Bathurst, Bishop of Norwich, for many years the only pro-catholic bishop in the Lords and an active fighter for emancipation. Another was the Rev. Sydney Smith, whose pithy pro-catholic arguments were exhibited in election addresses, at meetings of provincial clergy, and in the columns of the *Edinburgh Review*.

Enthusiasm often generates intolerance, and the products of the eighteenth-century religious revival were largely anti-catholic. This was especially true of the methodists, who formed a solid corps in the anti-catholic resistance. Among the low-church evangelicals there was more diversity. Most evangelicals in Parliament were pro-catholics, and William Wilberforce himself was one, but the latter could still say that 'all the religious people are on the other side'.[8] The older nonconformist denominations were distinct from the methodists in their attitude to emancipation, at least so far as their leaders were concerned. Many of their ministers petitioned for emancipation, largely as a *quid pro quo* for help given by pro-catholics towards the relief of dissenters. But the pro-catholic inclinations of dissenting ministers certainly did not extend to their flocks.[9]

In comparison with the large bodies which opposed Catholic emancipation, the support for it was meagre and fragmentary. The pro-catholic dissenting ministers could not compare numerically with the anti-catholic anglican clergy, and since they did not carry their congregations with them their support did not have much weight. Many lawyers were said to support emancipation, and the legal profession was sometimes represented as counterbalancing the established clergy. But there is not much evidence, beyond the wishful thinking of pro-catholics, to show that the lawyers as a body were enthusiastic for Catholic relief. It was the same with the politicians. No group of English (as distinguished from Irish) politicians championed Catholic emancipation as intensely as the ultras opposed it. The whigs on the whole were more whole-hearted pro-catholics than the liberal tories, but this distinction could scarcely be maintained (except

8. J. H. Hexter, 'The Protestant Revival and the Catholic Question in England, 1778–1829', *Journal of Modern History*, viii (1936), p. 306.
9. Sympathy for unitarianism was perhaps a deciding factor in the matter: 'The more sophisticated leaders of Dissent petitioned for Catholic Emancipation, while their trinitarian troops marched in the opposite direction.' Ursula Henriques, *Religious Toleration in England, 1787–1833* (London, 1961), p. 147.

on the theoretical level) when most whigs yielded to the 'open' system in 1827. The radicals upheld religious liberty on principle, but their support for Catholic emancipation was hardly more than lukewarm. Unbelieving utilitarians were naturally antipathetic to the Catholic creed, as is evident from Bentham's writings. Moreover, the radicals were interested in religious liberty only as an aid to their obsessive demand for political reform; and they were alienated when the Irish Catholics sometimes gave up supporting parliamentary reform in an effort to conciliate the tories. Bentham clearly stated that he was 'against Catholic Emancipation by any other instrument than radicalism';[1] and Cobbett, despite extravagant praise of the mediaeval Church in his *History of the Reformation,* promptly reversed his attitude in 1825 when the Catholic leaders accepted a policy which was opposed to the strict principles of parliamentary reform.

Anti-catholic opinion thus had a great advantage in the extent of its leadership. But in spite of this the anti-catholic masses were not sufficiently stimulated to make effective resistance to emancipation. The numerous anti-catholic societies—Orange associations, Pitt clubs, and later Brunswick clubs—were patronized mainly by the upper classes. The deep-rooted anti-catholic sentiments of the English masses remained, in contrast, unorganized and inert. The Gordon Riots of 1780 were the last great violent outburst of anti-popish sentiment, and the general election of 1806 was the last in which this sentiment had much influence. The 1826 election, in contrast, seemed only to show that it was possible for a great many pro-catholic candidates to succeed in spite of the prevailing opinion. Even in the final crisis of 1828–9 the ultras did no more than stir the surface of anti-catholic feeling. Mass opinion was still decidedly anti-catholic and remained so for many years. But it had changed gradually and imperceptibly from an aggressive movement into one of dormant impassivity. The ultra failure to revive the flame allowed the Government to carry emancipation without significant active resistance in the country.

1. Bentham to John Cam Hobhouse, 31 January 1821. J. Bowring (ed.), *Works of Jeremy Bentham* (11 vols., Edinburgh, 1843), x. 524. See also Bentham to O'Connell, 15 July 1828 (ibid., 594–5); and O'Connell to Bentham, 3 August 1828 (ibid., 597).

Any attempt to understand the Catholic emancipation struggle takes us back to the first years of Catholic exclusion. The object of the Tudor Supremacy Acts was not to deprive Catholics as such, but only those who countenanced the ambitions of foreign potentates and were therefore traitors to the realm. Catholics whose loyalty could be ascertained were sometimes advanced by Elizabeth I to the highest positions of state. Penalties became more stringent as a result of the great Spanish and Catholic menace of the 1580s, but this was only because religion was inextricably interwoven with politics. Under the early Stuarts, when the foreign threat had lifted, the pressure on Catholics eased and they enjoyed the favour of the court. But an attempt by Charles II to renew this favour in a form more dangerous to the anglican establishment proved disastrous to the Catholics. His desire to re-establish Catholicism, professed in the Secret Treaty of Dover (whether sincerely or not need not concern us here), was defeated by a staunchly anglican parliament which passed the Test Act of 1673. On account of the anti-catholic panic caused by Titus Oates's rumours of a Popish plot, the provisions of the earlier measure were extended in a second Test Act in 1678. Charles II had to accept these enactments in his last years, and the clumsy extremist efforts of James II to reverse this policy only produced the emphatically anti-catholic Revolution Settlement and the Penal Code.

The enactment of anti-catholic legislation continued for fifty years after the Revolution, but the main lines of Catholic exclusion were laid down in the last quarter of the seventeenth century. Basically its motives were the same as those which had produced the Elizabethan legislation—resistance to the menace of Catholic and foreign domination. The threat had been more dangerous under James II and consequently the ensuing settlement was more rigid. Even so, the law did not extend to the active suppression of Catholics until James II had made his attempt to rouse Ireland with French help. This was the last straw. After it came the Penal Code with its implicit assumption that every Catholic was a potential traitor. Its successive enactments, challenging religious faith, material security, professional advancement, and the unity of family life, deliberately sought to depress the Catholics to the lowest level of society. But for all its severity the Penal Code was only a temporary institution.

Relief measures began to vitiate its provisions in the early 1770s, and by the early nineteenth century most of the Code had vanished. There remained, however, the original measures excluding Catholics from parliament and government office. The Test Act of 1673 called on all office-holders and members of the House of Commons to take an oath against transubstantiation; the Act of 1678 extended this oath to peers, thus for the first time excluding Catholics from the upper House. It was against these Acts that the campaign for Catholic emancipation was directed.

In England a movement for Catholic emancipation first became active in the 1780s. The English lay Catholics formed committees to negotiate compromise solutions with the Government. The first of these, comprising five laymen, was founded in 1782, with Charles Butler as secretary;[2] and a larger committee was established in 1787–8.[3] This organization was inspired by a movement for the relief of dissenters which arose in the 1770s and gathered force in the following decade. Compared with the powerful dissenting movement, the English Catholics were a small and isolated body. They sought to compensate for their weakness by allying as closely as possible with the dissenters. It was apparently their object to give the impression that they were just another English nonconformist sect, rather than members of a universal Church which transcended national boundaries. Thus the second Catholic committee took the significant name of 'Protesting Catholic Dissenters'. Similarly in 1788 the committee drew up a 'Protestation', which denied temporal authority to the Pope and rejected papal infallibility. It was partly reproduced in an oath which was embodied in the Relief Act of 1791. These views survived in the Cisalpine Club, established in 1792, which boldly announced that it would resist any ecclesiastical interference which might obstruct the freedom of the English Catholics.

But in spite of their adaptability it is most unlikely that the English Catholics could have obtained emancipation by their own efforts. The main concessions, including the final one of 1829, were only made because Catholic emancipation was mainly

2. After a Relief Act of 1791 Butler became the first English Catholic barrister for over a century.
3. For further details, see Charles Butler, *Historical Memoirs respecting the English, Irish and Scottish Catholics* (4 vols., London, 1819–21), ii. 110–11.

an Irish question. Ireland provides the connecting link for the whole story of Catholic persecution and concession: the Irish situation explains both the repression of the later seventeenth century and the concession of the early nineteenth. On both occasions the reason was the same: Catholic Ireland was a standing threat to the unity and security of the British Isles. Catholic emancipation was a constant aim of Irish agitators in the eighteenth century, but the character of their demands was very different from that of the English Catholics. The latter were a small, largely aristocratic minority, but the Irish Catholics were a large majority, mainly peasant in composition. The English Catholics wanted only the removal of their civil and political disabilities. But the Irish Catholics had a whole range of grievances of which religious exclusion was only one; these grievances were basically social and economic, and ultimately nationalist. Catholic emancipation, a final objective to the English Catholics, was likely to be only one step towards satisfying the Irish. Moreover, whereas in England the Catholic laymen adopted extreme cisalpinism to forward their political aspirations, in Ireland religious orthodoxy was in the ascendant.[4] It may seem unlikely that the Irish attitude would win concessions. But the Irish had an all-important advantage: unlike the English, they could bring political pressure to bear on the Government, and this fact eventually proved to be decisive.

The conflict with revolutionary France in the 1790s again brought up the political dangers of the Irish situation. A French invasion of Ireland was threatened and was encouraged by the Society of United Irishmen. This body was largely composed of the presbyterians of the north. The Catholics at first avoided it, hoping that this show of loyalty would win them concessions from the British Government. A considerable concession was indeed obtained. By the Franchise Act of 1793 parliamentary suffrage was given to Irish Catholics who qualified as forty-shilling county freeholders—the same terms as were enjoyed by the Protestants in both Ireland and Britain. In Ireland a higher

---

4. The distinction was not quite clear-cut. There was a small group of aristocratic Irish Catholics, led by Lord Fingall, who sympathized with the views of English Catholics against those of the Irish Catholics. Conversely, the more militant of the English vicars-apostolic (the leading Catholic ecclesiastics) took the side of the Irish Catholic clerics and the majority of Irish Catholic laymen.

proportion of the population attained this qualification than in England.[5] This concession, however, was not enough for the Irish Catholics. They hoped that it would lead to the final repeal of their disabilities, but Pitt's Government clearly showed that it was not prepared to go any further. Moreover, when a pro-catholic Lord Lieutenant, Earl Fitzwilliam, indiscreetly attacked Protestant Ascendancy, he was quickly recalled from his post. Consequently the Catholics veered towards the United Irishmen, and joined in planning a rebellion with French aid in 1798. The famous uprising was put down. After its suppression Pitt resolved that similar threats must be guarded against in the future by eliminating the separate Irish parliament and thereby binding Ireland more closely to Britain. This was done in the Union Act of 1800, and with it the political struggles over Catholic emancipation began in earnest.

The Irish Catholics did not oppose the Union, since they thought that emancipation was more likely to be granted by the new united Parliament than the old Irish one. Indeed Pitt had given the impression that Catholic relief would follow the Union and the Catholics regarded this as a pledge. But George III stepped in. He was persuaded that consent to an emancipation measure would violate the Coronation Oath whereby he had sworn to uphold Protestant Ascendancy, and therefore refused to countenance any such measure. Pitt thereupon resigned in 1801 and the Irish Catholics were convinced that they had been duped. George III's action had emphasized the Crown's constitutional power; and in subsequent ministerial changes this power was again vindicated. Pitt returned to power in 1804 on condition that he would not raise the obnoxious question of Catholic relief. On his death in January 1806 he was succeeded by 'All the Talents'. The pro-catholic members of this ministry, such as Fox, did not want to raise the issue of emancipation at the cost of upsetting the King and destroying their Government. But the Irish Catholics were insistent: at the beginning of 1807 they presented a further petition for emancipation. In order to put off this awkward demand and secure their own position the whig ministers looked for a partial reform which would, they hoped,

---

5. This later became an argument against Catholic emancipation: it was said that if emancipation passed, irresponsible Catholic members would be returned by an irresponsible mob.

pacify the Catholics. They decided to try and extend to all Catholic soldiers a measure which had already applied to those serving in Ireland since 1793, giving them the right to hold commissions up to and including the rank of colonel. Sidmouth, one of the anti-catholic ministers, obtained the King's consent. But the whig ministers then tried to extend the measure to include staff appointments in the army. The King rejected this proposal. The whigs thereupon offered to drop the whole bill, but insisted that they should be free to extol the benefits of the abandoned measure, doubtless hoping in this way to save themselves from Catholic opprobrium. But the King wanted a promise that the matter should not be raised even in this form. The ministers refused to give the promise and in March 1807 they resigned.[6]

The tory ministries led by Portland and Perceval which held office between 1807 and 1812 contained Pittites who were nominally in favour of emancipation. But during this period the only active champions of Catholic relief were the whigs. The cause was obstructed by the popular no-popery feeling which had appeared in recent general elections and, more important, by the conflict between English and Irish Catholics. This had developed into a protracted dispute which bedevilled the political fortunes of the Catholic question for many years. The adaptable English Catholics were much readier than the Irish to agree to securities for the maintenance of the anglican establishment, as a means of winning emancipation. The chief and most controversial of these securities was known as the Veto. It provided that in return for Catholic emancipation the Government should have some control over the appointment of Catholic clerics in order to ensure their loyalty to the Crown. At first the Irish bishops had agreed to the Veto. Ten of them supported it in 1799; and in 1808 they consented that the Veto should form part of a pro-catholic motion advanced in Parliament by the whigs. But in that year the Irish Catholic laymen (apart from the aristocrats) protested against the Veto and thereupon the bishops reversed their attitude. This greatly embarrassed Dr. Milner, representative of the Irish Catholics in England and vicar-apostolic of the Midland district. Previously Milner had

6. For a detailed account of this crisis, see Michael Roberts, *The Whig Party, 1807–12* (London, 1939), pp. 7–34.

given the whigs to understand that he supported the Veto, but after the *volte face* of his Irish colleagues he turned round and vehemently opposed it.[7] The motion was defeated. Despite this set-back the whig leaders Grey and Grenville continued to advocate the Veto; and in 1810 they obtained the support of two out of the four vicars-apostolic, in addition to that of the English lay Catholics. This infuriated Milner and the Irish Catholics: the former abused his defecting colleagues and the latter once more condemned the Veto. To their gratification a motion embodying the Veto was again easily defeated in Parliament.

In 1811 George IV became Regent. His closest associates had been whigs and pro-catholics, and the whigs hoped to be called to office. They were disappointed. Perceval remained prime minister until his death in May 1812, and was succeeded by Liverpool, another anti-catholic. At the end of the month, however, Liverpool resigned over a vote of no-confidence. The Regent now considered appointing a ministry led by the pro-catholics Canning and Wellesley. Their stipulations included an immediate effort to settle the Catholic question. But the project broke down because Grey and Grenville refused a coalition. Liverpool then resumed his administration on the principle of government neutrality.

Meanwhile the anti-vetoist Irish Catholics, increasingly dominated by the militant O'Connell, were becoming more efficiently organized.[8] If the whigs continued to uphold the Veto they were likely to lose ground as champions of emancipation. In 1812, therefore, the whig leaders stated that they would give up the Veto if necessary. Suddenly the prospects for emancipation became very hopeful. Canning moved for an enquiry into the Catholic claims to take place in the succeeding parliamentary session, that of 1813. This motion passed by 112 votes in the Commons and was lost by only one vote in the Lords. But when 1813 came the Veto question once more intervened to destroy the Catholics' hopes. Grattan had formulated a relief bill including articles drawn up by Canning. These articles contained a lengthy cisalpine oath and a detailed plan for the Veto. The latter proposal was welcomed by the English Catholics. Three out of the four vicars-apostolic accepted it, the exception of course be-

7. For the details of Milner's behaviour see M. Roberts, op. cit., pp. 45–57.
8. See M. Roberts, pp. 81 ff.

ing Dr. Milner. Moreover, the bill was approved at Rome by the Secretary of Propaganda. But even the acquiescence of Rome could not break the inflexible opposition of the Irish Catholics. O'Connell and his followers simply began to regard themselves as the true guardians of the Catholic faith, as opposed to a malleable papacy which seemed to have betrayed it. 'I am sincerely a Catholic . . . but I am not a Papist,' O'Connell declared.[9]

In May 1813 the controversial bill was abandoned, but the vetoists and anti-vetoists continued to fight out their quarrel. When Pope Pius VII returned to Rome in 1814 representatives of each party presented their cases to him. The anti-vetoist delegation was led by Milner. The outcome of the mission was a papal letter of April 1815 rejecting the oath and Veto proposed in 1813, but suggesting instead a diluted form of veto which would enable the Crown to have a certain choice among candidates for Irish Catholic bishoprics. The compromise was rejected by the Irish Catholics, who denounced Milner and his colleagues for betraying them.

Thereafter the Veto conflict rested until 1821. Between 1813 and 1821 Grattan and others raised the Catholic issue several times in the Commons. Their motions were all defeated. But Grattan's motion of 1819 failed by only two votes. This near-success, together with the relaxation of internecine quarrels, may be regarded as heralding the better fortune which the Catholic claims were to enjoy in the coming decade.

The Catholic question, it has often been emphasized, was basically a political and not a religious matter. The extremely verbose arguments over Catholic emancipation, in pamphlet warfare and parliamentary debate, none the less contained much wrangling over Catholic beliefs. The Roman Catholic religion was attacked on grounds which were as old as the Reformation. It was accused of inculcating the idea that Catholics had an exclusive right to salvation and that they had no need to keep faith with heretics. Most important of all, Catholics were said to be subject to divided allegiance, since they attributed to the Pope a temporal authority which might conflict with that of the King.[1] These accusations were vigorously denied by the Catholics. In 1788

9. Quoted in E. Halévy, *Hist. Eng. People*, i (London, 1949), p. 484.
1. These charges are developed in Henriques, op. cit., pp. 148 ff.

the English Catholics obtained from five continental Catholic universities a firm declaration that the Pope could never dispense with the oath of allegiance which Catholic subjects, like all others, owed to the King;[2] and this denial was a persistent theme in pro-catholic arguments. But such declarations, no matter how often repeated, could scarcely do anything to undermine the ingrained prejudices of the English, and if Catholic emancipation had been simply concerned with religious toleration it must surely have been postponed for an indefinite period. That it was not such a question is shown by the small part which the abstract idea of toleration played in the controversy. A recent writer has noted that the argument over emancipation added but little to the theory of religious toleration.[3] The whigs, it is true, believed in toleration for its own sake; and their arguments in favour of emancipation, unlike those of the tory pro-catholics, were sometimes grounded on the ideal that civil equality was a natural right.[4] But such ideals were becoming out of date and were rendered largely ineffective by the whigs' own conservative attitude towards changes in Church and State, which they wanted to be gradual and not revolutionary.[5] As for the tory pro-catholics, some of them leaned over backwards to demonstrate their intolerance of Roman Catholicism. When one of them announced his conversion to the cause of emancipation he stated his conviction that the Catholic faith was 'a foul pollution of the word of God'.[6] That such men nevertheless supported Catholic emancipation clearly reveals their belief that it was primarily a question of political expediency, and that its concession was a matter of empirical necessity.

The champions of empirical concession found their chief obstruction in the anti-catholic belief that the Revolution Settlement was inviolable. In this view the settlement had provided the State with a fixed and perfect structure which had brought many blessings to England since its establishment; its alteration was bound to bring infinite harm. The quintessence of the Settlement was the anglican constitution—the union of Church and

2. Charles Butler, op. cit., ii. 110–11.
3. Henriques, op. cit., p. 138.
4. For this distinction in the attitude of whig and tory pro-catholics, see G. F. A. Best, 'The Whigs and the Church Establishment in the Age of Grey and Holland', *History*, xlv (1960), p. 109.
5. See G. F. A. Best, 'The Constitutional Revolution, 1828–32', *Theology*, 1959, pp. 228–9.   6. Quoted in Henriques, p. 155.

State, and exclusion of Catholics and dissenters from civil power. Such exclusion, argued one anti-catholic M.P., was as fundamental as Magna Carta.[7] But anti-catholics sometimes felt compelled to defend the continuance of Protestant Ascendancy on more immediate and practical grounds than reverence for a settlement which was over a hundred years old. They claimed that the Catholic threat which the settlement was designed to avoid was still in existence. Lord Chancellor Eldon, speaking in 1821, drew on current rumours to invoke the horrors of a former age:

We are led not to doubt that the present pope has re-established the order of the Jesuits—that the Inquisition was revived—we have heard of bulls against Protestant societies distributing the scriptures—we have heard of transactions respecting bishops in Belgium. We hear of Jesuits there, though we are told that the pope does not consent to their establishment in countries which are not willing to receive them.[8]

Other anti-catholics rejected the notion of a direct threat from the modern papacy, but held that it was not important whether such a threat were imminent or not. After all, the Pope had been politically powerless at the time of the English Revolution. 'It is asked', said Peel, 'where was the power of the Pope now? He would ask, where was it in 1688?'[9] To such men the point was that the Catholic threat was always liable to recur so long as the papacy retained powers over Catholics which could make it a rival to the authority of the English Crown. The Revolution Settlement must be maintained as a safeguard against emergency.

In pressing these arguments the anti-catholics were fighting a losing battle. They insisted that the Revolution Settlement was permanent and inviolable, and urged hypothetical dangers as a reason for maintaining it. But their opponents argued that the Settlement was transitory and had already been eroded, and that hypothetical dangers could be dismissed. First, the pro-catholics said that anglican exclusionism was not fundamental to the constitution at all. Seen in historical perspective the 130 years since the revolution seemed anomalous. It was pointed out that Elizabeth I had not debarred Catholics from high office. The Test Act of 1678 was dismissed as a panic measure hastily pushed through in a temporary crisis, hardly the kind of measure which could be regarded as a permanent feature of the constitu-

7. Hansard, iv. 1423.   8. Op. cit., v. 317.   9. Op. cit., iv. 1541.

tion.[1] Moreover, instead of remaining fixed since the revolution, the constitution had been both fluid and inconsistent. For many years the Penal Code had been undergoing repeal; Catholic emancipation would be merely the consummation of a liberalizing process and not a revolutionary change.[2] Further, the benefits which the constitution withheld from Catholics it inconsistently granted (through the Annual Indemnity Acts) to dissenters; so that there were admitted to parliament even unitarians, who denied the basic doctrine which Catholics accepted along with all other Christians.[3]

Next, the pro-catholics ridiculed the idea that a papal threat might revive. The Pope, said Sir Francis Burdett, 'was now considered as harmless as any old woman in Christendom'; [4] while W. C. Plunket denied 'that there was a spiritual, or a temporal, or any other jurisdiction on the part of the Pope, with respect to the constitution of the country'.[5] In this situation, argued Horace Twiss, it was futile to continue exclusion. 'If the founders of the constitution had been living now', he asked, 'would not they have been the first to apply that great maxim of all common sense, that the reason for the law ceasing, the law itself ceases also?'[6]

Finally, the pro-catholics were able to dwell on the darkening situation in Ireland. They regarded Catholic emancipation as the infallible remedy for all the Irish maladies—economic, political, and social. However, such beliefs were purely hypothetical and it was not through propaganda of this kind that the cause of emancipation succeeded. It succeeded because it seemed the only way of preventing civil war in Ireland. This was the practical necessity which was eventually responsible for carrying the relief measure in the face of resistance based on tradition and hypothesis.

Thus the anti-catholics had the worst of the arguments concerning the past and present. Were they nearer the mark in their

1. 'Who . . . could say', asked Sir James Mackintosh, 'that such an act was entitled to the weight which ought only to belong to measures deep and well digested for the public welfare?' Hansard, iv. 1006–7.
2. Canning said of the 1821 Relief Bill: 'It was another change in laws which had been continually changing; . . . a crowning measure of mercy to complete the improvements of half a century.' Op. cit., iv. 1543.
3. Speech of Sydney Smith at a meeting of the clergy of the archdeaconry of Cleveland in March 1825; *Works of the Rev. Sydney Smith* (1 vol., London, 1850), p. 549.
4. Op. cit., vii. 1074.   5. Op. cit., iv. 972.   6. Op. cit., iv. 1416.

opinions of what would happen in the future? The pro-catholics had idealistic expectations regarding the effects of emancipation. Sydney Smith firmly believed that emancipation would strengthen the established Church and national security:

My cry is, no Popery; therefore emancipate the Catholics, that they may not join with foreign papists in time of war. Church for ever; therefore emancipate the Catholics, that they may not help to pull it down. King for ever; therefore emancipate the Catholics, that they may become his loyal subjects. Great Britain for ever; therefore emancipate the Catholics, that they may not put an end to its perpetuity.[7]

The anti-catholics, however, had very different ideas about the results of relief. They feared that when admitted to parliament the Irish Catholics would form a large and tightly knit pressure group absorbed in the pursuit of its own ambitions. These ambitions it was thought would certainly include taking over the church establishment for Catholicism, and might well include the eventual severance of political ties with England.[8] Such fears were stimulated especially by the upholders of Protestant Ascendancy in Ireland, such as Lord Redesdale.[9] In opposition to this view it may be argued that disestablishment and national independence would have come earlier if emancipation had been postponed beyond 1829—that the longer emancipation was delayed the likelier were the other events to occur. It was for this reason that the pro-catholics wished to carry emancipation as quickly as possible; and they afterwards deplored the fact that it had not been carried soon enough to prevent the dangers which had been foreseen. 'What all the damned fools said would happen has come to pass', said Lord Melbourne when he surveyed the persistent Irish discontents of the 1830s.[1] The passage of emancipation in 1829 may have done a good deal to postpone the fulfilment of anti-catholic predictions, but the measure was too late to prevent the final realization of these prophecies. Seen

7. *Works*, op. cit., p. 579.
8. For the fears of Peel, for example, see N. Gash, *Mr. Secretary Peel* (London, 1961), pp. 591–2.
9. For the views of the Irish Protestant Ascendancy families see Henriques, op. cit., pp. 139 ff.
1. W. M. Torrens, *Memoirs of Viscount Melbourne* (new ed., London, 1890), p. 234. Melbourne clarified his remark by saying that emancipation was passed 'so tardily and insincerely as to falsify every reasonable anticipation'.

in perspective Catholic emancipation was only one of a series of Irish Catholic advances which later included both disestablishment and national independence, and many pro-catholics would not have agreed with either of these. But it would be unrealistic to emphasize later events when considering the problems of the 1820s. The statesmen of that era were faced with present dangers, beside which possible developments in the future seemed remote and unimportant.

CHAPTER II

THE CATHOLIC QUESTION, 1820 TO 1823

THE political atmosphere of 1820, the year after the Peterloo 'massacre' and the Six Acts, was not favourable to liberal demands. The Catholic leaders, however, were not particularly depressed. They were encouraged by the fact that in 1819 a pro-catholic motion had been defeated in the Commons by only two votes. O'Connell, moreover, hoped to consolidate the support of the pro-catholic tories by opposing or at least ignoring the question of parliamentary reform. He implied this when he wrote that emancipation could be secured in the next parliamentary session provided that the Catholics confined their efforts exclusively to their own question.[1] Hopes became more serious when, with the death of George III on 29 January, a major obstacle to emancipation was removed. The anti-catholics of course regretted the loss of a champion whose faithful attachment to their principles was in marked contrast to the well-known deceitfulness of his heir, and they feared that the new king might form a ministry of his old friends the whigs. But even if this were George IV's intention, any reshuffle would have to wait until after a general election which statutory law required should be held within six months of a change of sovereign.

In the 1820 election Catholic emancipation figured as one of the fixed principles of the whigs, as Lord Grey asserted that it was.[2] But it was only a subordinate issue in comparison with parliamentary reform, the Six Acts, and reduction of taxation, over which the struggles in the contested constituencies were chiefly fought. It is clear that pro-catholic candidates found their cause extremely embarrassing in view of the anti-catholic feelings of the mass of electors, and they preferred to keep it quiet as far as possible. In the Southwark election Sir Thomas Turton, the tory candidate, insisted that unlike his whig opponents,

1. O'Connell to the O'Connor Don, 21 October 1819; W. J. Fitzpatrick (ed.), *Correspondence of Daniel O'Connell* (2 vols., London, 1888), i. 61.
2. 'To Catholic Emancipation I consider myself so pledged', he wrote to Lord Holland, 'that I could not come in without it.' 18 February 1820; Grey MSS.

Charles Calvert and Sir Robert Wilson, he would never advocate Catholic emancipation; whereupon Calvert and Wilson denied that they had ever pledged themselves to support the question.[3] C. F. Palmer, the whig member for Reading, was notably evasive, saying that he did not know what the claims of the Catholics were at present, since they had not been raised in the last parliamentary session, and could not come to a decision until he did.[4] Certain candidates, moreover, concealed their pro-catholic leanings until safely elected. William Haldimand and T. B. Lennard, two whigs who were challenging the tory seats at Ipswich, declared before the poll that they were devoted to a sacred constitution. So vague a statement could easily have misled voters into thinking that the candidates wanted an exclusively anglican constitution. After they had achieved a narrow victory, however, Haldimand enlarged this devotion to include support of Catholic emancipation.[5] One of the few exceptions to this tale of evasion and concealment took place in the Devonshire election, where the whig candidate, Lord Ebrington, boldly proclaimed his faith in emancipation.[6]

In the election results government losses were neutralized by gains, and it seemed that ministerial strength in parliamentary divisions would not be materially altered. Huskisson's impression was that the ministry had lost nearly all its 'best and steadiest props', and that for these were substituted men of a more malleable kind, inclined to yield to 'the impression they had received at their elections'.[7] If this were true, the prospects for Catholic emancipation were dim, for pro-catholic M.P.s might continue to show as much respect for anti-catholic sentiment as they had done in the election. The Catholics could only hope that the new House of Commons would be more independent of its constituents than was expected.

There remained the question of whether the growing estrangement between the King and his ministers would lead to their replacement by a whig, pro-catholic government. When the affair of Queen Caroline arose it seemed that a whig ministry might grasp power by force rather than through the King's voluntary

3. *The Times*, 9 March 1820.   4. Ibid., 11 March 1820.
5. Ibid., 21 March 1820.   6. Ibid.
7. Huskisson to Charles Arbuthnot, 24 March 1820; Huskisson Papers, B.M. Add. Mss. 38742, f. 7. Quoted by A. Aspinall in his introduction to *The Diary of Henry Hobhouse, 1820–27* (London, 1947), p. vii.

invitation. For throughout 1820 popular hostility, which the whigs encouraged against the King's treatment of his queen, threatened to overturn the Government.[8] The more ambitious and active whigs, such as Brougham and Sir Robert Wilson, were encouraged by the Commons' support of the queen to hope that a coalition of whigs and liberal tories would replace the existing ministry. The older whigs, especially Grey and Holland, at first despised such a project as a visionary dream. But the Government obtained so small a majority on the third reading of the Bill of Pains and Penalties in the Lords that even Grey was impressed. It was now a serious possibility that he might be asked to form a ministry, and he began to consider his party programme, including the part which Catholic emancipation should play in it.

Grey considered himself pledged to emancipation, and in a letter to Sir Robert Wilson he said—rather oddly in view of the recent elections—that it was one of the measures through which a whig ministry might win confidence.[9] The King's attitude to a pro-catholic ministry was sounded by Lord Donoughmore at an audience whose substance was related by George Tierney to Grey on 21 November.[1] Donoughmore told the King that Grey would, if summoned to form a government,

... propose considerable reductions in most Departments both civil and military, & that concessions should be made to the Catholics. The impression made upon D's. mind was that . . . upon the subject of the Catholic Question the K. declared that he would at this moment give no opinion & would only say he was not committed one way or the other. I (Tierney) asked whether D. conceived, from his manner, that the K's. inclination was hostile to the Catholics & he assured me he did not collect from anything that passed that it was so.[2]

Although this interview is interesting in showing that George IV's attitude to the Catholic question was more flexible than that of his father, nothing tangible resulted from it. Canning's resignation from the ministry in December—to avoid, as he thought, being involved in its inevitable fall—was an error of

8. For a detailed account of this crisis see A. Aspinall, *Lord Brougham and the Whig Party* (Manchester, 1927), pp. 99–120.
9. 5 December 1820; quoted in Aspinall, *Brougham*, p. 115.
1. Grey MSS.   2. Ibid.

judgement. The 'queen's business' died away and the Government was left in the saddle.

Nevertheless, the crisis had revealed the high value which the whigs placed on Catholic emancipation as a plank in their platform. This was again exemplified in their attitude to W. C. Plunket, the Irish lawyer who had succeeded to the position of parliamentary champion of Catholic emancipation on Grattan's death in June 1820. Grattan had been a whig, but Plunket was associated with the Grenvilles, who had left the whigs in 1817. The whigs were dismayed that the leadership of one of their favourite causes should pass from a whig to one whom they regarded as an apostate, and they made an effort to regain his allegiance. Plunket made a conclusive declaration that all connexion between himself and Grey was at an end.[3] But Lord Lansdowne still tried to mend the breach in a letter whose reference to Ireland leaves no doubt of the importance which the whigs set on having the pro-catholic leader in their camp.[4] He wrote to Plunket that in conversation with Grey he had urged that

. . . under any circumstances that might lead to the formation of a new administration by the individuals connected with the present opposition, it would be most material, with a view to the great national interests, as well as those of Ireland locally considered, that your [Plunket's] asistance and co-operation should be secured; that there was no office to which your public and private character and conduct might not entitle you to look, and that nothing had occurred in the differences which had taken place in the preceding session . . . to prevent a political connexion which might, under such circumstances, become so desirable.[5]

However, as we have seen, the offer to the whigs did not materialize, and so the possibility that Plunket might be lured by office into the whig fold did not arise. In a year's time he had joined the tory government.

Plunket's assumption of Grattan's mantle also caused misgivings among the Irish Catholics. O'Connell was satisfied with Plunket as a champion of the Catholics' civil claims but doubted

3. In a long letter to Sir John Newport, an Irish whig, on 9 January 1821; David Plunket. *The Life, Letters and Speeches of Lord Plunket* (2 vols., London, 1867), i. 394–406.
4. Lansdowne to Plunket, 24 January 1821; Plunket, i. 406–9.
5. Ibid.

his suitability when it came to legislating for the Irish Catholic Church. He disliked Plunket's attachment to the Veto and other securities and accused him of entertaining 'conscientious objections to the allowing our ecclesiastical discipline to remain in its present state'.[6] Plunket on his side disliked O'Connell's extremism, fearing that he might ally with popular radicals and thereby alienate the pro-catholic tories.[7]

Thus the new parliamentary pro-catholic leader was distrusted by the whigs, hitherto the most dependable supporters of Catholic emancipation, and by O'Connell and the ultramontane Catholics who commanded a majority of Irish opinion. This was a further misfortune for the Catholics, who were already disappointed with the election results and the failure of a whig pro-catholic government to replace the 'open' system. It seemed therefore that the prospects for a pro-catholic motion which Plunket planned to bring forward in February 1821 were none too hopeful. On the other hand, George IV was planning a visit to Ireland later that year, and it was suspected that he would not be averse to encouraging Catholic emancipation in order to conciliate the Irish. Lord Liverpool, moreover, was supposed to have made some remarks favourable to Catholic relief.[8]

On 28 February Plunket brought forward his motion for a committee to consider the Catholic claims. He introduced it with a speech which Peel, his chief opponent in the debate, described over twenty years later as 'nearly the highest in point of ability of any ever heard in this House'.[9] Examining the topic from three standpoints—religious, constitutional, and political—he claimed in each case that concession was irresistible. The religious argument, he claimed, had been conceded already, since even anglican prelates had admitted that Catholics could not be excluded purely for their religious beliefs, so long as these beliefs were not

---

6. O'Connell to F. W. Conway, 17 June 1820; Fitzpatrick, *O'Connell*, i. 66–69. For an explanation of the Veto, see above, p. 13.

7. Plunket complained to Newport in his letter of 9 January 1821, op. cit.) that O'Connell had tried 'to involve the Roman Catholics in the Queen's question, and . . . to urge them towards revolutionary movements, and to abandon all applicaton to Parliament'.

8. The Marquess of Buckingham wrote to his cousin: 'The King's anxiety to go to Ireland immediately, and certain expressions lately dropt by Lord Liverpool induce many to believe that the ministers are not disinclined to wish the question carried.' Buckingham to Henry Wynn, 27 February 1821 (first letter); Williams Wynn MSS.

9. Plunket, ii. 16–17.

made a motive for intolerant or subversive action.[1] The argument
that exclusion of Catholics was fundamental to the constitution
he rejected on the historical grounds that the penal laws had
been designed to withstand specific dangers which were no longer
in existence.[2] As a matter of policy, Plunket declared that emancipation would remove Catholic hostility to the Government and
the established Church. The acceptability of this view depended
on whether the Catholics would guarantee not to subvert the
existing system. To this end Plunket proposed that two securities should accompany relief. One was that the State should
have knowledge of all correspondence between Catholics in the
United Kingdom and Catholics abroad, and the other was the
Veto. The latter security ultimately helped to wreck the pro-
catholic effort of 1821. But for the moment optimism reigned, for
Plunket's motion passed by a majority of six.

A comparison of this division with others in the 1820 Parliament amply shows the heterogeneous nature of party politics at
this period. Plunket's motion had the support of many whigs,
but also of many tories who did not support the usual whig
motions such as those favouring Queen Caroline or those advancing parliamentary reform. If the division on Plunket's
motion is compared with the whig Lord Tavistock's motion
favouring the queen (6 February 1821), it is found that 120
M.P.s voted in favour of both, and these comprised the majority
of the whigs; sixty-six, being pro-catholic tories, voted for
Plunket but against Tavistock; and 177, being anti-catholic tories,
voted against both motions. In addition there was a small
group of twelve whigs who supported Tavistock but opposed
Plunket, being for various reasons unable to vote with their
pro-catholic fellows.[3] A similar picture emerges when Plunket's
division is compared with the vote on Lord John Russell's parliamentary reform motion on 9 May 1821. On this occasion, however, the situation was further complicated by the fact that
Russell was supported by two tories who had opposed both
Plunket's and Tavistock's motions—ultra-tories, that is, who

---

1. Hansard, iv. 965.
2. Ibid., 970 ff.
3. These whigs were: T. H. H. Davies (member for Worcester), W. Dickinson (Somerset), G. P. Jervoice (Hants.), J. H. Langston (Woodstock), Sir W.
Lemon, Bt. (Cornwall), J. Maberly (Abingdon), W. Rickford (Aylesbury), A.
Robarts (Maidstone), Samuel Smith (Wendover), Lord C. V. F. Townshend
(Tamworth), E. Webb (Gloucester), and Henry Bright (Bristol).

favoured parliamentary reform.[4] Persistent deviation of this
kind well merits the conclusion that it was individual issues
rather than party labels which divided politicians at this time.

Plunket had obtained the first pro-catholic majority since
1813. This was a surprise to many, and not least to Plunket himself, who had prepared no detailed relief measure beforehand.[5]
The pro-catholics were optimistic. After the victory Lord Grenville wrote a long letter to the King trying to win his support for
the Catholic cause. Plunket's success, he claimed, had convinced
the public that emancipation was inevitable. George III's conscience was no longer an obstacle, and George IV should seize
the opportunity provided by Plunket's victory to proclaim his
support of emancipation, thereby earning the undying gratitude
of the Irish.[6] The royal reply was brief and non-committal.[7]
Nevertheless, rumour had it that the King was favourable to the
Catholics. It was said that he had not used his personal influence
to secure anti-catholic votes as had been done on previous
occasions.[8]

Soon, however, opposition did arise to Plunket's relief measure,
and it came from the Catholics themselves. Early in March a
pro-catholic committee proposed two bills for consideration in
parliament. The first was a general relief measure, seeking to
modify the Oath of Supremacy by including an 'explanation' of
its terms in order that the Catholics might take it with an easy
conscience.[9] The second bill comprised the two proposed securities. Each security was to be enforced by a commission: one was
to certify the loyalty of all newly appointed Catholic bishops and
deans, and the other was to examine all communications from
Rome. Thus in each bill there was room for the old Catholic
objections, and the Catholics reacted according to their degree

4. These were Sir Charles Burrell, Bt. (New Shoreham), and William Hey-
gate (Sudbury).
5. Diary of Henry Hobhouse, 11 April 1821; ed. Aspinall, op. cit., p. 53.
6. Grenville to the King, 8 March 1821; A. Aspinall (ed.), *The Letters of
George IV* (3 vols., Cambridge, 1938), ii. 419–21.
7. Ibid., ii. 422.
8. Countess Cowper to the Hon. Frederick Lamb, 13 March 1821; Mabell,
Countess of Airlie, *Lady Palmerston and her Times* (2 vols., London, 1922),
i. 85–86. See also the diary of John Cam Hobhouse, 11 March 1821; Ld.
Broughton, *Recollections*, ii. 142.
9. The object was to minimize the denial of the Pope's spiritual authority
which was demanded in the original Elizabethan oath.

of militancy. The English lay Catholics, ever the most amenable, were ready to accept all the proposals. But Dr. Poynter, spokesman of the English Catholic clergy, was highly dubious about the 'explanation' of the Supremacy Oath. He did not approve it until Plunket had made considerable alterations, and even then he only acquiesced in order to give official religious backing to the English Catholics who accepted the clause.[1] From the ultramontane Dr. Milner came a complete refutation of both bills. He published a pamphlet censuring the 'explanation' clause and the securities[2] and organized a petition against the bill from the Catholics of his own Midland province.

The pro-catholics were dismayed at this revival of the dispute which had ruined their chances in 1813. They now had a majority in the Commons, as they had eight years earlier, and they feared that this advantage would be ruined once more by a quarrel between vetoists and anti-vetoists. It is no surprise, therefore, that Milner was bitterly condemned by Plunket and the pro-catholic Press. One thing was lacking, however, to complete the pattern of 1813, and that was a unified body of Irish opinion in Milner's support. The leading clerics, whose moving spirit was James Doyle, Bishop of Kildare and Leighlin, did not exactly approve of the securities yet did not preach outright hostility. They sought to effect a compromise by getting their parliamentary friends to amend the securities before they were debated in the Lords. The views of these moderate clerics were reflected in the resolutions of the Dublin clergy passed on 26 March, which welcomed the Relief Bill and its modified Supremacy Oath, but mildly disapproved of the securities and expressed the hope that they would soon be modified. Soon, however, harsher anti-vetoist sentiments appeared among the provincial priests. The resolutions of the clergy of Limerick, Tuam, and Waterford breathed a spirit of hostility to the bills which was extremely embarrassing to Doyle. If Milner should find a large following for his views in Ireland, Doyle thought that 'our cause is not only lost this session, but probably will make no progress

1. 'I threw myself', he wrote, 'with an official approbation of the Oath amongst them, as a life-boat to save them.' Poynter to Edward Jerningham, 5 April 1821; B. Ward, *The Eve of Catholic Emancipation* (3 vols., London, 1911), iii. 60.
2. *The Theological Judgement of the Divines of the Midland District*, dated 13 March 1821.

for several years to come'.[3] The opinion of Catholic lay leaders was also divided over the bills. O'Connell issued an address welcoming the Relief Bill but roundly condemning the securities; while Richard Sheil, another prominent lay leader, could not find enough praise for either bill.

The anti-vetoist Irish Catholics found sympathizers in the whig family of Hutchinson, whose head was Lord Donoughmore. A member of this family, the Hon. Christopher Hely-Hutchinson (M.P. for Cork City), brought their demands into the Commons where he championed the views of the extreme Catholic clergy. It was thought that this onslaught might have 'sunk the whole concern'.[4] However, several other pro-catholic Irish members opposed Hutchinson, saying that most Irish Catholics were willing to accept the securities. Although this was not the end of the matter, disagreement no longer prevented the progress of the bills in the Commons. The second reading passed by eleven votes, the individual clauses were all carried in committee, and the third reading was carried by nineteen votes on 2 April.

Meanwhile pro-catholic progress was alarming the ultras. They seem to have feared that the Government might yield to the pressure and concede emancipation. On 22 March the ultra Duke of Newcastle published a pamphlet against the bills in the form of a letter to Lord Liverpool.[5] For two reasons, he wrote, encouragement of Catholic relief was an injustice to the nation. First, the country was preoccupied with its own domestic problems and consequently had little interest in the Catholic question; if the Government took it unawares and conceded emancipation this would amount to a betrayal. Secondly, Newcastle held that the 'open' system of government neutrality was unconstitutional, and supported this claim with the following reasoning. If a relief bill passed both Houses, the King would be compelled to withhold his assent by his Coronation Oath, which bound him to uphold a Protestant constitution. If the King were to do this alone, without the advice of his ministers, it would be an unconstitutional act, since the constitution only recognized acts

3. Doyle to Sir Henry Parnell, 30 March 1821; W. J. Fitzpatrick, *The Life, Times and Correspondence of Dr. Doyle* (2 vols., new ed., Dublin, 1880), i. 158–9.

4. Dr. Phillimore, one of the Grenville party, to Buckingham, 29 March 1821; Second Duke of Buckingham (ed.), *Memoirs of the Court of George IV* (2 vols., London, 1859), i. 145–6.

5. An original draft of this pamphlet is in the Newcastle MSS.

which the King undertook after ministerial advice. With the present neutrality system, however, the ministers had no co-ordinate advice to offer on the Catholic question. In order to preserve constitutional consistency it was necessary both that the ministers should be able to offer co-ordinate advice on this question, and (in order to coincide with the Coronation Oath) that this advice should be of an anti-catholic nature. In other words, the ministers must abandon the 'open' system and unanimously declare themselves against emancipation.

Newcastle's tendentious philosophizing was out of touch with reality. In actual fact he could trust the anti-catholic integrity neither of Liverpool nor the King. Liverpool, thinking it possible that the Lords might not resist the bills, suggested to Lord Sidmouth that the anti-catholic ministers should try and amend them as much as possible and finally allow them to pass.[6] He even advised the King not to commit himself to any declaration on the matter at this stage. At Liverpool's bidding Charles Arbuthnot wrote to Sir Benjamin Bloomfield, Keeper of the Privy Purse and confidant of the King, saying:

... he [Liverpool] is aware that there is an increasing spirit in favour of the Catholics, and he is therefore most anxious for the sake of the King's own quiet that His Majesty should not be prevailed upon to commit himself in any way upon the subject. If the Bill should pass both Houses, it would ... save His Majesty from much embarrassment if he should be able to look at the question quite calmly, and without its being possible for anyone to quote His Majesty's private sentiments and opinions, whatever they may be.[7]

The King appears to have vacillated for a time, but he was kept on anti-catholic lines by the strong ultra influence of the Duke of York.[8] Similarly, Sidmouth's anti-catholic resolution persuaded Liverpool to remain firm.[9] Nevertheless, the ultras' suspicions had been aroused, and this made them doubly determined to throw out the bills (which had now been amalgamated into one) when introduced into the Lords. Lord Kenyon, an ultra peer, wrote at this time that he trusted for protection to 'a higher power than the King'.[1]

6. *Diary of Henry Hobhouse*, pp. 54–55.
7. 29 March 1821; *Geo. IV Letters*, ii. 424–5.
8. *Diary of Henry Hobhouse*, p. 55.
9. Ibid.
1. Lord Kenyon to his aunt, 9 April 1821; Kenyon Papers.

Before the bill was debated in the Lords, a last effort was made to modify the securities through negotiation between the leading Irish Catholic clerics and prominent pro-catholic peers. This was unsuccessful, and the advocates of the bill decided that the anti-vetoist desires of the Irish Catholics must be granted. Lord Donoughmore opened the Lords' debate on 16 April with a speech condemning all the proposed securities as an insult to the Catholic clergy; and Lord Grenville, who had previously advocated securities, also implied that he now held this opinion. But this last-minute reconciliation of differences could not prevent the pro-catholics' defeat. After Lord Chancellor Eldon had given a classic exposition of the anti-catholic case the Lords threw out the bill by thirty-nine votes. Liverpool had now ceased vacillating and spoke warmly against the bill. Even more effective was the anti-catholic speech of the Duke of York, since he was expected to outlive George IV and provide England with a thoroughly anti-catholic monarch. Eldon wrote that York had 'done more to quiet this matter than everything else put together'.[2]

Despite its failure the pro-catholic effort of 1821 was in some ways a landmark in the history of the question. It was the last occasion when quarrels over the Veto played a prominent part in the struggle, and it was the first time that several recurring features of the question appeared. It set the pattern for the 1820s of a small pro-catholic majority in the Commons whose wishes were rejected by a large anti-catholic majority in the Lords. The pro-catholics might persuade themselves that their majority in the Commons made eventual triumph inevitable, but the Lords continued to reject relief by consistently large majorities until 1829. Other features of the 1821 struggle were repeated in later years. The voice of the ultras was heard in Newcastle's pamphlet, and it was to be raised much louder before Catholic emancipation was passed. Moreover, Liverpool's anti-catholic scruples had been shaken, and even though he had spoken against the bill the ultras could trust him no longer. 'He will not stir a step [against Catholic relief] beyond pronouncing in words his speech', wrote Eldon.[3] Lastly, the influence of the Duke of York continued to be felt until his death in 1827. The 1821 defeat also owed something to the Irish situation. Instead of being

2. Eldon to Sir William Scott, April 1821; Twiss, ii. 416.
3. Eldon to Sir W. Scott, 27 April 1821; op. cit., ii. 418.

united, the Irish Catholics were deeply divided over the Veto. Until they could present a unanimous and forceful front it was unlikely that their cause would succeed.

The pro-catholic effort had failed, but its strength had impressed the Government. Plunket had attracted their attention with his greatly enhanced reputation. As a Grenville he was a member of a floating body which might return to the whig fold whence it came, and to avoid this danger Liverpool hoped to bring Plunket and his fellow-Grenvilles into the Government. This accompanied similar approaches to Canning and Peel, prominent tories who were then out of office. Their attachment would strengthen the Government, particularly in the Commons, and rescue it from the unpopularity caused by the 'queen's business' and a coercive home policy.

This idea had also occurred to the King, and perhaps helps to explain his conciliatory attitude to the Catholics and to Plunket when he visited Ireland in August 1821. Although royal gestures were abundant and were received loyally by the Catholic leaders, no promises of relief accompanied them. Nevertheless, the pro-catholics were optimistic about the outcome,[4] and the visit left a deep impression on Ireland. The more sentimental Irish Catholics were left with the false conviction that their emancipation was the King's personal desire. The ultras, on their side, were alarmed at the King's apparent encouragement of the Catholic claims. Eldon thought that unless some explanation for the King's attitude were given the Government could not go on. 'I understand', he went on, 'the King was particular and lavish in his attentions to Plunkett [sic]; he certainly means, if he can, to bring him into office—another Papist.'[5]

Liverpool had already shown his desire to liberalize the Irish Government. In July he wanted to remove Saurin, the Irish Attorney-General and a noted anti-catholic bigot, in order to give his office to Plunket. But Talbot, the anti-catholic Lord Lieutenant, opposed any such change, and it was clear that as long as Talbot held office any infiltration of pro-catholics into the Government would be difficult to effect. Events came to Liverpool's aid. Disturbances broke out in Ireland in November and

4. Frederick Ponsonby wrote to Viscount Milton that the King had 'given a blow to the Orange faction from which . . . it will not easily recover'; 3 September 1821 (Fitzwilliam MSS.).

5. Eldon to Lord Stowell, August 1821; Twiss, ii. 435.

revealed a deep division in the Irish Government. Talbot wished to enforce the Insurrection Act against the rioters, but this was opposed by Charles Grant, the pro-catholic Chief Secretary, who thought it would offend the Catholics. On account of the dissensions between Grant and his anti-catholic colleagues and the increasing disturbances in Ireland, the Cabinet decided to change the whole Irish Government. Both Talbot and Grant were dismissed; Wellesley, a pro-catholic, was appointed Lord Lieutenant, and Henry Goulburn, an anti-catholic, was appointed Chief Secretary. Thus the balance of power between pro- and anti-catholic was nominally maintained. But the ultras disliked the arrangement because they thought that Wellesley would dominate Goulburn. Moreover, Liverpool still intended to give office to Plunket and the Grenvilles, and this was a further irritation to the anti-catholics.

In considering Liverpool's advances the Grenvilles were beset by conflicting views. If they joined the Government they would lose much of their effectiveness as pro-catholics, for they would have to conform to the 'open' system. They might, of course, persuade themselves that they could do more to influence the carrying of Catholic emancipation if they were in the Government than if they remained outside it; but this argument would not convince the whigs, who derided all pro-catholics who yielded to the 'open' system. The final negotiations between Liverpool and the Grenvilles took place at the end of 1821. Liverpool offered to make Plunket Attorney-General for Ireland and to give an office with Cabinet status to Charles Wynn, a leading Grenville. The Marquess of Buckingham, virtual leader of the Grenvilles, was anxious to lead his followers into the Government camp because he coveted office and a dukedom for himself. He praised the appointment of the pro-catholic Wellesley and the approach to Plunket. But Lord Grenville, Buckingham's uncle, was not anxious for office and remained sceptical about the recent changes. Wellesley's appointment, he thought, would be neutralized by the anti-catholic appointments. For Goulburn was to be Chief Secretary for Ireland, Peel Home Secretary, and Sidmouth, whom Peel replaced, was to remain in the Cabinet without portfolio. Well might Grenville write: 'Charles [Wynn] is to go alone into the Cabinet at the very moment that is studiously chosen for making it more orange in its complexion *than it was before.*' [6]

The Grenvilles' objections to Sidmouth and Goulburn were raised in discussions with Cabinet ministers. The Marquess of Londonderry (formerly Lord Castlereagh) did his best to reduce their objections to Sidmouth by saying that, though himself a pro-catholic, he had been more anxious than anyone to retain Sidmouth in the Cabinet:

... as long as the Government was constituted upon its present principle ... I attach very little importance whether the votes in Cabinet were equal on the [Catholic] question, or on which side they preponderated; that the members of it should be selected with a view to the efficient administration of the counry in matters on which we could agree, and not with reference to a question on which it was notorious we could not.[7]

The upshot was that the Grenvilles agreed to enter the Government but made certain reservations about their pro-catholic principles. In a letter to Liverpool, Charles Wynn made three demands. He required the fullest liberty not only to support but to originate a measure of Catholic emancipation in Parliament or Cabinet. He declared that, as 'the hope of contributing to the success of this measure had been my principal inducement to accept office', he would immediately give up his post if he thought such a step would be more helpful to the cause than staying in the Government. Finally he stated that whereas the appointments of Wellesley and Plunket were his main encouragement to join the Government, he must if necessary disavow that he had any connexion with the appointment of Goulburn. It was clear that the Grenvilles only advanced these reservations to save their faces.[8] Liverpool, in consequence, readily accepted them. The actual distribution of offices was delayed, since Liverpool wanted to have Plunket's appointment settled and he thought that this would be hastened if he could say that the whole matter of the Grenville connexion must be suspended until

6. Grenville to Buckingham, 4 December 1821; Buckingham's *Memoirs,* op. cit., i. 243.

7. Londonderry to Liverpool, 6 December 1821; C. D. Yonge, *The Life and Administration of the Second Earl of Liverpool* (3 vols., London, 1868), iii. 160–2.

8. As Londonderry put it: 'In order to satisfy their principles of consistency, they will make the reserves which past opinions require.' Ibid.

Plunket had secured office. Saurin proved difficult to eject from the Attorney-Generalship and it was not until January that the appointment of Plunket and of the other Grenvilles was made official. Charles Wynn replaced an anti-catholic as Secretary to the Board of Control, so the pro-catholics gained one Cabinet place. The anti-catholics retained the same strength in the Cabinet, for Peel joined it, and the composition of the Cabinet was now 8:6 in favour of the anti-catholics. Through the Grenville connexion the Government also gained the support of several pro-catholics in the Commons, the outstanding acquisition being Plunket.

The junction with the Grenvilles aroused the anger of all other political groups. Among the tories Wellington, Londonderry, and Charles Arbuthnot were all, according to Mrs. Arbuthnot, indignant at the Grenvilles' pretentiousness.[9] But there was at least the appointment of Peel to alleviate their indignation. The whigs had no such compensation. They were disappointed that the Government was strengthened and that the 'open' system had acquired new support. The pro-catholic reservations made by Charles Wynn were ridiculed. Grey regarded them as 'mere hypocrisy'.[1] Indeed, it appeared that the Catholic cause was being drawn ever further from the grasp of the whigs and was coming to rest within the comfortable bounds of the Government, where its champions, lulled by office, would be content to let the conditions of stalemate continue. From this standpoint it seemed that Wellesley and the Grenvilles had decided to abandon their support of the Catholic claims. On the other hand it might be said that they could advance the Catholic cause by taking office, even if only in a tentative and indirect manner. In Ireland, Wellesley and Plunket could strive by impartial administration to allay the Orange-Catholic conflict; while at home the Grenvilles might hope to infiltrate their principles into the Government. For all this the Grenvilles were henceforth useless as pro-catholic champions. They lost the respect of the whigs, as did all pro-catholic tories who joined the Government, and as ministers the only pro-catholic action they took was to raise an occasional protest against the behaviour of their anti-catholic colleagues.

9. *Journal of Mrs. Arbuthnot*, i. 132–3.
1. Grey to Holland, 30 December 1821; Grey MSS.

The opinion of the whigs was vindicated by the attitude of Wellesley and Plunket in their new offices. Wellesley proceeded to deal with the Irish disturbances in the old coercive way. The whigs thought that these disturbances had made emancipation more pressing, but Plunket considered that to bring forward a Catholic motion in the 1822 session would be ruinous. He repeated this opinion when, on 29 March, Canning gave notice of his intention to introduce a motion for allowing Catholic peers to sit again in the House of Lords.[2] Plunket's conduct was condemned at a whig dinner-party, and Henry Fox wrote: 'Plunket has quite fallen this year, and has behaved most shabbily in a true *Hibernian* manner.'[3] But Plunket was not the only procatholic to urge deferment of the question. Lord Grenville said that the differences over securities which had marred the 1821 Bill must be ironed out before the matter was brought forward again. A pause was necessary while an effort at compromise was made. But, lest undue delay should place the initiative in more extreme pro-catholic hands, clear notice should be given of an intention to move emancipation next session. In the meantime, Grenville approved of Canning's motion concerning Catholic peers since this would help to keep the question alive.[4]

Canning introduced his Catholic Peers' Bill on 30 April. He said that such a measure was bound to benefit the main issue since it would reduce the number of obstacles to be overcome.[5] Peel replied that Canning's idea of partial reform would increase the anomalies in the law rather than abolish them, that such a measure could scarcely effect that pacification of Ireland which so many expected from Catholic emancipation, or please those who supported emancipation as part of the broad question of individual liberty.[6] The whigs were certainly not very enthusiastic about this partial measure, and besides this they distrusted Canning. However, instead of the substantial decrease in procatholic votes which was expected, a majority of five carried the motion in the Commons. Following the previous pattern, it was defeated by forty-two votes in the Lords.

2. Hansard, vi. 1389–90.
3. *Journal of Henry Fox*, 19 June 1822; ed. Sixth Earl of Ilchester (London, 1923), p. 126.
4. Grenville to Sir John Newport, 14 April 1822; Plunket, ii. 100–2.
5. Hansard, vi. 211–45.
6. Ibid., 246–60.

Lord Londonderry's suicide in August 1822 brought fresh alterations in the Government. The anti-catholics wished that his successor as Leader of the Commons should be one of their own kind. The ultra Newcastle told Liverpool that he wanted a Leader who would 'undeviatingly oppose all Roman Catholic innovations',[7] and in a letter to Eldon he made another onslaught on the 'open' system: 'I wish for a Ministry composed of persons thinking alike on all great and constitutional questions, especially on the Roman Catholic question. . . . At present no one knows what to do, the principles of the administration are not known on account of their mixed nature.'[8]

The ultras wanted Peel as the new Leader. But his appointment would have upset the delicate balance in the Government; in the Cabinet's view, a person of Londonderry's pro-catholic opinions was more desirable, and the obvious choice was Canning. There were also more compelling reasons for appointing Canning. These were summarized by J. W. Croker in a long letter to Peel on 25 August.[9] If he were not given office Canning might form a powerful opposition group. Croker calculated that in the Commons he could count on the support of 'all the dissatisfied of all sides', and would be 'at the head of the most powerful floating party which has existed for near a century . . . I do not think I underrate their probable amount when I state them at 40'. This was a much more formidable combination than the Grenville party, and the Government would neglect it at their peril. It could form the nucleus of an opposition which might attract both Wellesley and the Grenvilles, or Canning might join the whigs and make the Catholic question an issue whereby the Government would stand or fall. These fears, however, proved groundless. Canning was quite ready to join the Government and was even prepared to compromise his views on Catholic emancipation. Charles Wynn summarized, as follows, a conversation he had with Canning on this point:

He dwelt so much on the disposition of the Duke of York, if he succeeded to the throne, to stake his Crown entirely upon opposition to [the Catholic claims], and talked so much on the advantages of a compromise, which should secure [for the Catholics] everything

7. Newcastle to Liverpool, 16 August 1822; published in Newcastle's *Thoughts in Times Past* (London, 1837), pp. 10–12.
8. 18 August 1822; ibid., pp. 13–14.
9. L. J. Jennings (ed.), *The Croker Papers* (3 vols., London, 1884), ii. 229–32.

except Privy Council and Parliament; professing willingness himself, if that was conceded, to oppose any agitation of the question for a considerable time, that I am myself convinced that he is disposed to consider it as a millstone, to which he is not absolutely pledged, and which he will for his own interest shake from off his neck.[1]

Canning's flexibility on the question was made clear in his public speeches at the end of August. One speech at Liverpool, in particular, in which Canning declared his readiness to accept a 'liberal compromise' on Catholic emancipation, aroused the anger of the whigs and the sarcasm of the *Edinburgh Review*.[2] Grey, Canning's arch-enemy, wrote that his speeches 'shew, at least in an equal degree, a strong desire to take every chance of power at home, by the use of every topic best calculated to recommend him to the powerful Tories, to the ministers & to the Court; even to the extent of an offer of compromise on the Catholick question. And I think he will succeed.'[3] Canning succeeded. In September he became Foreign Secretary and Leader of the House of Commons. It seemed to the whigs that yet another prominent pro-catholic had sacrificed emancipation for office, thus encouraging the policy of stalemate.

The deadlock was first challenged and then strengthened still further by events towards the end of 1822 and their effects in the following year. In November the faction-fights of Orangeman and Catholic in Ireland took an ugly turn. Since the King's visit and the appointment of Wellesley, the Orangemen were convinced that the Catholics were the favoured party, and they unleashed their chagrin in provocative acts. In defiance of a proclamation by the Lord Mayor of Dublin, they made preparations to decorate the statue of William III in that city, to commemorate the defeat of James II. But authority prevailed and the attempt was not made.[4] Responsible anti-catholics in the Government, like Peel and Goulburn, disapproved of all such attempts. But it was otherwise with Manners, Lord Chancellor of Ireland, who disagreed with the Government's refusal to allow the statue to be decorated and was thenceforth at loggerheads with Welles-

---

1. Charles Wynn to Buckingham, n.d.; Buckingham, i. 397.
2. Vol. lxxiv (November 1822), pp. 386–7. For Canning's own view of his compromise, see A. Aspinall, 'Canning's Return to Office in September 1822', *EHR*, lxxviii (1963), p. 543.
3. Grey to Brougham, 5 September 1822; Brougham's *Life and Times* (3 vols., Edinburgh, 1871), ii. 451–4.
4. Goulbourn to Peel, 2 and 4 November 1822; PP, 40328, ff. 166–8, 180–2.

ley. Much more serious was a riot by Orangemen in a Dublin
theatre, when Wellesley was present, on 14 December. Bottles
and 'a large wedge of timber' were thrown at his box.[5] On
account of this Wellesley believed, quite without foundation,
that a systematic plan to murder him was in progress, concerted
by Orangemen. The rioters were committed, with Plunket acting
as prosecuting counsel. Orangemen were furious, and Catholics
exulted. 'Party feeling', it was reported, 'is worked up to the
highest pitch.'[6]

All parties in England disliked Wellesley's action. To the right
of the Government, the ultras condemned Wellesley outright,
ridiculing his accusations against the Orangemen. To the left
of the Government, the whigs lamented the increase of bitter-
ness in Ireland which would retard, as before, discussion of the
Catholic question. Within the Government Wellesley's impetu-
ous behaviour was thought to be utterly out of keeping with the
delicate balance of the 'open' system. The danger of the new
situation was revealed in rumours that the Government would
break up under the strain. In Ireland it seemed that either
Wellesley and the pro-catholics or Manners and the Orangemen
must give way to the other, and it appeared that the corresponding section of the Government in England must also yield. Grey
summarized the probable ramifications in a letter to Lord
Holland :[7]

The state of things in Ireland appears to me ... [a] probable cause
of division. Peel & his friends ... talk without reserve against both
Wellesley & Plunket. .... The Duke of Wellington, tho' not a friend
to the Catholick Question, would probably wish to support his
Brother's [Wellesley's] 'Person & Government', & in this matter he,
Canning & the Grenvilles would naturally be placed in opposition to
the ultra Tory & High Church part of the government. This too
would lead to a state of things in which Canning might look to the
means of strengthening those interests by new connections, & ultimately of forming a new government, if he can carry the King with
him.

The Government, however, survived intact, partly because the
Catholic question was temporarily 'shelved'. In the existing un-
settled conditions, discussion of the question in parliament would

5. *John Bull*, 23 December 1822, quoting the *Irish Freeman's Journal*.
6. Goulburn to Peel, 21 December 1822; PP, 40328, f. 302.
7. 22 January 1823; Grey MSS.

only have exacerbated matters, so the Government postponed it.
This aroused opposition amongst some of the whigs. Many of
them had by this time become so hostile to the Government
pro-catholics that it seemed that when the question was revived
in parliament it could be of no practical effect. On the eve of
renewed parliamentary discussion, in April 1823, it was thought
that the question would be lost through the 'intentional absence'
of its usual supporters, namely the whigs.[8] The causes of this
alienation included all the Government acquisitions of the past
eighteen months. In the cases of Wellesley, the Grenvilles, and
Canning, the whigs argued that prominent pro-catholics had
deserted their principles and that acquiescence in the Catholic
stalemate was incompatible with sincere support of emancipation.
In these circumstances it is not surprising that when the question
was discussed in the Commons on 17 April the debate became
merely an opportunity for the pro-catholics who were 'out' to
charge with treachery those who were 'in'. The accusers and the
accused followed each other, alternately attacking and defend-
ing the conduct of pro-catholic members of the Government.
The debate soon degenerated into an extremely personal affray.
Plunket was openly accused of deception; and Brougham made
a famous attack on Canning, described his taking office (and
thus, as Brougham thought, sacrificing the Catholic question) as
'the most incredible specimen of monstrous truckling, for the
purpose of obtaining office, that the whole history of political
tergiversation could furnish'.[9]

These recriminatory interchanges ended with a division among
the whig pro-catholics themselves. Jealousy of the pro-catholic
tories had decided the English whigs to withhold their support
from the motion which Plunket was to introduce. The Irish
whigs, however, believed that the Catholic cause was vital to their
country, and one of their number declared that they would continue to debate the question in whatever form it arose, no matter
how few members they could muster.[1] Several of the English
whigs—including Sir Francis Burdett, John Cam Hobhouse, Sir
Robert Wilson, and Thomas Creevey—left the House during the

---

8. Colchester's diary, 11 April 1823; Colchester, iii. 278.
9. Hansard, viii. 1091. Professor Aspinall has ascribed this attack to
Brougham's intense disappointment at the destruction of his hopes of a whig-
Canningite coalition (*Brougham*, p. 130).
1. Speech of T. Spring-Rice; Hansard, viii. 1105–6.

debate. Plunket persisted in delivering the speech he had prepared and in moving for a committee of the whole House to
consider the Catholic claims. But this was a forlorn effort, and
he was forced to abandon his motion through lack of support.

Thus, two years after Plunket had triumphed in obtaining
the first majority for Catholic emancipation since 1813, his
former supporters had become so divided that it was pointless
to press his motion in the Commons. This showed how far the
prospects of Catholic emancipation had fallen in three parliamentary sessions. A large part of the explanation for this phe-
nomenon is the fact that in 1823 Plunket was in the Government,
whereas in 1821 he was outside it. When Catholic relief was
introduced by a member of the Government all the scorn of a
frustrated opposition was unleashed against the 'open' system. In
the eyes of the whigs this system was not so much an 'open' one
as one of paralysis. All the prominent pro-catholics who joined
the Government between 1821 and 1823 were bound to accept the
stalemate, despite protestations that their support of emancipation was as strong as ever. They entered the Government at the
price of weakening their principles, and a great deal of their
influence as pro-catholic leaders vanished when they took office.
They became targets for the abuse of the whigs who, sharing
the same pro-catholic views, remained free and uncommitted.

The tory pro-catholics could argue that the administration
gained in stability and the country in leadership from their
accession to office. Indeed, while the Catholic question could
be subordinated to other matters of statecraft these politicians
were perhaps justified in acting as they did. And at this time it
seemed that not even in Ireland was Catholic emancipation regarded as a matter of vital importance. There was no great
popular demand of sufficient pressure to challenge the 'open'
system. Until this appeared it seemed that the Catholic question
must remain dormant.

CHAPTER III

THE CATHOLIC ASSOCIATION
AND THE CRISIS OF 1825

THE decline in the prospects of Catholic emancipation brought a sullen despondency to the Irish Catholics, but soon this mood gave way to one of fresh hope and renewed determination. At a meeting of O'Connell and R. L. Sheil in the spring of 1823 a scheme for a new association was suggested. The plan was unanimously approved at an aggregate meeting of Irish Catholics, and soon the new body was provided with a constitution and an annual subscription. Thus was established the Catholic Association, a body which in its six years of existence was greatly to influence English politics and eventually persuade the Government that Catholic emancipation could no longer be withheld. But at first the Irish themselves regarded it with indifference, and its early meetings were ill-attended. Not until the end of 1824 was it seriously noticed by English politicians. Until then the Catholic cause remained in the doldrums. The division between whig and Government pro-catholics, so clearly revealed in 1823, meant that there was no parliamentary discussion of the full question in the following year. Canning clearly stated in 1824 that he would not consider joining the whigs to form a pro-catholic ministry. In a letter to Plunket he blamed the Opposition for the situation, because in 1823 they had separated themselves from the Government pro-catholics and made the question a party one. Because of this he thought that Catholic emancipation was now as little likely to succeed as parliamentary reform.[1]

The Catholics, however, were not completely ignored at this time. Partial measures for relief were introduced in 1823 and 1824. The chief of these was Lord Nugent's motion to give certain benefits to the British (as opposed to the Irish) Catholics. The British Catholics had not been granted the same concessions as the Irish, since they were far less numerous and far less of a

1. 27 December 1823; Plunket, ii. 142-4.

menace to the Government. They had not been included, for example, in the benefits of the Franchise Act of 1793. Nugent now proposed to give them the parliamentary franchise and the same eligibility for civil office as the Irish Catholics. Introducing his motion on 28 May 1823, he argued that privileges which the Irish Catholics had been given in 1793 in an attempt to stop them allying with the French could not justly be withheld from British Catholics whose demeanour had been constantly loyal and peaceable. Moreover he pointed out that, although Catholics could not vote in parliamentary elections, some of them had parliamentary seats in their pockets;[2] and although they were not legally allowed to vote in elections, they sometimes did so through the indulgence of election officers who did not administer the Supremacy Oath.[3]

The debates on Nugent's motion revealed a growing rift between the anti-catholics within the Government and the ultras outside it. Liverpool and Peel were ready, on certain conditions, to acquiesce in Nugent's plan, perhaps because they wished to placate the new pro-catholic members of the Government.[4] Peel agreed to the measure, provided that it was divided into two—one bill to deal with the elective franchise (with which he was satisfied) and the other to concern offices, in which he wanted the Supremacy Oath to be included. On the other hand, several ultras flatly opposed the Elective Franchise Bill in the Commons. The bill passed that House by fifty-nine votes on 30 June; in the Lords it was supported by Liverpool and Westmorland, opposed by the ultras, and defeated by seven votes.

Lansdowne had deferred the second bill (concerning civil office) until the next session, and in May 1824 he took the opportunity to bring up both measures once more. Again there was a division between the ultras and the Government anti-catholics. Liverpool and Westmorland supported both bills, while emphasizing that this did not alter their resistance to the larger question of emancipation. The main ultra speech was that of Colchester,

2. Hansard, ix. 579–80. The Catholic Duke of Norfolk influenced the return of eleven members in 1816; this shows the contrast between the unprivileged legal position of the English Catholics and the political power which they sometimes wielded. A. Aspinall and E. A. Smith (eds.), *English Historical Documents*, vol. XI (London, 1959), p. 225.

3. Op. cit., ix. 580–1.

4. This suggestion is made by Halévy, *Hist Eng. People*, ii. (second ed., London, 1949), p. 220.

who insisted that partial measures like these were insidious approaches to gaining the full question.[5] The Elective Franchise Bill was lost by thirty-eight votes and the bill concerning offices by thirty-four. But the anti-catholics had agreed that one Catholic, the Duke of Norfolk, should be allowed to perform his office of Earl-Marshal in person, instead of by deputy as hitherto. The Earl-Marshal's Bill which followed was very much a formality. Its second reading passed by twenty-four votes to ten; and the King, having been assured that no disadvantage to the anti-catholic cause would result, gave his assent. But this did not prevent two ultra peers, Newcastle and the Earl of Abingdon, from entering a protest. They said that the constitution would be violated by allowing a Catholic to dispense with the Supremacy Oath and to hold high office near the King. They further complained that the division had taken place at a late period of the session and at an awkward time of day, so that many peers were absent and the House was taken unawares. Eldon, however, gave his judicial opinion against the protest, and it was withdrawn.[6]

The Catholic debates of 1823 and 1824 thus showed a distinction between the anti-catholic ministers who temporarily unbent to support partial concessions, and the ultras who were adamant in their opposition to all concessions—a division analogous to that between the Government pro-catholics and the whig opposition. Moreover, when the question became one of merely allowing a single Catholic to perform his office, there was a division among the ultras themselves. Eldon and Colchester were willing to allow this concession, whereas Newcastle remained inflexibly against it. Consequently, the extreme 'no-popery' man who was against any concession to the Catholics might regard Newcastle as his champion rather than Peel or even Eldon. Already there were vague signs of combination between the extra-governmental ultra peers, and perhaps they were already beginning to regard themselves as leaders of anti-catholic public opinion.

Wellesley as Lord Lieutenant was struggling to improve the condition of Ireland, and towards the end of 1824 he could report

5. Hansard, xi. 823–9.
6. Ibid., xi. 1484–92. Eldon stated that 'after a bill had once passed the sense of the House must be considered as having been distinctly pronounced upon it'.

a considerable lessening of disturbances and an increase in efficient government. He would have liked to complete his work by making far-reaching concessions to the Catholics, but he was prevented from doing this by the Government at home and by the anti-catholics in his own administration. Thus the rumbling discontent of the Irish Catholics grew in volume. Parallel to the enhancement of public order and national prosperity ran a tremendous expansion of the Catholic Association. The original coterie of devotees had been transformed into a nation-wide movement, and this was mainly due to the inauguration, in February 1824, of the Catholic Rent. This was a levy of a penny a month which all Catholics were urged to subscribe. Priests were used to superintend its collection, and in this way O'Connell gave a strong religious complexion to his political movement.[7] It was said that many Catholics joined the Association because they had given up hope of emancipation being carried in the united parliament.[8] It was thought that they might demand a separate parliament for Ireland, and even that they might want to separate from England altogether. Seen in this light, the struggle seemed basically nationalist. It also seemed basically democratic. The ultra Lord Redesdale thought that, in the event of a popular Irish uprising, the Irish Protestant would suffer because of his religion, the English Catholic because of his nationality, and the aristocratic Irish Catholic because of his property.[9]

These fears were not entirely groundless. Lord Cloncurry, for one, entertained the hope that the Association would seek not merely Catholic emancipation but a repeal of the Union.[1] But this was not the desire of most Catholic leaders. Their immediate object was to obtain emancipation through parliamentary channels, and they wanted to win English opinion for their cause rather than alienate it with a campaign against the Union. Archbishop Curtis, the Catholic primate, assured the Duke of Wellington that the Irish Catholics were thoroughly constitutional in their attitude.[2] In the same spirit O'Connell issued an

7. A detailed account of the Catholic Association is given in J. A. Reynolds, *The Catholic Emancipation Crisis in Ireland, 1823–9* (New Haven, 1954).
8. Hansard, xii. 168.
9. Redesdale to Eldon, 31 December 1824 and 11 January 1825; Twiss, ii. 530–2.
1. *Personal Recollections of Lord Cloncurry* (Dublin, 1849), pp. 323–4.
2. Curtis to Wellington, 6 December 1824; WND, ii. 364.

address to the Irish people in December 1824, urging them to abstain from outrages and secret societies.

O'Connell wanted to propagate the Catholic Association's proceedings amongst the English. With this purpose he stimulated English pro-catholic newspapers and encouraged the English Catholics to form associations. Important business of the Catholic Association was inserted in English newspapers at advertisement rates; certain pro-catholic papers received subsidies from the Catholic Rent; and finally there was established the *Truth Teller*, an English paper wholly devoted to the Catholic cause.[3] O'Connell had a London agent, Eneas McDonnell, and one of his duties was to keep an eye on the metropolitan Press. In the provinces perhaps the most devoted pro-catholic newspaper was the *Liverpool Mercury*, which was described as one of the 'unpensioned, unpaid champions of the rights of Irishmen'.[4] The English Catholics began to emulate the Irish association. In June 1823 they founded their own association in London. Towards the end of 1824 branches were being formed amongst the provincial Catholics, largely through the activities of a Catholic barrister named John Rosson, a member of the metropolitan body. There were soon several branches in Lancashire, probably on account of the high proportion of Catholics in that county. Preston led the way with a meeting of 500 Catholics, who set up a committee; and the example was followed at Manchester, Liverpool, Wigan, and Blackburn.[5] By December branches had spread over the Pennines to York, Sheffield, and Pontefract.[6] In the Midlands, on the other hand, there appears to have been only one branch, at Birmingham, to represent the Catholics of four counties.[7]

The aims of the English association were very similar to those of the Irish body. Unlike the old Catholic Board, which had been aristocratic, exclusive, and willing to concede the Veto, the new association was popular, anti-vetoist and anxious for unity with the Irish Catholics. Its objects were to repel any attacks by the anti-catholic Press; to bring to justice anyone who injured the

3. A. Aspinall, *Politics and the Press* (London, 1949), pp. 321–4.
4. Quotation from the *Belfast Irishman* in the *Liverpool Mercury* of 17 December 1824.
5. *Preston Chronicle*, 18 September 1824; *Liverpool Mercury*, 8 October, 1824.
6. *The Times*, 4 December 1824.
7. *Birmingham Chronicle*, 25 November 1824.

persons or property of Catholic clergy; and to support the publication of pro-catholic pamphlets and the petitioning of Parliament.[8] The provincial branches were similar in structure to the central association, and doubts arose as to whether so close a correspondence might be a contravention of the Act of 1799 to suppress corresponding societies. It was O'Connell himself who pointed out this danger,[9] and the Catholic leader thereby revealed his sensitive regard for constitutional principles and for the reactions of English politicians.

The Catholic Association aroused various reactions, and its impact sharpened the current division of opinion on the Catholic question between English political groups. The radicals and the anti-catholics respectively welcomed and denounced the Association. Between these, the whigs sympathized with it and the pro-catholic tories wanted to suppress it as a menace to orderly government and to a quiet settlement of the Catholic claims. The division lay not between pro- and anti-catholics but between whigs and tories.

The ultras argued that the Association wanted to dissolve the Union and replace the anglican establishment in Ireland with a Catholic one. Because the Government did not take immediate action against the Association, the ultras decided to use pressure themselves, and at this time there are hints of a movement among ultra peers to form a group which would by-pass the Government in demanding repressive action. John Cam Hobhouse was informed that Newcastle, the Earl of Lonsdale, and others 'are said to disclaim the present Administration on account of its Liberalism'.[1] Newcastle does not appear to have been very successful in obtaining recruits for this group, which was frowned on by Government anti-catholics and by the Duke of York. The Marquess of Hertford thought that any movement which was not sanctioned by Peel and York 'could only do mischief & if (it) were powerful enough in numerical force only divide & distress

8. *Liverpool Mercury*, 8 October 1824. For some of these duties, local societies already existed. In Preston, for example, there was a Catholic Defence Society whose function was to correct the erroneous opinions and accusations of anti-catholics.

9. *Manchester Guardian*, 6 November 1824.

1. Letter to J. C. Hobhouse from his cousin Henry Hobhouse, 25 January 1825 (Broughton Papers, Add. Mss. 36464, ff. 197–8). This Henry Hobhouse was not the author of the contemporary political diary.

the Government'.[2] Hertford also firmly stated that he had entire confidence in Peel and would continue to support the Government.[3] The radicals, in contrast, enthusiastically supported the Association. They saw it as a popular combination and a guarantee that the Irish Catholics were no longer striving to succeed by compromising with the tory government. Cobbett, whose extravagantly pro-catholic *History of the Reformation* had been appearing in instalments in 1824, welcomed the Association; Bentham gave £5 to the Catholic Rent; and Sir Francis Burdett declared that he sympathized with all the Association's views and feelings. Hitherto the radicals had been suspicious of O'Connell because he had refused to support parliamentary reform, and they now expected him to adopt it. The radicals were deceived. O'Connell wished to avoid any course whereby he might be accused of acting unconstitutionally. He saw that success depended on winning over more anti-catholics, particularly those in the Cabinet, and these were all against Parliamentary reform. O'Connell, therefore, continued to oppose it also; and when he said he was a disciple of Bentham he made it clear that this was only with regard to Bentham's projects for legal reform. The radicals did not immediately grasp this, but when at last they did so they angrily showed their disillusionment.

The two main pro-catholic bodies were sharply divided in their attitude to the Association. The whigs half-heartedly approved of it. They were conscious of the revolutionary clamour it might lead to, but considered immediate emancipation to be an essential homœopathic means of avoiding this; consequently they would only consent to the suppression of the Association if it were accompanied by full Catholic relief. The tory pro-catholics, on the other hand, would not consider granting emancipation unless the Association was previously suppressed. Some of them thought that the danger of the Association had been exaggerated, but many others were as alarmed as the ultras at the threatened destruction of the Protestant constitution. The whigs

2. Hertford to Peel, 24 November 1824; PP, 40370, ff. 201–2. Hertford enclosed a letter from Newcastle, but this is unfortunately not in the Peel Papers. He also said he had previously received letters from Newcastle offering him his interest if he put up a parliamentary candidate at East Retford, a constituency influenced by Newcastle. These letters, said Hertford, contained 'many lamentations on the state of the country' (ibid.).
3. Ibid.

suspected that the Government pro-catholics were making an excuse of the Catholic Association to abandon the cause of emancipation. Grey wrote as follows:

I am prepared for measures against the Catholic Association, & for Canning's taking advantage of the alarm occasioned by it, & for which it is made a pretence, to relieve himself of the embarrassment of the Catholick Question. He will of course be for coercion, increase of army & all its consequences, & our friends I suppose will go on praising him for his liberality. . . .[4]

As a result of the Association's activities, the King was persuaded by York and Lady Conyngham to discourage the impression, which still persisted, that he was favourable to Catholic relief.[5] He told Peel that if these activities continued, he could no longer allow the question to remain an 'open' one in the Cabinet:

This indulgence was originally granted on the ground of political expediency, but that expediency dissolves when threatened rebellion calls upon the King for that which the King will never grant. . . . The sentiments of the King upon Catholic Emancipation are those of his revered and excellent Father; from those sentiments the King never can and never will deviate.[6]

But the Government anti-catholics realized that an exclusively anti-catholic ministry could only be formed with difficulty and was unlikely to last. Wellington told the King that the best chance of defeating the Catholic claims was to let them remain an open question.[7] Both pro- and anti-catholics in the Government agreed that the Association must be suppressed. The construction of a suppression bill was placed in the hands of Goulburn, the anti-catholic Chief Secretary of Ireland. Goulburn, being an extremist, would have liked a measure directed only against the Catholic Association, but the Government wanted to appear impartial and insisted that it should apply to Orangemen as well. The measure adopted, therefore, was a general one against all unlawful societies in Ireland. Further, the bill was to

4. Grey to Holland, 3 February 1825; Grey MSS.
5. In his address of December 1824 O'Connell had exhorted the Irish to be peaceable for the sake of 'the affectionate reverence you bear for the gracious Monarch who deigns to think of your sufferings with a view to your relief'; *Liverpool Mercury*, 17 December 1824.
6. 19 November 1824; C. S. Parker, *Peel*, i. 349.
7. *Journal of Mrs. Arbuthnot*, 26 November 1824 (i. 357).

last only two years with the possibility of re-enactment, instead of being permanent as Goulburn wished.

The Government could be confident of a parliamentary majority for its bill, since both the anti-catholics and the tory pro-catholics supported it. However, the Catholic Association had by this time secured considerable power over Irish electors, and it was possible that this would cause some tory pro-catholics representing Irish constituencies to oppose the bill through fear of losing their seats.[8] The Opposition, moreover, was expected to put up a strenuous fight against the measure. Indeed, the debate on Goulburn's bill, which was introduced on 10 February, lasted four days—the longest debate within memory, according to John Cam Hobhouse, on a bill which had been recommended in a King's Speech.[9] The supporters of the bill wanted the Association suppressed as a menace to public safety; their opponents argued that the Association was only trying to defend Catholics against attacks by Orangemen and asserted that the only cure for Ireland was Catholic emancipation. The debate turned into a full discussion of the Catholic question. The whigs were markedly hostile to the Government pro-catholics and the bitter atmosphere of the 1823 session was revived. George Tierney accused Plunket of deserting the Catholic cause by taking office, and Brougham attacked Canning for not using his talents to carry the Catholic question.[1] Nevertheless, the bill passed easily through parliament. The first reading in the Commons passed by 155 votes, the second by 146, and the third by 130. In the Lords the second reading passed by 102 votes and the bill received the royal assent.[2]

Parliamentary divisions on the bill showed the expected cleavage. In the first division in the Commons most of the minority were whig and pro-catholic. But there were nine exceptions. Six of these were whigs who had hitherto voted anti-catholic but now opposed the suppression of the Association. This could mean that they disliked the suppression of a popular associa-

8. Goulburn wrote at this time: 'Whenever an election shall take place the people will be placed in opposition to their landlords & such members only returned as shall please the Association'; Goulburn to Peel, 27 October 1824 (quoted by J. A. Reynolds, p. 94).

9. Diary of J. C. Hobhouse, 15 February 1825; Broughton, *Recollections*, iii. 88.

1. Hansard, xii. 340–1, 513–14.
2. 6 Geo. IV, c. 4.

tion, even though it conflicted with their anti-catholic sentiments. The other three exceptions were tory pro-catholics, all of whom sat for Irish counties. One of them was Richard Martin, member for county Galway, who had been expected to oppose the bill on account of the Catholic Association's influence in his constituency.[3]

Several speakers against Goulburn's bill had warned that the Catholic Association would take advantage of loopholes in the measure to revive it in a different form.[4] Peel had also foreseen this at an early stage, but said that what he chiefly desired from a suppression bill was not so much the extinction of the Association as an opportunity to expose its danger and to prove that the Government was aware of it.[5] That the Association would seek to circumvent the new law was shown when the Irish Catholics protested that the Act had been passed by trickery and that they would be justified in evading it.[6] For the moment, however, it was advisable that the Catholic leaders should appear conciliatory. A Catholic deputation led by O'Connell and Sheil had come to England ostensibly to defend the Association against Goulburn's bill. They had failed to obtain a hearing in parliament, but this had not been their only object in crossing the seas. O'Connell hoped to raise the question of emancipation in parliament before the session ended, and to enlist the sympathies of the English people in preparation for this.

It was uncertain whether Catholic emancipation had much chance of success in the current session. O'Connell perceived that its chances depended on the good behaviour of the Irish. As the leader of the Association he had assumed a threatening attitude, and this had succeeded in riveting the attention of parliament on the Catholic claims. The time had now come for conciliation to replace threats. O'Connell hoped that a conciliatory policy might induce the Government to grant emancipation. Thus there is no real puzzle in O'Connell's change of attitude, as has sometimes been imagined. He was the politician throughout. If at one period he appeared as a fearsome demagogue and at

3. In a short speech Martin clearly conveyed that his true sentiments were in favour of the bill; Hansard, xii. 300–1.
4. Hansard, xii. 192, 286.
5. Peel to Goulburn, 6 November 1824; Parker, *Peel*, i. 346–8.
6. Extract from the *Dublin Weekly Register*, in PP, 40374, ff. 317–18.

another as a conciliatory diplomat wooing English authority, he was doing what seemed best at different times to achieve the consistent object of emancipation. We have no need to accept Sheil's explanation of his conduct, which claims that he was overawed by the grandeur of metropolitan society into humble acquiescence to compromise.[7]

So determined was O'Connell to conciliate that he was ready to agree to certain securities which became the 'wings' of the 1825 Relief Bill. He told a parliamentary committee which was considering the state of Ireland that he favoured a scheme for paying the Catholic clergy out of State funds. The priests might accept this in return for Catholic emancipation, and it would ensure their loyalty to the Crown. The other proposed security was the disfranchisement of the Irish pauper forty-shilling freeholders. This would provide that if Catholic M.P.s were allowed into parliament they would at least not be dependent for their election on the votes of the mob. It seems that O'Connell had come to a previous understanding with Plunket and Sir Francis Burdett to advance these securities.[8] He was confident that he could persuade the Irish Catholics to accept them. Moreover, it was likely that many pro-catholic whigs would also acquiesce. If this compromise were reached, the parliamentary prospects for Catholic emancipation would be more promising than for many years. There would be no division among the Irish Catholics as in 1821, and the disastrous rift of 1823 among the pro-catholics would be healed. Certain anti-catholics might even agree to emancipation if it were accompanied by securities. Mrs. Arbuthnot hinted that the Duke of Wellington might accept emancipation if adequate securities were given to the Protestants. She confided to her private diary:

7. 'His deputation to England', wrote Sheil, 'produced a temporary effect on him. As we advanced [into England], the din of Irish assemblies became more faint; the voice of the multitude was scarcely heard in the distance' (quoted by J. A. Reynolds, p. 39). Reynolds takes this view a stage further: 'The genteel atmosphere of the lobby of the house [of Commons] and of dinner parties at the Duke of Norfolk's was far removed from the boisterous clamour. . . . Flattered by the polite attention shown him, he appeared less the demagogue and more the politician, amenable to the compromise which seemed so essential' (p. 40). O'Connell may have been impressed by pomp and circumstance, but he was too shrewd a man to let this change his policy.

8. This at least is what O'Connell himself asserted. 'If I had not been here nothing would have been done,' he told his wife. 'I forced Sir Francis Burdett to bring on his motion.' O'Connell to Mrs. O'Connell, 4 March 1825; Fitzpatrick, *O'Connell*, i. 107.

He feels the full importance of the case & is most anxious to settle it, but ... he will not grant political power to the Catholics till he knows what protection will be granted to the Protestants. ... If the King of England ... had the nomination of the Popish priesthood, if they received a salary from the Govt., it wd. become their interest to preach peace to the misguided peasantry. ... The arrangements wd. then be facilitated, but till the King is head of their Church no step can be with safety adopted.[9]

On 28 February Burdett introduced in the Commons a motion for a committee of the whole House to consider the Catholic claims. He supported his motion with a mild, conciliatory speech exhorting the Irish Catholics to meet with restraint the favourable opinion which he insisted the English people felt for their cause.[1] The motion passed by thirteen votes. The pro-catholics were delighted, and Plunket hoped that the introduction of securities would procure rapidly increasing majorities. The anti-catholics were alarmed, and many thought that the Government was becoming increasingly pro-catholic. It was rumoured that Lord Liverpool would incline towards letting the question pass, as in 1821. Eldon told Lord Colchester that it was universally believed that the premier would bring in a relief bill,[2] and this rumour brought alarm to the anti-catholic stronghold of Oxford University.[3] It was necessary to quash the rumour immediately. Liverpool sent a rebuttal to the *Courier* (a government newspaper) and denied the rumour privately to his colleagues.[4] Peel asserted that there was no danger of Liverpool giving way.[5] Nevertheless, some pro-catholics appear to have cherished the hope until Liverpool quelled it in a strong anti-catholic speech later in the session.[6] The value of Liverpool's apostasy to the Catholic cause was doubtful in any case, considering the firm anti-catholic attitude of the House of Lords. 'I doubt', wrote Lord Grenville, 'even whether Liverpool's vote in favour of the Catholics would convert more than two Peers.'[7]

The anti-catholics hit back at the pro-catholics by saying that

9. *Journal*, i. 377–8.
1. Hansard, xii. 764–84.
2. Colchester's diary, 10 March 1825; Colchester, iii. 372.
3. Dr. Lloyd of Christ Church to Peel, 11 March 1825; PP, 40342, ff. 213–14.
4. Colchester, iii. 373–4; Liverpool to Peel, 10 March 1825 (PP, 40305, f. 20).
5. Peel to Dr. Lloyd, 12 March 1825; PP, 40342, f. 216.
6. Edward Maltby to Viscount Milton, 19 March 1825 (Fitzwilliam MSS.); Frederick Ponsonby to Earl Fitzwilliam, 31 March 1825 (ibid.).
7. Grenville to E. J. Littleton, 30 March 1825; Hatherton Papers.

their majority in the Commons did not represent English feeling on the question, and soon public opinion substantiated their protest. For the next two and a half months the Catholic question dominated politics, and during that time the public were given many opportunities for recording their views in petitions to parliament. The result was most encouraging to the anti-catholics, since over 400 anti-catholic petitions were said to have been presented in the Commons.[8] Many of these were sponsored by the established clergy, who summoned meetings through circular letters. The opinions of the lesser clergy, however, seemed to coincide remarkably with the views of the higher ecclesiastics, whether these were anti-catholic or pro-catholic. For example, a petition presented in the Lords by the anti-catholic Bishop of Chester was signed by forty-one out of the forty-two clergy resident in Manchester;[9] and at a meeting of the clergy of the archdeaconry of the East Riding, in another anti-catholic diocese, Sydney Smith was the only pro-catholic present.[1] On the other hand, one of the extremely rare pro-catholic petitions from the clergy came from the archdeaconry of Norwich, in the diocese of one of the two pro-catholic bishops at that time.[2] Thus it seems that the convictions of the clergy on Catholic emancipation were reinforced by self-interest; their views became all the stronger when they coincided with the opinions of their superiors who were responsible for giving the testimonials necessary for their promotion. Another influence which now revealed itself was that of the magnates, who used their territorial power to have petitions drawn up in favour of their own views. The Duke of Newcastle sponsored an anti-catholic petition from Retford.[3] In Northamptonshire the whig Earl Fitzwilliam and his son Viscount Milton tried to start a counter-action to anti-catholic expressions, but they were obstructed by the passive resistance of the Bishop of Peterborough.[4] Sometimes large manufacturers used their influence on behalf of the anti-catholic cause. The *Manchester Guardian* reported that at an anti-catholic meeting at Ashton-under-Lyne on 6 May 'Mr. Saxon, an extensive spin-

8. *Preston Pilot*, 23 April 1825.
9. Hansard, xii. 1334.
1. *Works of the Rev. Sydney Smith* (1 vol., London, 1850), pp. 547-51.
2. Hansard, xiii. 20-21.
3. Op. cit., xii. 1336.
4. *Cambridge and Hertford Independent Press*, 16 April 1825; extract in Fitzwilliam MSS.

ner, ordered the men out of his factory to take post in the room where the meeting was assembled, and "support the cause of their church and country" '.[5]

Among the dissenters a cleavage of opinion was shown between the methodists and the leaders of the older denominations. The former were largely anti-catholic, the latter largely pro-catholic. An incident at Manchester hints at the different attitudes to Catholic emancipation among dissenters. Copies of an anti-catholic petition were sent to methodist, congregational, and baptist ministers, who were asked to leave them at their chapels in order to be signed. The methodist ministers agreed to do this, but the others refused. Sometimes the methodists appeared more anti-catholic than the anglicans: at a meeting at Spitalfields, where violence developed, the anti-catholic speakers were mainly methodist and the pro-catholics largely anglican.[6]

Far more anti-catholic petitions were presented in parliament than pro-catholic ones. But it should not be assumed from this that English opinion was unanimously against Catholic relief. Many places produced counter-petitions in favour of concession, and these had considerable popular support. Most of these petitions came from the larger cities like Liverpool, Birmingham, and Manchester. As in other matters the cities were more liberal than the rural areas, where the established clergy possessed a great deal of influence. The anti-catholics, on their side, complained that not enough had been done to stir up no-popery feeling, even by the clergy.[7] Nevertheless, the bulk of public opinion lay with them.

After his motion for enquiry had passed the Commons, Burdett prepared a Relief Bill with the help of Plunket and O'Connell. Its centre was an emancipation measure, in which were embodied a provision for control of Catholic ecclesiastics and a modified version of the Oath of Supremacy for Catholics to take. The two 'wings' lay on either side of the measure. The provisions

5. 14 May 1825.
6. *The Times,* 13 April 1825.
7. Wordsworth wrote to the ultra Earl of Lonsdale: 'The laity were unwilling to take the lead . . . in a matter . . . eminently ecclesiastical; and the clergy are averse from coming forward except in a corporate capacity, lest they should be accused of stirring up the people for selfish views; and thus the real opinion of the nation is not embodied' (May 1825). E. de Selincourt (ed.), *Letters of William and Dorothy Wordsworth, 1821–30* (Oxford, 1939), p. 207.

for a diluted oath and a modified form of Veto had their opponents, and Dr. Milner was among them. But his protests were a shadow of his former efforts, and it soon appeared that the 'wings' would give more trouble. O'Connell did his best to quieten the apprehensions of the Irish Catholics. In a letter of 7 March to the Catholic Association he insisted that nothing in the proposed securities was inconsistent with the doctrine or discipline of the Church, and advised his followers to withhold any protests 'until the Bill was printed, or until my arrival amongst you'.[8] In another letter O'Connell sought to sweeten the pill of the securities by assuring his followers that 'emancipation is certain and speedy'.[9] John Lawless, an Irishman then in England, did not take O'Connell's advice, and heartily denounced the 'wings'. His attack temporarily undermined O'Connell's reputation among the Irish Catholics; while in England Lawless had the support of Cobbett, whose desire for parliamentary reform was affronted by the proposed disfranchisement of the Irish forty-shilling free-holders. Cobbett was particularly angry with Burdett, whom he accused of betraying the cause to which he had given lifelong support, and of advocating instead the 'complete Anti-Reform of Parliament'.[1]

Cobbett, as an extra-parliamentary radical, could do little direct harm to the Relief Bill. Much more dangerous was the reaction of certain whig M.P.s to the disfranchisement measure. Although many whigs were able to reconcile it with the principles of parliamentary reform, a few found this impossible. John Cam Hobhouse noted that Burdett's measures were well received by the dukes of Devonshire and Norfolk and other 'great whigs', but that alarm was shown by Grey, who was supported by Lord Sefton, Sir Robert Wilson, J. G. Lambton, and Thomas Creevey.[2] In order to avoid hindering the main question with this division of opinion, it was decided to detach the 'wings' from the Relief Bill and propose them as separate measures. The Relief Bill was therefore introduced without the 'wings' for its second reading in the Commons on 19 April. Because of this,

8. Published in Cobbett's *Political Register*, 19 March 1825, cols. 710–15.
9. To the acting secretary of the Association, 14 March 1825; Fitzpatrick, *O'Connell*, i. 108–9.
1. *Pol. Reg.*, 12 March 1825, cols. 681–2. Cobbett continued his attack on O'Connell and Burdett in subsequent issues of the *Register* (23 July, 13 August, 3, 10, 17, 24 September).
2. Diary of J. C. Hobhouse, 9 March 1825; Broughton's *Recollections*, iii. 98.

the support of at least one pro-catholic tory was jeopardized;[3] but this was far outweighed by the conversion of several Irish members to the Catholic cause, notably that of Charles Brownlow (member for Armagh) who had formerly been regarded as an extreme Orangeman. The second reading passed by twenty-seven votes, but the whigs, apprehensive about the 'wings' which were to follow, were not very happy with the result.[4]

The 'wings' were then introduced as separate measures. E. J. Littleton, a Canningite, introduced the controversial Disfranchisement Bill on 22 April, and its second reading was debated on the 26th. The division of whig opinion clearly emerges from the debate. Even those whigs who were prepared to vote for the measure could not defend it with any enthusiasm : and the whigs who could not tolerate disfranchisement forcefully denounced it. Brougham argued lengthily against it, saying that the Irish peasantry whom it proposed to disfranchise would be turned against Catholic emancipation.[5] Many anti-catholics also opposed this 'wing', either because they disliked its basic conception as an aid to Catholic emancipation, or because they regarded the parliamentary franchise as constitutionally inviolate. However, the bill's opponents were outnumbered by its supporters. The latter included the pro-catholic tories, the whigs who managed to reconcile it with their consciences, and the anti-catholic tories who wanted to see the Irish Catholic mob disfranchised. The second reading passed by a majority of forty-eight. The other 'wing', concerning State payment of the Catholic clergy, was introduced in the form of a resolution on 29 April.[6] It passed by a similar margin, but it had created a similar division among the whigs. Creevey denounced it because it would mean levying taxes on Protestants to pay Catholic priests.[7]

3. This was Lord Ennismore, member for county Cork. He promised, however, to vote for the third reading if the 'wings' were reattached; Hansard, xiii. 57.
4. Diary of J. C. Hobhouse, 21 April 1825; Broughton, iii. 96.
5. Hansard, xiii. 195–213, especially 203–4. Professor A. Aspinall has stated that Brougham wanted the whigs to agree to the Disfranchisement Bill, as a means of drawing closer to the liberal tories in order to form a coalition with them (Brougham, p. 136); but I have found no evidence to support this view.
6. It could not be introduced as a bill, since money could not be voted without the prior consent of the King.
7. Hansard, xiii. 332.

The pro-catholic force was somewhat weakened by the whig division over the 'wings'. But the success of these measures was very annoying to the anti-catholic ministers, and had tended to alienate them from their pro-catholic colleagues in the Cabinet. For all the pro-catholic cabinet ministers in the Commons, except Canning who was absent through illness, had supported the 'wings'; the anti-catholics made out that this action was not essential to a consistent pro-catholic viewpoint and was therefore a gratuitous breach of the 'open' system.[8] Liverpool became very alarmed. The Relief Bill was now almost certain to pass the Commons. The Lords could still throw it out 'by a small majority', but Liverpool thought this would be 'an expiring and possibly inexpedient effort'.[9] He considered it inevitable that the present government would dissolve and be succeeded by a pro-catholic ministry which would carry emancipation. He was certain, moreover, that he could not acquiesce in this arrangement: '. . . impossible . . . that I should be a party to the *new system* much less the instrument of carrying it into effect'.[1] Mrs. Arbuthnot noted that the King would be quite happy if Liverpool resigned, and this may have meant that George IV was vacillating on the question too.[2]

It was possibly a desire to steady both the premier and the King which inspired a momentous declaration in the Lords on 25 April by the staunchly anti-catholic Duke of York. He stated that the Coronation Oath eternally prevented the royal assent being given to a Catholic relief bill, and implied that should he succeed George IV (as seemed likely at that time), such assent would never be given in his lifetime.[3] The speech dampened

8. 'Thus', wrote Henry Hobhouse indignantly, 'did these gentlemen augment the embarrassment of the Cabinet by advancing the Catholic pretensions without any necessity for so doing, and when they might with perfect consistency have voted the other way.' Diary, 24 May 1825; ed. Aspinall, p. 114.
9. Liverpool to Wellington, 1 April 1825; WND, ii. 435.
1. Ibid.
2. Journal, 23 April 1825 (i. 389).
3. Hansard, xiii. 138–42. Some thought the speech had been composed by Eldon, but he denied it (Twiss, ii. 544–5). The speech was greatly appreciated by the anti-catholics. *John Bull* said it should be printed in letters of gold (2 May 1825), and the inhabitants of Chester presented York with an enormous decorated Cheshire cheese (*Preston Pilot*, 11 June 1825). Certain anti-catholics were, however, uneasy at the finality of the convictions which York expressed; and Henry Hobhouse wrote that York was prepared, if attacked in the Lords, to disavow 'all intention of pledging himself to the line he shot, take in case of his succession to the Crown. This', he added, 'I know from one of his private friends' (28 May 1825; Aspinall, p. 116).

the enthusiasm of the pro-catholics but did not do much to strengthen the confidence of the anti-catholic ministers. Admittedly, it seemed to have an immediate effect on George IV, for two days later York told Sidmouth that the King had declared he would never assent to a relief bill.[4] But the effect on Liverpool was less decisive. He now said that he would take no public action until the Lords had come to a decision on the Relief Bill;[5] but he still thought that a compromise would have to be made on the Catholic question, even if they rejected the bill, and he would resign rather than be a party to it. Liverpool said this at a meeting with Wellington, Bathurst, and Peel on 1 May. At this meeting the anti-catholic ministers received a further jolt, for Peel said he must resign too.

Peel's opinion strengthened Liverpool's decision to resign. This conjured up a most unhappy prospect for the Government, for whereas Peel's resignation would only weaken it, Liverpool's might destroy it altogether. Bathurst and Wellington, two anti-catholics whose overriding desire it was to hold the Government together, set about trying to dissuade Liverpool from resigning. In a letter of 4 May Bathurst pointed out to Liverpool the difference between his position and that of Peel. Peel had a strong case for resignation, since he was in the extremely difficult position of being the only anti-catholic cabinet minister in the Commons, where he had been beaten on the main Catholic question and on related proposals. All these questions, moreover, belonged to the sphere of his own Home Department. Liverpool, on the other hand, was surrounded by anti-catholic colleagues in the Lords, and a majority of that House was against emancipation. The question did not lie within his immediate responsibility. The Government, moreover, had been formed on the understanding that the Catholic question would be an 'open' one; and if Liverpool threatened to resign over the issue he would be bitterly reproached by those who had joined his ministry on that understanding. 'Your Government', wrote Bathurst, 'was formed upon it: your friends have trusted their political fortunes upon it, and you now without notice turn round and consider it as a vital question.'[6] Bathurst concluded by advising Liverpool

4. Colchester, iii. 380.
5. Liverpool to Bathurst, 30 April 1825; Bathurst Papers (HMC, 1923), p. 579.
6. Bathurst to Liverpool, 4 May 1825; ibid., pp. 579–80.

to dissolve parliament and await the result of fresh elections before coming to a decision. This personal appeal to the premier did not, however, have the desired effect. Liverpool first insisted that his ministry could not do without Peel. Secondly he asserted that his own anti-catholic opinions had already been overruled in the Commons, and he could not expect to be able to defend them much longer in the Lords: 'the *crisis* cannot be averted for many months. Whenever the *crisis does come*, the *Protestants* must go to the wall.'[7]

The next effort by those who were determined to preserve the existing government, was an attempt by Wellington to prevent Peel's resignation. In a conversation of 7 May he stressed the vital nature of Peel's threat, in view of the fact that Liverpool's resignation would follow: it was 'completely throwing up the Protestant cause'.[8] But Peel was unmoved: he would only concede that, in order to avoid embarrassing Liverpool, he would delay his resignation until the Lords had thrown out the bill. The anti-catholics therefore had to envisage the possibility of the Government's dissolution and its replacement by a coalition of Canning and the whigs which would be committed to carrying Catholic emancipation. However, they had other resources left, and the man who produced them was Wellington. The duke strongly urged that, rather than forfeit office, the ministers should agree to a Catholic settlement on the basis of compromise. He had already formulated a plan whereby Catholic relief should be passed in return for a concordat with the Pope, which would give the King partial control over the appointment of Catholic bishops and vicars-apostolic in the British Isles.[9] Wellington's guiding aim was to preserve the Government, and he only intended that his plan should be put into action if Liverpool and Peel could not be persuaded to remain in office as anti-catholics. But there was also the possibility that Peel and Liverpool would not adopt his plan of compromise. The pragmatical duke had an answer to this too: if necessary, he would form a government and carry the plan himself. He implied this final course of action when he assured the King that he would stand by him to the

7. Liverpool to Bathurst, 4 May 1825; Bathurst Papers, p. 581.
8. *Journal of Mrs. Arbuthnot*, 8 May 1825 (i. 393–4).
9. For a detailed draft of this scheme, see WND, ii. 592–607.

end;[1] and it was suspected that George IV, for his part, would not be averse to a Catholic settlement.[2]

Wellington's intimate friends, being aware of his thoughts, became excited at the possibility of his becoming premier. Mrs. Arbuthnot wanted him to make his position clear when the bill was debated in the Lords. 'As it is possible he may be called upon to pass a Bill of Relief for the Catholics upon his own view of the case', she wrote, 'I am very anxious he shd. state his opinion publicly that it may be impossible hereafter to say that he changed his opinions in preference to quitting office.'[3] Wellington did not adopt this attitude in the debate, and the ensuing events removed all thoughts of such behaviour. But it is interesting to speculate on the stir which an announcement of the duke's conversion to Catholic emancipation would have made.

Meanwhile the Relief Bill was going through its final stages in the Commons. The third reading was debated on 10 May. The 'wings' were not included, but it was known that they would be added if the main measure were carried. Certain whig M.P.s were assumed to have abstained from voting for this reason, and the third reading passed by only twenty-one votes, a decrease of six since the second reading. It was suggested that the support which the 'wings' won for the bill was neutralized by the lost votes of whig pro-catholics who disliked them.[4] The result was comforting to the anti-catholics and must have encouraged the Lords in their determination to resist the bill. The Upper House debated the measure before a large audience on 17 May. Liverpool expected that the bill would only be rejected by a narrow majority, such as would not justify further resistance to the Catholic claims. He was anxious to emphasize that his own conscience would not allow him to participate in a pro-catholic ministry, and he therefore made a more inflexibly anti-catholic speech than any which had yet come from him. Delivered in the tones usually adopted by the ultras, the speech was an unyielding condemnation of Catholic relief mainly on religious

1. Summary of a conversation between Wellington and the King in the *Journal of Mrs. Arbuthnot*, 12 May 1825 (i. 396); see also Charles Arbuthnot to Bathurst, 13 May 1825 (Bathurst Papers, p. 582).
2. *Mrs. Arbuthnot*, 23 April 1825 (i. 389).
3. 12 May 1825 (ibid., 397).
4. John Cam Hobhouse thought that 'little was gained and something was lost by the sacrifices made by Burdett and his friends'; Broughton, iii. 98.

grounds, and it contained no hint of compromise.[5] The effect was very surprising to Liverpool. His oration, which had been intended as a final personal protest against the inevitable grant of emancipation, helped to stiffen the anti-catholic resistance of the Lords and made emancipation anything but inevitable. The bill was thrown out by forty-eight votes, about twenty more than Liverpool had expected;[6] and it was said that this result was very largely due to his own speech.[7]

With this, the pro-catholic effort of 1825 ended in failure. Public rejoicings were held by the anti-catholic populace and church bells rung. Liverpool's reasons for threatening resignation seemed at first sight to have vanished. The precarious condition of the Government, however, was not immediately resolved, for its pro-catholic members would not bear their defeat in silence. Canning declared that the Catholic question must now be settled one way or the other. This appeared to threaten once again the existence of the Government, and Liverpool's fears were revived. He told Bathurst that, should the Catholic question again be discussed in Cabinet, the Government must dissolve unless some compromise could be reached between the pro- and anti-catholic ministers. If this could not be done, he would have to inform the King that the formation of an exclusively anti-catholic government was 'absolutely impracticable, whereas the formation of a government upon the opposite principle . . . is within his power'.[8] In a pro-catholic government, he repeated, he could have no place, especially after his decisive speech in the Lords. Bathurst once more tried to steady the quaking premier and urged him not to be put off by Canning's demand for a settlement. If Canning should be driven to resign, he wrote, it was doubtful whether anyone else would resign with him; Liverpool could not desert the Government simply because of Canning's single resignation, particularly when the ministry was popular in the country.[9] Bathurst's exhortations proved to be unnecessary, for Canning's behaviour was completely innocuous. He summoned a meeting of the Cabinet on 20 May; and, if we

5. Hansard, xiii. 739–52.
6. Colchester, iii. 386.
7. Lord Binning thought that 'the speech has had more effect than any I remember any man to have made'. Binning to Sir Charles Bagot, 27 May 1825; Josceline Bagot, *George Canning and his Friends* (2 vols., London, 1909), ii. 281.
8. Liverpool to Bathurst, 22 May 1825; Bathurst Papers, p. 583.
9. Bathurst to Liverpool, 23 May 1825; ibid., pp. 584–5.

can believe an observer who received his information third hand, he made only the following declaration: 'If, in consequence of refusing the Catholic claims, Ireland should be agitated at any future time, and it should be asked to create fresh penal enactments, I will not give my consent; sooner than do so I will retire from office.'[1] Canning, in fact, made it clear that he had no intention of sacrificing office in order to make an extremely risky attempt to set up a pro-catholic government. In a debate in the Commons a few days later, he said that he thought his resignation would do nothing to assist the progress of Catholic emancipation, and stressed the fact that he was free to raise the question for discussion in Cabinet at any time.[2]

Thus Canning declared his undeviating allegiance to Liverpool's 'open' system. By the end of May the *status quo* was completely restored and the crisis of 1825 had come to an end. Yet while it lasted it had gravely endangered the Government. At one stage it had seemed that the 'open' system might be destroyed by its own latitude. Pro-catholic ministers had firmly supported the Catholic claims in the Commons, with the result that Peel, the only anti-catholic cabinet minister in that House, had been driven to the verge of resignation, and Liverpool had seriously imagined that his own ministry would have to be replaced by one committed to Catholic emancipation. But this was before the Relief Bill was debated in the Lords. In that House the verdict of the Commons was reversed. If the pro-catholic majority in the Commons had been promising, the anti-catholic majority in the Lords was decisive. After their defeat the pro-catholics tried to console themselves with the reflection that the Lords did not represent the people.[3] But this was an unrealistic protest, in view of the overwhelming number of popular anti-catholic petitions recently presented in parliament.

Against the impenetrable anti-catholic barrier provided by the Lords and the Crown, any attempt to form a pro-catholic

---

1. Diary of J. C. Hobhouse, 27 May 1825; Broughton, iii. 103–4. Hobhouse was given the information by Lord Nugent, whose informant was Buckingham, who in turn had it from Charles Wynn. The date of the cabinet meeting can be gauged from a letter of Canning to Liverpool, 18 May 1825 (E. J. Stapleton, *Canning Corresp.*, i. 269). This states that Canning intended to summon the cabinet, in order to discuss its position on the Catholic question, on 'Friday'. The next Friday after 18 May was the 20th.

2. Hansard, xiii. 889–90.

3. e.g. *The Times*, 19 May 1825.

ministry seemed bound to fail. Canning well realized that the 'open' system must continue for an indefinite period, and he therefore made no effort to overturn the existing ministry. The deadlock between pro- and anti-catholics in the Government could only be broken by a vital external movement, namely an irresistible Irish demand for Catholic emancipation. The Catholic Association had at first appeared to provide this demand, and O'Connell's conciliatory policy following its suppression would have been a masterly corollary if only this policy had not aroused whig opposition. In the end its effect was to advance the Catholic cause only in the Commons. The Lords' victory made it clear that the Irish Catholics must find a new and more potent means of agitation. Meanwhile the *status quo* had received a fresh mandate.

CHAPTER IV

THE GENERAL ELECTION OF 1826

IN June 1825 Parliament was approaching the end of its sixth
session. If allowed to last for another session it would be the
first parliament since the Septennial Act to run for its whole
legal period. A dissolution was therefore expected in 1825.
General prosperity, tranquillity in Ireland, and the popularity of
the ministry made the time most suitable. But the Catholic
issue came to exercise a more decisive influence on the question
of dissolution than any other factor. The whig pro-catholics
favoured an early dissolution. If a House of Commons with a
majority of pro-catholics was returned in a general election, it
would gain strength at the expense of the Lords, who would be
less justified in rejecting a relief bill in a new parliament than
one which was sent up to them in the last session of an old one.
Moreover, the pro-catholic M.P.s had supported Burdett's bill
in defiance of the anti-catholic opinion of the country, even
though it seemed likely that parliament would be dissolved soon
afterwards. This suggests that they thought it unlikely that a
strong anti-catholic Commons would be returned at that time.
The ultras seemed to agree with this view, for they opposed an
early dissolution.[1]

Wellington differed from the ultras in advocating an early
dissolution. Having more faith in the anti-catholic strength of
the electorate than they had, he urged an immediate dissolution
before anti-catholic ardour had time to cool.[2] Wellington's
object was still that of holding the Government together. For
this reason he had been ready to adopt, in an emergency, a compromise settlement of the Catholic question. But now, after the
defeat of Burdett's bill, it seemed that an appeal to popular anti-
catholicism offered a less drastic method of preserving the *status
quo*. Liverpool rejected Wellington's advice with the reply that
there was no precedent for a dissolution in July, but said that

---

1. Grey to Viscount Howick, 9 September 1825; Grey MSS.
2. Wellington to Liverpool, 22 June 1825; WND, ii. 463-5.

he strongly favoured a dissolution in September.[3] When September came, however, the Government pro-catholics protested against a dissolution, and in this they showed themselves once more at variance with the whigs. In a letter to Liverpool on 5 September, Canning discouraged a dissolution on the grounds that it would seem a deliberate attempt to harm the pro-catholic cause.[4] This argument had been suggested to Canning by Huskisson on the previous day, on the grounds that the Canningite M.P.s, having voted for Burdett's bill, were frightened of facing the electorate. Huskisson wrote: 'Our Friends exaggerate, perhaps, the irritation which exists against them in many places in consequence of their votes of last Session, but, be that as it may, they certainly dread *No Popery* cries and contests. They see no *special* reason for dissolving now except this appeal. . . .'[5]

Huskisson's argument may have been superficially convincing, but on closer examination it seems groundless. The whig pro-catholics were not afraid of facing an election, while the ultras were against one. This would not have been the case if the anti-catholic electorate had appeared really formidable. The reason behind Huskisson's argument was probably a desire on the part of the Government pro-catholics to preserve peace and quiet and keep the ministry free from the worry of the Catholic question. Indeed, Huskisson demanded in the same letter that the Catholic question should not be moved during the next session: the Government pro-catholics should resist any attempt by the Irish Catholics to bring it forward. Other Canningites made similar suggestions, and Canning wrote again to Liverpool on 12 September urging that the dissolution be postponed.[6] Liverpool preferred Canning's view to Wellington's, saying that he was ready to postpone the dissolution until the following year on condition that the issues of Catholic emancipation and the Corn Laws, particularly the former, were suppressed for a session.[7] Canning gave this undertaking, and on 23 September the Cabinet decided to postpone the dissolution. In making its deci-

---

3. Liverpool to Wellington, 23 June 1825; ibid., 465.
4. E. J. Stapleton (ed.), *Some Official Correspondence of George Canning* (2 vols., London, 1887), i. 289–91.
5. Huskisson to Canning, 4 September 1825; Huskisson Papers, Add. Mss. 38747, f. 78.
6. Canning to Liverpool, 12 September 1825; Stapleton, op. cit., i. 294.
7. Liverpool to Peel, 15 September 1825 (PP, 40305, ff. 86–87); Liverpool to Wellington, 16 September 1825 (WND, ii. 499).

sion the Cabinet was swayed by letters from certain anti-catholic peers asking for a postponement.[8]

Complete victory lay with Canning. Not only was the dissolution postponed in accordance with his wishes, but it looked as though it had been done to please the anti-catholic magnates. As in May, Canning had obtained security for the Government without abandoning his position as a pro-catholic. The decision to postpone the dissolution and Canning's temporary undertaking to suppress discussion of the Catholic question meant that the Government would enjoy an untroubled session; and it could be hoped that when the session closed the question would have been so long in abeyance as to cause much less irritation.

Canning's policy, however, did not please his colleagues in the Irish Government, who had favoured an immediate dissolution because popular ardour in Ireland seemed likely to return more pro-catholic members at an election. Wellesley, in particular, had wanted a September dissolution for this reason.[9] The pro-catholics in the Irish Government also did not take kindly to Canning's insistence that there should be no agitation of the Catholic question. Ireland was fairly tranquil until October. The Catholic leaders, taking advantage of the loopholes in Goulburn's Act, revived the Catholic Association in July, but for the present it was a shadow of its former self. Towards the end of 1825, however, there were renewed disturbances. Although these were not obviously political or religious in nature, Canning complained to Plunket about the irresponsibility of the Catholic leaders. He insisted that Catholic turbulence in Ireland would increase anti-catholic exertions in Britain, and said that the Catholic question could not be raised, even in the new Parliament, if the disturbances lasted.[1] Plunket disagreed. Although he acquiesced in a temporary postponement of the Catholic question, he could not agree that a question which vitally concerned Ireland should be indefinitely put off in deference to English feelings.[2] Not even the tory pro-catholics attached to the home Government agreed completely with Canning's views. Buckingham did not think

8. Mrs. Arbuthnot, i. 414. Letters were read at the cabinet meeting from the Duke of Rutland, the Earl of Lonsdale, and the Duke of York.

9. Canning to Liverpool, 5 September 1825; Stapleton, i. 289–90.

1. Canning to Plunket, 16 November and 13 December 1825; Plunket, ii. 219–23.

2. Plunket to Canning, 18 December 1825; ibid., 224–6.

that the abeyance of the Catholic question would affect the ensuing election, nor indeed that the English public was much concerned with the matter.[3] Charles Wynn annoyed Canning by proposing to introduce a minor matter concerning Catholics in the Lords.[4]

The whigs were divided in their reaction to Canning's policy. From some of Brougham's correspondence we gather that he took the initiative in trying to persuade the whigs to do as Canning wished; and this is not surprising, since Brougham was often hankering after a coalition between the 'moderate' whigs and the Canningites.[5] Lord Grey, on the other hand, argued vehemently against suppressing the Catholic question: 'It may be convenient to *us*, to have no Catholic Question; but is it equally good for the Irish? Have they ever got anything except what has been extorted in the hour of distress? Is it not then *their* interest, to keep alive & to inflame a spirit of discontent for that reason?'[6]

Canning, however, had his way. The Catholic question, except for the presentation of petitions, made no appearance in the final session of the 1820 Parliament, which lasted from 2 February to 31 May 1826. If the pro-catholics hoped that their cause would benefit from a session without discussion, the hiatus also gave their opponents a chance to stir up anti-catholic feeling. In August Brougham was looking for effective new pro-catholic candidates;[7] but the anti-catholics seem to have prepared more actively for the forthcoming elections. The pro-catholic members had been warned, during the progress of Burdett's bill through the Commons, that they were incurring the hostility of their constituents. In some constituencies the warning was well justified. The borough of Taunton was successfully canvassed in August by two anti-catholic candidates who were hoping to profit from the unpopularity of the sitting members, both of whom had supported Burdett's bill.[8] The pro-catholic mem-

3. Buckingham to Plunket, 15 January 1826 (Plunket, ii. 228–9). From his own experience, Buckingham thought that the established clergy were less zealously anti-catholic than they had been in the past (ibid.).
4. Canning to Plunket, 25 October 1825; Plunket, ii. 218.
5. Burdett to Brougham, 13 December 1825; Brougham Papers.
6. Grey to Brougham, 21 December 1825; Brougham's *Life and Times* (3 vols., Edinburgh, 1871), ii. 473–5.
7. Brougham to the Duke of Norfolk, 24 August 1825. Norfolk Papers; HMC, Various collections, ii. (London, 1903), pp. 346–7.
8. *John Bull*, 29 August 1825.

bers for Coventry, Edward Ellice and Peter Moore, were deserted by their agent, who proceeded to advertise on behalf of the freemen of the city for two candidates who would pledge themselves to oppose Catholic emancipation.[9] George IV said he would withdraw the royal patronage from Sir Edward Disbrowe, member for Windsor, who had voted pro-catholic.[1] At East Retford an Independent True Blue Club was formed, with the object of preventing the return of pro-catholic members, and before the end of 1825 the no-popery cry had been raised in Yorkshire, Devon, and Cornwall. The pro-catholics seem to have realized the importance of remaining quiet so as not to exacerbate anti-catholic feeling. In February Lord Althorp discouraged holding a county meeting in Northamptonshire, in order to avoid the slightest possibility of arousing anti-catholic zeal, even though it seemed unlikely that Catholic emancipation would be discussed at the meeting.[2]

The general election of 1826 was fought with unexpected eagerness. One hundred constituencies were contested, twelve more than in 1820.[3] Among the issues in the election were economic retrenchment, parliamentary reform, abolition of slavery, and industrial unemployment. But the two main issues were the Corn Laws and Catholic emancipation. In this chapter there will be given, first, a general survey of the Catholic question in the elections; secondly, a more detailed study of some elections where the question was particularly important, and lastly an assessment of the effect of the Catholic issue on the election results.

Anti-catholic candidates boasted of the overwhelming support they expected to muster, and when election meetings began the crowds made their anti-catholic feeling evident. Henry Crabb Robinson was heckled at Maldon when he made a pro-catholic speech in favour of the whig candidate.[4] Only rarely, however,

9. *Historical Sketches of the Coventry Election, 1826*, pp. 11–13.
1. Sir Herbert Taylor to Sir William Knighton, 15 October 1825; *Geo. IV Letters*, iii. 126–7.
2. Althorp to Viscount Milton, 11 February 1826; Fitzwilliam MSS.
3. This and all other calculations concerning the elections come from H. S. Smith, *Register of Parliamentary Contested Elections* (second ed., London, 1842).
4. T. Sadler (ed.), *The Diary, Reminiscences and Correspondence of Henry Crabb Robinson* (3 vols., London, 1869), ii. 330–1.

does partisan zeal appear to have led to actual rioting during the elections. Furthermore, anti-catholic fervour was sometimes stimulated artificially as a 'blind' for other aims and interests. At Coventry, Ellice and Moore were defeated, primarily it appeared because of their pro-catholic views. Moore, however, had contrived to express these views for twenty years in the Commons without being challenged by his constituents; and this sudden concern for the Protestant constitution in Coventry was really on account of other reasons. The corporation wished to obtain the nomination of the members, and the two corporation candidates were both billed as anti-catholics in order to attract popular support. In addition, the corporation persuaded the weavers of the town that Moore and Ellice were on the side of their employers against a wage claim they were making.[5] Alongside the conviction of the electors that Moore and Ellice were against them, the fact that they were pro-catholics was purely incidental. But it provided a useful rallying-cry, and no-popery was aroused with unprecedented fervour in the borough. At Leicester, too, the corporation encouraged anti-catholic zeal for ulterior reasons. It was feared that, if Catholic emancipation were granted, full civic rights could no longer be withheld from the dissenters, who might then be able to gain control of the corporation.[6] At Nottingham, on the other hand, a corporation of dissenters and pro-catholics was already in control. Anti-catholic sentiments were used against the corporation candidates by a nominee of the county aristocracy, who wanted to rob the corporation of their influence over the representation.[7] The cry was raised with some success, but not sufficient to turn out the corporation candidates.

Thus it seems that anti-catholicism was a useful and effective cry for supporting various kinds of interests. Candidates realized that an avowal of anti-catholic principles was certain to appeal to most English electors. In some cases this avowal was responsible for winning a seat. In Bedfordshire a tory and anti-catholic candidate named T. P. Macqueen, who was challenging the Duke of Bedford's interest, was said to have gained the support of 137 out of 168 freeholders living at Bedford 'upon the assur-

5. *Coventry Election Sketches*, op. cit., pp. 17–18.
6. A. Temple Patterson, *Radical Leicester* (Leicester, 1954), pp. 147–9.
7. *Nottingham Mercury*, 14 June 1826; *Nottingham Journal*, 24 June 1826.

ance that he would "oppose the further encroachments of the Roman Catholics" '.[8] Lord John Russell reported that Lord Tavistock and Francis Pym, the whig members elected for Bedfordshire in 1820, were 'fighting an uphill game. ... The people cry No Popery.'[9] The poll was headed by Macqueen, whose tory predecessor had come bottom in 1820; Tavistock was a poor second and Pym was ousted. Lord John Russell himself lost his seat at Huntingdonshire; Lord Mandeville, who gained it, was said to have reversed his former pro-catholic opinions in order to curry favour with the electors.[1]

Candidates who were known pro-catholics were often at a disadvantage in this election. At London, the pro-catholic alderman Matthew Wood fell from head of the poll in 1820 to fourth in 1826. In the Cambridgeshire election, the pro-catholic views of Lord Francis Godolphin Osborne were said to have materially weakened his interest.[2] In the Cornwall contest it was predicted that the whig Pendarves would lose much support because he would not promise to oppose concession.[3] Some candidates who could otherwise expect to attract popular support were badly hindered by their pro-catholic views. One candidate whose fortunes were affected in this way was Brougham, who was challenging the great Lowther interest in Westmorland for the third time. His campaign commenced hopefully, for in 1820 he had lost by only sixty-three votes. But this optimism was soon threatened by popular anti-catholicism. The Lowthers stimulated this feeling in addresses and speeches, suggesting on one occasion that Brougham was in receipt of an annual payment to support the Catholics.[4] Wordsworth, an active Lowther supporter, thought that Brougham's pro-catholic opinions had harmed his chances of success, and this was borne out by the attitude of the voters. Eighty county freeholders who had supported Brougham at the last election published a declaration that, because of the recent progress of pro-catholic measures, they must now desert him.[5] Altogether, anti-catholic feeling had no small

8. *John Bull*, 6 February 1826.
9. Russell to Viscount Milton, 23 June 1826; Fitzwilliam MSS.
1. 'W. G.' to Viscount Milton, 3 February 1826; ibid.
2. *The Times*, 1 July 1826.
3. W. B. Elvins, *The Reform Movement and County Politics in Cornwall, 1809–52* (unpublished thesis), c. iv. p. 19.
4. *The Times*, 1 June and 1 July 1826.
5. *John Bull*, 26 June 1826.

part in placing Brougham, at the close of the poll, much farther behind his opponents than in 1820.

The fact that many other pro-catholic candidates were not defeated was because of the indulgence of anti-catholic electors who did not feel sufficiently strongly to make a vital issue out of their difference of opinion. In other cases it was because they were able to evade or conceal their views. There were several means of doing this. Candidates could give an assurance, as William Evans did at Leicester, that they would not agree to any concessions which threatened the position of the established Church. Or it could be insisted that their attitude on more important questions outweighed their pro-catholic tendencies. A supporter of J. B. Monck, a whig candidate at Reading, implored the whig electors not to withhold their support from him just because he was a pro-catholic:

> . . . in what a situation must parties in this country be, if they were to split upon this single point, when they agreed upon all other leading points of public policy. Why not imitate the conduct of the ministers who agreed to differ on this question? . . . What was to become of reform in Parliament, what of the corn laws, if the men who were ready to do the good work were not to be supported, because of their mode of thinking on Catholic Emancipation?[6]

If he were given to more dubious modes of evasion, the pro-catholic candidate could try to delude his electors by issuing confusing manifestoes, or by declaring different opinions at different times. In the Northumberland election the Hon. H. T. Liddell, a pro-catholic tory, caused doubts about his attitude on the Catholic question by making declarations on both sides. Lord Grey wrote to his son, Viscount Howick, who was another candidate at this election:

> . . . will anybody pretend to say what [Liddell's] opinions are on any one of the subjects, which most nearly affect the Publick Interests at this moment—He has got votes from the Catholicks, by private promises to support their cause—His most active & powerful supporters . . . are the most uncompromising opposers of the Catholick Claims—Has he given them any assurances which may relieve their minds from the pious apprehensions which they entertain of the power of the Pope? In publick what he has said sets at defiance all

6. *The Times*, 13 June 1826.

understanding—He has especially refused to sign any pledge—He has spoken about it . . . but when you catch one sentence which seems to announce . . . an opinion or principle, you find it in the next so completely undone by some qualification or reserve, that you have never yet been able to find any assurance . . . of what his conduct will be on this important question.[7]

Liddell replied to these accusations by saying that he was strongly pro-catholic, but only after he was safely elected. Concealment of pro-catholic opinions was, indeed, as widespread as it had been in the 1820 election. It was sometimes taken so far that candidates who were really pro-catholics posed as anti-catholics. R. E. Heathcote, a nominee of the Coventry corporation, was proclaimed an anti-catholic during the election. But when his return was considered certain he declared that he neither had given nor would give a pledge on any particular question;[8] and in the new parliament he voted pro-catholic. At Leicester Robert Otway Cave, who had the support of the corporation, declared that 'he had yielded to the general opinion of the electors, and pledged himself not to vote for Catholic Emancipation'.[9] Yet in the next few years Cave showed himself a very enthusiastic pro-catholic. Perhaps the most blatant deception was that practised by E. B. Sugden, an unsuccessful candidate for Shoreham, where one seat was controlled by the Catholic Duke of Norfolk. Sugden posed as an anti-catholic in order to attract the support of the anti-catholic electors. But to his annoyance a letter was published which showed that he had avowed just the opposite opinion only a year before in order to win the support of Norfolk. He had been particularly anxious that this fact should be concealed lest it should alienate the freemen of Shoreham. As *The Times* stated: 'The whole proceeding is a fair picture of the political honesty with which watchwords like this [no popery] are on most occasions made use of by men who seek for seats in Parliament . . . as fields of profitable enterprise.'[1]

It would not have been necessary to resort to such tactics if anti-catholic opinion had not been overwhelming amongst the electorate of 1826. However, the picture is not entirely one of

7. 23 June 1826; Grey MSS.
8. *Coventry Election Sketches*, pp. 48–49.
9. *Nottingham Journal*, 17 June 1826.
1. 13 June 1826.

anti-catholic ascendancy. There were exceptions to the disadvantages suffered by declared pro-catholics. Sir James Graham was successful at Carlisle, although full relief for Catholics and dissenters was a principal topic of his address. J. G. Lambton, at his nomination for county Durham, made a clean breast of his principles but was none the less elected. E. J. Littleton did the same in Staffordshire and was acclaimed by his audience. In the Northumberland election Grey advised Howick not to hide his opinions, since 'nothing is ever gained by ambiguity and concealment'.[2] Indeed, when Liddell's deceptiveness was revealed Grey suggested that even honesty might pay electoral dividends: 'For your own part I hope you will always despise such equivocation, & rather lose twenty elections, than succeed by concealing or disguising the opinions which you really hold. If it should come to a regular set to with Liddell, this seems to be the line which you might take with certain advantage.'[3]

A more detailed study of certain elections where the Catholic question loomed large will reveal additional points of interest, as well as further illustrating those already mentioned. In a county where a pro-catholic magnate had considerable but not exclusive influence he was likely to find his interest threatened by the anti-catholic feelings of rival influential gentry. So it was in Caernarvonshire, where much influence was in the hands of the Paget family of Plas Newydd, of which the Marquess of Anglesey was then the head. Anglesey had generally voted pro-catholic, but in the Lords' debate of May 1825 he had strongly denounced the Catholic Association. This must have won him considerable popularity in North Wales. The area had become something of a Protestant stronghold, its anti-catholicism no doubt hardened by the prevalence of methodism. On the other hand, Anglesey's electoral influence was committed to the support of Sir Robert Williams, a whig who had represented the county for thirty-five years. Sir Robert had alienated a great many of his constituents by his radicalism in general and his support of Catholic emancipation in particular. In September 1825 Lord Newborough, a large landowner in North Wales, unexpectedly announced that he would oppose Williams. In a contest it seemed that New-

2. Grey to Howick, 16 February 1826; Grey MSS.
3. Grey to Howick, 23 June 1826; ibid.

borough was bound to win, since he would obtain the support of all the anti-catholic interests in the county. A memorandum sent to Lord Anglesey by his chief political agent, John Sanderson, showed how slender were Williams's chances of victory. Sir Robert could count only on his own influence and that of Plas Newydd. Newborough, on the other hand, could rely on his own influence and that of many lesser gentry in the county, especially that of the Assheton Smith family, as well as the support of the established clergy, who were affronted at what they believed to be William's threat to Church and constitution.[4]

Not surprisingly, in these circumstances, Anglesey supported Sir Robert in only a half-hearted manner and tried to persuade him to withdraw from the contest. He wrote: 'My principle upon this subject is this. The representative must act on all *publick* questions upon his own judgement. If that judgement coincides with the opinion of the Electors, then all is smooth and as it should be. But when the Reverse is the case, then the member is bound to withdraw.'[5] Williams refused to withdraw for a long time. At the last minute, however, he yielded to reality and resigned from the contest. Newborough was returned unopposed and Williams was seated for the Paget pocket borough of Beaumaris. Williams claimed in later years that he had been dismissed from his seat because he was a pro-catholic. This was not strictly true, since the opinion of the electorate was never officially given. But there can be little doubt that, had he proceeded with the election, Williams would have been defeated. His withdrawal acknowledged the strength of anti-catholic feeling in an area which was particularly addicted to it.

An election which aroused national interest was the contest in Yorkshire, where for the first time there were four seats to be filled. Considerable weight was always attached to the opinions which were expressed by the great body of Yorkshire freeholders in their voting, and from the first it was thought that this would be of particular importance to the Catholic cause. Viscount Milton, the long-standing whig member for the county who was about to seek re-election, was told by a correspondent:

. . . perhaps the declared opinion of the Freeholders of Yorkshire on . . . Catholic Emancipation, would be considered by the King &

4. 12 October 1825; Plas Newydd Papers.
5. Anglesey to Williams, September 1825; ibid.

the anti-Catholic Members of his present Cabinet, as a truer Test, than any that could be obtained, of the prevailing opinion in this Kingdom on the subject of the Test Laws; & might therefore lead to very important results in the subsequent formation of the King's Cabinet, during the remainder of his Reign.[6]

For this reason Milton was urged to unite in a strenuous canvass with Lord Morpeth (the other whig candidate in the early stages of the struggle) and to try and arrange that they should split votes with the two tory pro-catholic candidates, James Stuart-Wortley and Richard Bethell. These could not hope to succeed with the support of the pro-catholic tory freeholders alone, and had to come to an arrangement with either the whigs or the anti-catholic tories. If the whigs could persuade them to form an alliance, success was likely to be theirs.[7]

But whig optimism diminished when the bogy of anti-catholicism reared its head. The anti-catholic tories refused to agree that the two tory seats should go to pro-catholics. Meetings were held at leading West Riding towns to promote the return of more congenial members. A meeting at Leeds chose Richard Fountayne Wilson as a candidate on anti-catholic principles. At Bradford fourteen anti-catholics, led by the local vicar, requisitioned a meeting to choose candidates of their own persuasion. At a meeting at Ripon on 1 December 1825, resolutions were passed which expressed concern at the prospect of having all four members in favour of Catholic emancipation, resolved to support only candidates who were known anti-catholics, and provided for a committee of eight to act with other committees in the county in order to achieve their purpose.[8] The chief of these meetings was held at York on 3 December to propose William Duncombe as an anti-catholic candidate in addition to Wilson. Although only a hundred were present, the speakers claimed that six hundred freeholders wanted not only the tory members but all four representatives to be anti-catholics. The anti-catholics then proceeded to consolidate their attack. A meeting at Leeds on 19 December appointed a 'Committee for the Protestant Cause'. Anti-catholic influence was exercised by magnates: in January the Duke of Newcastle was informed by

6. J. W. Tottie to Viscount Milton, 12 December 1825; Fitzwilliam MSS.
7. Ibid.
8. *John Bull*, 12 December 1825.

his agent at Boroughbridge that all his freeholder tenants resid-
ing there were engaged in favour of the anti-catholic candidates.[9]

As to the composition of the Yorkshire anti-catholics, Milton
was told by one of his supporters, Sir Francis Wood, that their
power lay not in the mob but in the middle classes and yeomanry.
Since many of this class had votes or could wield influence in
the county, Wood suggested that the whigs' wisest policy was
to yield to the anti-catholic storm and agree that Wilson and
Duncombe should be returned together with them.[1] It appears
from this that the whigs did not think their seats were seriously
challenged by the anti-catholic candidates; they thought it was
the tory candidates rather than themselves who would suffer in
the face of the anti-catholic attack. The whigs were confident
largely because of Milton's great personal power, which was
firmly grounded on the wide Fitzwilliam estates. No other whig,
it was thought, could withstand the anti-catholic attack. When
it was rumoured in May that he might resign from the county,
Sir Francis Wood wrote pleading with him not to do so: 'In the
present No Popery fever I firmly believe no other Whig than
yourself can come in without severe Contest & incalculable
Expense.'[2] Milton did not withdraw. But his partner Lord
Morpeth was thought to be too young and inexperienced to
help fend off the anti-catholics; he was persuaded to withdraw,
and for a while it was expected that Yorkshire would return only
one whig against three tories. Towards the end of May, however,
another whig candidate was adopted. This was John Marshall,
a Leeds manufacturer whose liberal economic principles and
wide local repute made him very popular in the West Riding.[3]
Marshall's adoption coincided with Stuart-Wortley's promotion
to the House of Lords, which left only one pro-catholic tory in
the fight.

There were now five candidates, and a contest seemed necessary. A final canvass was therefore undertaken and a poll was
commenced. It appears that canvassers for the whigs had
previously gained many promises of support through concealing

9. William Hirst to Newcastle, 9 January 1826; Newcastle MSS.
1. Sir F. Wood to Milton, 20 May 1826; Fitzwilliam MSS.
2. 23 May 1826; ibid.
3. It was said that Marshall possessed every qualification for entering parliament except speaking talent. E. Baines, jun., *Life of Edward Baines* (London, 1851), p. 140.

the pro-catholic views of the candidates. After Milton had made open avowals of these principles in his pre-polling speeches, several freeholders expressed themselves deceived and declared that they would vote for Wilson and Duncombe.[4] Whether this would have seriously weakened the whigs at the poll must remain hypothetical, for Richard Bethell, the remaining tory pro-catholic candidate, withdrew at the last and the contest was abandoned. The outcome of the Yorkshire election, then, was a compromise between the whigs and the anti-catholic tories—a result of the former being able to command much support in spite of their pro-catholic views and of the latter being unable to produce additional anti-catholic candidates.

There was a contested election at Preston, where a wide franchise and a large Catholic population gave peculiar interest to the struggle. At the beginning there were three candidates— the Hon. Edward Stanley, representing the interest of the whig Earl of Derby; John Wood, a whig appealing to the corporation against the Derby interest; and the radical William Cobbett. All these candidates were pro-catholics. Cobbett even had the financial support of certain Irish Catholics.[5] Until the poll was about to start there was no anti-catholic opposition, and Catholic emancipation was not a principal issue in the canvass. There was, however, competition between the radicals and the whigs for the support of the Catholic townsmen, with the former urging the Catholics to vote for Cobbett and the latter urging them to reject him. A whig election bill of 5 June stated that Cobbett would dishonour the Catholic cause. The *Political Mountebank*, a paper published every morning during the election with a view to excluding Cobbett, devoted its second number to reprinting extracts from Cobbett's writings which had denigrated various aspects of the Roman Catholic Church, hoping in this way to discourage Catholics from supporting him.[6]

At the last minute some anti-catholic members of the corporation promoted as an additional candidate an anti-catholic tory, Captain Barrie. Barrie insisted that the Oath of Supremacy should be administered to all electors. This would prevent

4. *The Times*, 10 June 1826.
5. Extracts in a collection of literature on the Preston election in the Lancashire Record Office.
6. Ibid.

conscientious Catholics from voting. It was a blow to Cobbett, who thought that most of the Catholic electors would vote for him, and he accused Stanley of acquiescing in Barrie's scheme:

Stanley began by most solemnly protesting against putting the Catholic Oath; but Barrie comes and puts it; and though he does this, *Stanley splits votes with him*! What shameful hypocrisy! And now mark the *piety* of Stanley. He protested against putting the oath; but he knew well that his friend [Barrie] would put it; and *knowing this*, he, in his speech, . . . BEGGED AND PRAYED OF THE CATHOLICS NOT TO TAKE THE OATH!!! . . . he knew that nearly, if not quite all, the Catholics would have voted for me, not many of them for him, and none for any body else.[7]

Cobbett's allegations were without foundation, since Stanley in fact refused a coalition with Barrie.[8] His accusations seem to have been an attempt to excuse his own lack of success. On the ninth day of the poll he retired from the contest. Barrie was scarcely more successful, although he tried to attract the maximum popularity on the hustings, where he avowed himself '. . . a Man of no Party, neither Whig, Tory, nor Radical, but thought, spoke, and acted for himself . . . he was an enemy to the Slave Trade, wished for a great alteration in the Corn Laws, a Friend to Civil and Religious Liberty, favourable to Dissenters, but opposed to the Catholic Emancipation'.[9]

Despite such efforts Barrie was bottom of the poll. In Stanley and Wood, the successful candidates, Preston had two pro-catholic members in place of one. A combination of the Derby and corporation interests had won the day, despite the fact that the administration of the Oath of Supremacy had robbed them of Catholic support. The local priests recognized that Stanley and Wood had been ready to dispense with the Oath and urged their flocks to join the procession of the victorious candidates.

The Government was officially neutral in the matter of dispensing patronage in this election. There are hints that Liverpool had agreed not to give government support to anti-catholic candidates, provided that Canning exercised a similar restraint with

7. G. D. H. Cole, *Life of Cobbett* (London, 1924), p. 310.
8. Ibid., p. 300.
9. Preston election literature.

regard to pro-catholic candidates. Lord William Bentinck wrote that Liverpool and Canning were the most strictly neutral of all the ministers in this matter, and that Canning would probably consider giving assistance to pro-catholic candidates as a departure from his 'engagement'.[1] Accusations were later made by Lord Tavistock that Canning had even connived at assisting anti-catholic candidates at the election, but no reasons were disclosed for this view.[2]

Despite government neutrality, difficulties over treasury patronage were liable to arise at elections where a pro-catholic and an anti-catholic were standing, both of them being friends of the Government. The problem arose with peculiar intensity at Cambridge University, where Lord Liverpool's neutrality was so rigid as to give the appearance of paralysis and the whole 'open' system in the Government was infringed. Lord Palmerston, a university representative since 1811, was opposed by two of his colleagues in the Government, J. S. Copley (Attorney-General, afterwards Lord Lyndhurst) and Henry Goulburn, in addition to W. J. Bankes, who had been returned for the university in 1822. Palmerston was the only pro-catholic of the four. In a letter to E. J. Littleton, Palmerston blamed Liverpool for permitting a contest in which three candidates were members of the Government and the fourth (Bankes) was the premier's supporter and relative.[3] He expressed his indignation more fully in a long letter to Liverpool himself.[4] He started by saying that for colleagues in the Government to contest each other's seats could only imperil government cohesion. On such occasions, he contended, the differences of individual members of the Government on the Catholic question should be forgotten. The sole criterion in contested elections should be whether a candidate was a government supporter or not. At Cambridge, however, his colleagues intended to arouse opposition against him on the grounds that he was pro-catholic. Palmerston's second grievance concerned the allocation of treasury patronage. He argued that even if an inter-ministerial contest were allowed to commence, at least the minister who was already in possession of the seat,

1. Bentinck to Milton, 21 January 1826; Fitzwilliam MSS.
2. Tavistock to John Cam Hobhouse, 9 and 10 March 1827. A. Aspinall (ed.), *The Formation of Canning's Ministry*; Camden Soc., third series, lix (London, 1937), pp. 36, 38.   3. 9 January 1826; Hatherton Papers.
4. 19 January 1826. A. Aspinall and E. A. Smith (eds.), *English Historical Documents*, xi (London, 1959), pp. 105–8.

namely himself, had an indisputable claim on the fullest support
which the Government could offer. The fact that Palmerston
was standing as a solitary pro-catholic was another reason for
giving him immediate and unequivocal government support, as
a proof that the ministry still respected the 'open' system.[5] Yet
when he had sought this support, Liverpool had pleaded
neutrality, and other anti-catholic ministers had said they must
primarily consider the claims of Copley and Goulburn when
bestowing their influence. Further, Palmerston claimed that one
of the Secretaries to the Treasury and a Lord of the Treasury were
giving active help to one of his opponents.

Deserted by the Government to which he belonged, Palmerston also suffered the disadvantage of being a pro-catholic in the
face of preponderating anti-catholic feeling in the university.
It was possible that certain tories would, for personal and other
reasons, support him in spite of his pro-catholic views, but it was
unlikely that this aid would be sufficient for victory. His only
hope of success, therefore, was an appeal to the whigs. He warned
Liverpool that if he were returned to parliament through the
support of the Opposition this would be a situation forced on
him against his own wishes.[6] The university whigs, for their
part, were able to overcome their dislike of a tory minister for
the sake of Catholic emancipation. The Rev. Adam Sedgwick,
Professor of Geology, wrote to John Cam Hobhouse:

A defeat [for Palmerston] will be a complete triumph to the *no
popery* faction, it will consolidate their interests, & the noise of it
will ring thro' every corner of the kingdom. If the Catholic question
be an important question it is important for us to defeat the Country
Parsons & the bigots who at this moment are dishonouring the land
we live in.[7]

Outside the university the whigs were similarly enthusiastic
in Palmerston's cause. Lord John Russell called him 'the Whig
candidate for Cambridge'. He was also helped by the fact that
three anti-catholics insisted on standing. Since there were only
two seats to fill, one of these candidates was bound to lose. The

5. Palmerston had told E. J. Littleton that Liverpool's views on the Catholic
question 'ought to have made him as a Point of Delicacy peculiarly anxious
to prevent his Protestant office men from attacking his Catholic ones on that
ground'. 9 January 1826; Hatherton Papers.
6. Palmerston to Liverpool, 19 January 1826; Aspinall and Smith, p. 108
7. 8 January 1826; Broughton Papers, Add. Mss. 36461, ff. 389–90.

splitting of votes between three of them might allow Palmerston to steal a victory, whereas the concentration of support on two might have kept him out.[8] Palmerston commenced an energetic canvass at the end of November 1825. He was well received in the university and openly stated his pro-catholic views. He was confident that he had powerful support among London lawyers and resident members of the university, and that he would receive the majority of votes in St. John's, his own college, and in Trinity, where whiggism was strong. Nevertheless the predominance of clergymen among the electors made him apprehensive. He wrote to E. J. Littleton: 'The Anti Catholic Fever is raging among the Country Parsons . . . the great majority of the Electors are rural Reverends and if they come up in mass against me their charge will be as formidable as that of the black Hussars.'[9]

On the eve of the election Palmerston was more hopeful, and this was very largely on account of the whigs. 'The Whigs', he told his brother, '. . . have given me cordial and hearty support, and, in fact, bring me in.'[1] This support, he continued, was a snub for Liverpool, whom he charged with behaving 'shabbily, timidly, and ill'. On the day of the parliamentary dissolution (31 May) he wrote to Liverpool, threatening to resign from the Ministry if he lost the election. This step, however, proved unnecessary. In the poll he was returned second to Copley. His return was regarded as a triumph by the pro-catholics, and Copley's by the anti-catholics.

Palmerston's success was a severe blow to anti-catholic feeling in the university. He himself thought that such feeling was broken for good. He said that many of the Johnians and others who had supported him because of college loyalty or personal regard were anti-catholics, and they could scarcely retain their opinions with the same fervour thereafter.[2] The result also had an important effect on Palmerston's own political position. Liverpool had allowed his scrupulous upholding of the 'open' system to lapse, and had driven Palmerston to seek support from the

8. The anti-catholic candidates also clashed in the matter of seeking support from their college. All three were Trinity men.
9. 2 January 1826; Hatherton Papers.
1. Palmerston to the Hon. W. Temple, 5 June 1826. H. W. Bulwer, *Life of Palmerston* (2 vols., London, 1870), i. 154.
2. Palmerston to the Hon. W. Temple, 17 July 1826; Bulwer, i. 170.

whigs. Palmerston's indebtedness to the whigs and his enmity towards the anti-catholic ministers who opposed him made him realize that the liberal tories had much more in common with the Opposition than with the ultras who were their official colleagues. He wrote to his brother:

. . . in truth the real opposition of the present day sit behind the Treasury Bench; and it is by the stupid old Tory party, who bawl out the memory and praises of Pitt while they are opposing all the measures and principles which he held most important . . . that the progress of the Government in every improvement which they are attempting is thwarted and impeded.[3]

In retrospect Palmerston described the election as 'the first decided step towards a breach between me and the Tories, and they were the aggressors'.[4] It was the beginning of his move towards the whigs. Henceforth he acted with the Canningites and with them joined Grey's government in 1830.

So far we have dealt with the impact of Catholic emancipation on elections in Britain, but more important for the Catholic cause were the Irish elections. In England Catholic emancipation was only one of several important issues, whereas in Ireland it completely absorbed electoral attention, as was natural in a country where the cause was becoming increasingly vital. In previous elections the Catholic lay leaders, supported by the priests, had already taken issue with the anti-catholic landlords in the crucial county constituencies, where they tried to win the support of the forty-shilling freeholders enfranchised by the Act of 1793. The landlords had had the worst of the struggle. In the general election of 1818 pro-catholic freeholders had beaten the landlord interest in Wexford, Leitrim, and Sligo, and they were again successful in a by-election in County Dublin in 1823. In 1826, therefore, it was widely expected that the revived Catholic Association would make an all-out effort to assail the landlord interest in elections where that interest was anti-catholic. But this was not the case. The Catholic leaders were slow to organize the masses advantageously in the elections. It is true that the Waterford branch of the Association, led by Thomas Wyse, had been preparing since August 1825 to fight the well-

3. Ibid., p. 171.   4. Op. cit., p. 155.

established interest of the anti-catholic Beresford family in that county. But O'Connell refused Wyse's suggestion that he should intervene personally to encourage the freeholders.[5] Only in June, just before the poll, did the Catholic leaders realize that H. Villiers Stuart, the pro-catholic candidate in the county, was likely to succeed. When, to the surprise and jubilation of the Irish Catholics the Beresfords were overthrown, the Association made amends for its inactivity by assisting Alexander Dawson to a similar victory in Louth. A third pro-catholic victory against the landlord interest was in Monaghan.

Halévy, among others, has exaggerated the effect of the Catholic successes in Ireland in saying that the pro-catholics gained 'a very considerable number of seats'.[6] J. H. Hexter has contradicted this assertion, showing that the net gain of pro-catholic seats in Ireland was only three.[7] But neither of these historians gives a satisfactory interpretation. Hexter rightly corrects Halévy, but he himself fails to point out that out of six pro-catholic gains three were hotly contested popular victories in the counties, whereas all three anti-catholic gains were in uncontested boroughs. Further, he says nothing of the effect of the victories on Catholic morale and the future prospects of the Catholic cause. The bare results, it is true, could not significantly alter the balance in the new parliament, but the successes were of immense potential advantage to the Catholic cause. O'Connell now had in his hands an aggressive force which, if exploited in the future, was likely to bring emancipation far quicker than renewed attempts at conciliation on the 1825 model. Villiers Stuart said after his success in County Waterford: 'I look to the next general election, and then we shall see if there will be a city or county in Ireland from which one member shall be returned who openly avows his determination to vote against Catholic Emancipation.'[8]

5. An idea was generally held that the Irish pro-catholic victories of 1826 were the result of a well-prepared and organized effort by O'Connell. Halévy, for example, wrote: 'O'Connell organized the revolt of the free tenants against their Protestant landlords' (*Hist. Eng. People*, ii. 240). This idea is mistaken, and has been banished from recent works.

6. *Hist. Eng. People*, ii. 240.

7. 'The Protestant Revival and the Catholic Question in England, 1778–1829', *Journal of Modern History*, viii (1936), p. 312, n.

8. *The Times*, 1 July 1826.

The pro-catholic victories in Ireland were the most impressive results of the 1826 election. Alongside the positive pro-catholic efforts of the Irish, attempts to raise the cry of 'no popery' in Britain appear negative and apathetic. They were simply no match for the electoral zeal of the Irish Catholics, even in its embryonic state of 1826. Our consideration of British elections has suggested that anti-catholicism was by no means universally successful, and this is borne out by the results of these elections.

In the constituencies of Great Britain (excluding Ireland) whose elections were not contested, only forty-eight new members were returned who held different views on Catholic emancipation from those of the members they replaced. Twenty-seven of these were anti-catholics and twenty-one pro-catholics.[9] Most of these changes, however, probably represented the opinions of individual parliamentary patrons rather than the public. A clearer indication of popular feeling on the Catholic question is provided by the results of contests. In the eighty-four contests in Great Britain only twenty-eight members were returned whose views on Catholic emancipation differed from those of their predecessors. Eighteen of the changes were anti-catholic and ten pro-catholic. This does not indicate that popular anti-catholicism was a very effective force in the elections. Even in constituencies where the franchise was comparatively free from influence, there was no indication that anti-catholic feeling was strong enough to sway many results. Hexter found, from a study of the forty-two 'free' constituencies of England (seven counties and thirty-five boroughs), that only twelve of these constituencies returned one new member each whose views on Catholic relief differed from those of their predecessors. Seven of these new members were anti-catholic and five pro-catholic. Only five of these popular changes, moreover, were made at contested elections, although there were twenty of these 'open' contests altogether, and in three of these the change was anti-catholic. This marginal anti-catholic gain of one from the popular contests shows how ineffective was the popular anti-catholic cry in English elections.

Many of the members in the above assessments were 'new' only to the places where they were elected; they had sat in the

9. *Members of Parliament, 1705–1874* (Official Return of the House of Commons). In these assessments I have incorporated the various changes which took place, as a result of election petitions and by-elections, before the next Catholic division in the Commons (6 March 1827).

old parliament for other constituencies. There were, however, 144 members who were entering parliament for the first time. Several of these may not have decided how they were going to vote on the Catholic issue, or may have avoided expressing pro-catholic opinions because of the sentiments of their electors. Nevertheless, it may be assumed that the views expressed by most of these new members in parliamentary divisions in 1827 or 1828 were the same as their opinions in 1826. It may be imagined that their views were more subject to the anti-catholic climate than were the opinions of older and more hardened members. But no such conclusion can be drawn. Seventy-three of the new members were anti-catholic, sixty-seven pro-catholic. As for the comparative age of these members, the statistics are similarly equivocal; they give no support to the pro-catholics' contention that they had a majority of youngsters. Of the youngest new members, born in 1800 or after, twenty-two were anti-catholic and eighteen pro-catholic.[1]

Taking the parliamentary divisions in 1827 and 1828 as the basis of assessment, calculations of gains and losses show that in Great Britain the anti-catholics had a net gain of sixteen seats, and when the Irish results are counted in, this gain is reduced to thirteen.[2] This meagre advantage shows that the no-popery cry had had some effect, though nothing like as great as the anti-catholics had hoped. The pro-catholics, for their part, were far from downcast by the results. Palmerston wrote, with some exaggeration:

... the grand point is that the No Popery cry had been tried in many places and has everywhere failed; and we may now appeal to the experience of facts to show that there does *not* exist among the people of England that bigoted prejudice on this point which the anti-Catholics accused them of entertaining.[3]

J. H. Hexter has asserted that the small anti-catholic gain 'hardly indicates a serious division of sentiment between Parliament and

---

1. See below, Appendix (b). The approximate ages of all except one of the 144 new members are known. The most useful source is Gerritt P. Judd IV, *Members of Parliament, 1734–1823* (New Haven, 1955).
2. See below, Appendix (a). In the Irish results, the Hon. H. R. Westenra has been treated as a 'new member' for Monaghan, although he had represented the county in the old parliament. He had become a pro-catholic, and stood on completely different principles.
3. Palmerston to the Hon. William Temple, 17 July 1826; Bulwer, i. 170–1.

the nation' on the Catholic question.[4] Nevertheless, after his study of the elections he still states that anti-catholic feeling was chronic throughout British society.[5] How are we to reconcile the apparent conflict between indecisive election results and strong popular anti-catholic feeling? The answer is that anti-catholic sentiment was not a sufficiently burning motive to influence the results as a whole. Our consideration of the election has shown that pro-catholic views were an unpleasant disadvantage to many candidates in British elections. Some of the candidates were sub- jected to rigorous criticism by their electors because they held pro-catholic opinions, and some had later to answer charges of having deceived their constituents on this point. However, if the candidate were personally popular, if his views on other topics were acceptable, or if he simply concealed his opinions, the disadvantage of being a pro-catholic could be circumvented. Popular anti-catholic feeling, although abundantly expressed, was too passive to inspire a positive and co-ordinated movement like the Catholic Association in Ireland. In the short run, it achieved a small anti-catholic majority in the new parliament, which was a temporary set-back to the Catholic cause. In the long run, the apathy and disorganization of no-popery sentiment made it ineffective in the final crisis of Catholic emancipation.

4. Hexter, op. cit., p. 311.   5. Ibid., pp. 316–19.

CHAPTER V

THE CATHOLIC QUESTION IN 1827

THE pro-catholics were not unduly discouraged by the general election. Soon afterwards they were saying that, if their cause received the mandate of the Commons in a new parliament, its advocates could urge the Lords to reconsider the Catholic claims as a new question.[1] Meanwhile they were frankly heartened by the grave illness of the Duke of York, whose intervention had done much to ruin the prospects of the 1825 Relief Bill. One pro-catholic wrote that York's demise would be a great public benefit.[2] Other observers thought that Liverpool's Government was so dependent on York's support that the latter's death would break it up.[3] Such people did not realize that York's political influence had recently suffered a sharp decline. On 9 November 1826 he sent a paper to the King, claiming on the strength of the election results that Great Britain was overwhelmingly anti-catholic and demanding vigorous measures to quell the turbulent spirit shown at Irish elections.[4] A further letter of 11 November suggested no less than the formation of an exclusively anti-catholic government.[5] So blatant an ultimatum was highly embarrassing to the anti-catholic ministers who were schooled in the discreet co-operation of the 'open' system. Peel expressed his disapproval.[6] Wellington, anxious as ever to preserve the *status quo*, drew up a memorandum for the King in which he defended the system of neutrality in the Government, emphasizing the restrictions which this system imposed on the expression of pro-catholic sentiments by ministers.[7] Liverpool also advised the King to consider 'whether it would not be as impracticable, at least *now*

1. Charles Wynn to Plunket, 24 September 1826; William Wynn MSS.
2. John Campbell to George Campbell, November 1826; Mrs. Hardcastle, *Life of John, Lord Campbell* (2 vols., London, 1881), i. 437.
3. Sir George Warrender (member for Westbury) to the Duke of Buckingham, 27 December 1826; Newcastle MSS.
4. *Geo. IV Letters*, iii. 180.
5. Ibid., pp. 180–1.
6. Peel to Bathurst, 16 November 1826; Bathurst Papers, p. 616.
7. Dated 20 November 1826; WND, iii. 462–3.

as in 1812, to form an administration upon the exclusive Protestant principle, and whether the attempt to do so must not infallibly lead to an administration of an opposite character'.[8] Faced with this hostile body of opinion, and realizing too that the King had been influenced against him, York was compelled to climb down. He now protested that his original object had been misunderstood, that he had merely wanted to set down the alarm he felt about recent threats to the Protestant constitution, and that his fears had become exaggerated through protracted illness and the consciousness of approaching death.[9] Nothing more was done about the matter, and the only result was York's political humiliation. Even if he had rallied, it is unlikely that he would have enjoyed his former influence, and it was a greatly exaggerated view which held that his removal would ruin a government.

Nevertheless, rumours of change persisted after York's death on 5 January, and they came to a head on 17 February, when Liverpool was felled by an apoplectic stroke which ended his political career. This event precipitated the crisis which had been expected after York's decease. Two motions, on the Corn and Catholic questions, were awaiting debate in the Commons. The Cabinet persuaded the King that Liverpool's illness should be regarded as temporary, so that the choice of a new premier would not be made until after the debates. The choice would be particularly influenced, it was thought, by a division on the Catholic question. A large pro-catholic majority might produce a government in which Canning had unquestioned leadership. A decided anti-catholic majority would mean the continuance of the present Government; Canning would probably lead it but would have less power than in the former case.[1] It was therefore very important to Canning that the result should be known before he began to form a government. Consequently he showed considerable anxiety about the exact timing of the debate. The appointment of a new premier could only be delayed so long as the pretence about Liverpool's possible recovery could be kept up. This could not be for long, and Canning therefore wanted the debate to take place before too much time elapsed. Only

8. 10 November 1826; C. D. Yonge, *Liverpool*, iii. 435–6.
9. York to the King, 18 November 1826; *Geo. IV Letters*, iii. 182–4.
1. Joseph Planta to Stratford Canning, 23 February 1827; Aspinall, *Canning*, pp. 20–21.

with reluctance did he agree to a postponement of the motion until 5 March.[2] He feared that the whigs—one of whom, Sir Francis Burdett, was to introduce the motion—might want to delay further still, beyond the deadline when an appointment must be made.[3]

It appears from Canning's correspondence on this matter that he wanted to continue the Government on its 'open' basis. This was certainly suspected by the whigs. They again raised the cry of betrayal against the pro-catholic ministers, and they wanted a further postponement of the Catholic debate because this might reduce the chances of the arch-traitor Canning. Grey told Lord Holland that to bring forward the question at this time would be to 'favour Canning's views, if he wishes to compromise, i.e. to betray the question'.[4] The Duke of Bedford said that the whigs were retarding the Catholic cause 'by giving in to, and becoming parties to, the juggle of Canning, Plunkett & Co.'.[5] Certain whigs wanted to shelve the question for other reasons. Their confidence in a pro-catholic majority was undermined by two recently amended parliamentary returns which replaced four pro-catholics with four anti-catholics.[6] Despite these doubts, the question was introduced on 5 March, after resolutions on the Corn question had been discussed—favourably from Canning's point of view—on the first of that month.

Canning himself was optimistic about the result. But he admitted that this feeling was founded on no very accurate data,[7] and the pro-catholics in general cannot have been very sanguine after the discouragement of the amended returns. It was, indeed, possible that some new members would cast aside an anti-catholic cloak which they had assumed to please their electors, and stand forth unashamed as pro-catholics. But Viscount Tavistock, Bedford's heir, took the reverse view: 'Many people, friendly to the Catholics in their hearts, [but] with hostile constituents, wd. willingly keep away [from Parliament], but if forced to come up ... will vote in compliance with the wishes of their con-

---

2. Canning to Huskisson, 21 February 1827 (first letter, Aspinall, p. 9).
3. Canning to Huskisson, 21 February 1827 (op. cit., p. 7); also Canning to Huskisson, 23 and 25 February 1827 (op. cit., pp. 17, 26).
4. 28 February 1827; Grey MSS.
5. Aspinall, op. cit., p. 4.
6. See Huskisson to Canning, 25 February 1827 (ibid., pp. 24–25).
7. Canning to Huskisson, 25 February 1827 (second letter, op. cit., p. 26).

stituents.'[8] The ultras, for their part, were reasonably hopeful about the debate. It was said that those who had examined the lists of members were sure of an anti-catholic majority strong enough to counteract the loss of York and Liverpool. In preparing their motion, the pro-catholics showed that they had learnt from the 1825 crisis the lesson that collateral measures might alienate supporters. Several months before, it was considered advisable that the distracting 'wings' of 1825 should not be revived.[9] The motion was finally introduced without specific securities, and not as a bill but as a general resolution.

In his introductory speech Burdett dwelt on three past events in which, he claimed, great hopes of Catholic emancipation had been held out—the treaty of Limerick, the Irish Union Act, and the King's visit to Ireland in 1821. His emphasis on the last-named event shows how deeply rooted was the impression that George IV was in favour of the Catholic claims. Burdett quoted from Sidmouth's official letter at the time of the royal visit, which stated that the King wished to remove every cause of irritation in Ireland, and remarked:

He [Burdett] hoped that such language must be considered as the statement of his Majesty's sentiments upon the subject [of the Catholic claims]; and it would be in the highest degree unbecoming to suppose that his Majesty had elevated with one hand the hopes of the people of Ireland, in order to enjoy the miserable pleasure of dashing them to the earth with the other.[1]

On the whole the debate was encouraging for the pro-catholics. One conversion and one re-conversion were declared in their favour.[2] But when the division was taken at 5 a.m. on 7 March, their hopes were dashed. The motion was defeated by four votes, 276 to 272. For the first time since 1819 a pro-catholic motion had failed to pass the Commons.

The main cause of this result was the anti-catholic gain of thirteen seats in the general election and in ensuing amendments to the returns. Pro-catholic observers, however, ascribed their defeat to other reasons. Some said it was due to abstentions. Others blamed the machinations of the anti-catholic Secretaries

8. Tavistock to John Cam Hobhouse, 11 February 1827; Broughton Papers, Add. Mss. 36463, f. 260.
9. Plunket to Canning, 10 October 1826; Plunket, ii. 232–4.
1. Hansard, xvi. 847.
2. Ibid., 904–5, 1008–9.

to the Treasury, S. R. Lushington and J. C. Herries. The latter
were accused of trying to gather together all known anti-catholic
members to vote in the division, and of using all the influence
they could to win votes from the pro-catholics.[3] It was not only
the Catholic question but the character of the future ministry
which was at stake in the division; and it was said that the
Secretaries had disseminated the impression that a vote against
the Catholics was a vote for Peel as premier, while a pro-catholic
vote was one for Canning.[4] Seen in this light, the anti-catholic
majority was too small to have a decisive effect on the formation
of a new government. However, the Catholic defeat was un-
doubtedly a reverse for Canning's chances of gaining the premiership, and the prospect of an anti-catholic being appointed was
somewhat improved.

The ministerial hiatus lasted until 10 April. For over a month
of intrigue, rumour, and negotiation, three anti-catholics were
mentioned as rivals of Canning—Wellington, Peel, and Bathurst.
Wellington and Bathurst were never really serious candidates.
Wellington was pushed forward against his own will by friends
such as the Arbuthnots. However, from correspondence relating
to Wellington at this time there emerges the interesting fact that
some thought he was ready and able to settle the Catholic
question on a compromise basis. Hints of this were seized on
by a few interested parties. The Earl of Clare declared his wish
that Wellington would insist on the Catholic question being
made a Cabinet measure and carry it without yielding to the unqualified concession which the Catholic Association demanded.[5]
Similarly the Duke of Buckingham, who was on the verge of
bankruptcy and thought he might regain solvency by obtaining
a lucrative post in a Wellington ministry, urged Wellington to
take office and settle the question.[6] Wellington sharply discouraged Buckingham's self-seeking, but did not deny that he was
still thinking of a compromise settlement.[7]

Canning remained the leading candidate, and speculation

---

3. Sir Robert Wilson to Grey, 9 March 1827 (Aspinall, *Canning*, p. 37);
Lord Binning to Sir Charles Bagot, 6 March 1827 (ibid., p. 32); Canning to
Wellesley, 22 May 1827 (*Wellesley Papers*, ii. 161).
4. Agar Ellis to Ralph Sneyd, 10 March 1827; Sneyd MSS.
5. Clare to Ralph Sneyd, 27 February 1827; ibid.
6. Buckingham to Wellington, 21 February 1827; Aspinall, *Canning*, pp.
10–11.
7. See the correspondence in Aspinall, p. 12 and pp. 44–56.

abounded as to what form his Government would take. It was anticipated that he could do no more than continue the 'open' system and that the Catholics would gain no more than a premier with favourable inclinations. This seemed to satisfy Canning's followers.[8] But the question had arisen as to whether the whigs would support and possibly join a government formed on this basis. Grey was decidedly against it from the first. Overtures from Canning to the whigs, he wrote, could only be entertained if the new government guaranteed to adopt Catholic emancipation.[9] Elsewhere he repeated whig objections to the 'open' system, and continued: 'I declare most seriously & conscientiously my firm conviction, that an administration decidedly anti-Catholick, would be infinitely less mischievous [than the 'open' system]. . . . In short nothing will satisfy me that Canning is sincere & in earnest, but his bringing forward the question.'[1] Grey received some support for these views, notably from Viscount Tavistock;[2] but many whigs seemed ready to join Canning whether Catholic emancipation were adopted or not. Prominent among these was Brougham, whose intermittent desire for some years had been a coalition with the liberal tories. A leading article in *The Times*, which Brougham influenced at this period, advised the Marquess of Lansdowne (who was expected to lead a whig junction with Canning) not to insist on Catholic emancipation as an indispensable condition.[3] Similarly, some whigs resolved at a meeting towards the end of February that they were satisfied with Canning's pro-catholic sincerity whether or not he insisted on carrying emancipation when he formed his government. At the end of March Canning enquired whether the whigs would give him time to erase the King's anti-catholic sentiments before pressing emancipation, and whether they would insist on taking office as a body. Again the whigs showed their determined

8. Lord Dudley wrote to E. J. Littleton: 'I do not think that he is by any means bound to stipulate for Catholick Emancipation. It would be a sufficient advantage to the Romans to have a first minister favourable to their claim, and who would not employ the patronage of the crown . . . against them.' 20 February 1827; Hatherton Papers.
9. Grey to Viscount Howick, 18 February 1827; G. M. Trevelyan, *Lord Grey of the Reform Bill* (London, 1929), p. 374.
1. Grey to Holland, 7 March 1827; Grey MSS.
2. Tavistock to J. C. Hobhouse, 9 March 1827 (Aspinall, *Canning*, p. 18) and 10 March 1827 (A. Aspinall, 'The Canning and Goderich Ministries', *EHR*, xlii (1927), p. 222).
3. 20 February 1827; Aspinall, *Brougham*, pp. 141-2.

amenability. Lansdowne made only the negative stipulation that Canning should not pledge himself to the King to abandon emancipation, and required that he should use treasury patronage to advance the Catholic cause. Further, the whigs would not demand office as a body but would be content with the introduction of individuals into the ministry.[4] Grey and Lansdowne had thus taken up contrasting attitudes, and materials were laid for a split in the whig party which took place the following month.

Meanwhile there were the anti-catholics to be considered. It was predicted (wrongly, as it turned out) that the anti-catholic ministers would agree to serve under Canning for the sake of keeping their places. The anti-catholic sentiments of George IV were expected to provide a more formidable obstacle. Years afterwards, Princess Lieven claimed that she had a conversation with Canning in February 1827, in which he said that the chief obstacle to his becoming premier was the King's anti-catholicism. He wanted therefore to allay the King's fears on the matter. He was encouraged by the whigs' recent declaration that they would not insist on Catholic emancipation being adopted. He continued:

If the king made him his first minister, he would neither make it a Cabinet question nor a subject of discussion, in a word emancipation would not pass, and he had the right to count on his own power to keep that promise, for the whole Liberal part of the Lower Chamber and of the country was his.[5]

It is doubtful whether Canning actually pledged himself not to adopt Catholic emancipation. Princess Lieven's account cannot be relied on, since she did not write her diary before 1833. In any case, the account contains no proof that Canning made a declaration to the King. George IV later professed in private that Canning had given him a pledge on the subject, but the *confidances* of that monarch were not noted for their trustworthiness.[6] Canning, moreover, wrote to the King at the end of March that he 'must be free as air with respect to the question', and that 'he could give his Majesty no pledges of any kind

4. Aspinall, *EHR*, xlii (1927), p. 205.
5. H. W. V. Temperley, *The Unpublished Diary of the Princess Lieven* (London, 1925), p. 117.
6. *Private Diary of the First Duke of Buckingham* (3 vols., London, 1862), i. 13–14.

respecting it'.[7] This letter was written a month after Canning's conversation with Princess Lieven. It is possible that he had in the meantime received sufficient assurance of his strength at court to indicate that he did not need to make an anti-catholic pledge.[8] On the other hand, Canning's past record on the Catholic question was certainly not one to inspire pro-catholic confidence. In his anxiety to enter the Cabinet in 1822 he had made declarations which dangerously compromised his pro-catholic sentiments. In the crisis of 1825 he had made only a half-hearted and innocuous protest against the continuance of the *status quo*; and he had done all he could to suppress discussion of the Catholic question during the session of 1826. All these acts revealed Canning as a faithful follower of the 'open' system, and none of them had endeared him to the more single-minded champions of the Catholic cause. It may perhaps be assumed that George IV had little cause to fear Canning's pro-catholic sentiments, pledge or no pledge.

Canning may have succeeded in reconciling the King, but it was clear that he would find difficulty in persuading the anti-catholic ministers to serve under him. Wellington, who deeply distrusted Canning, said he was determined not to be his colleague.[9] Peel too, though not personally hostile to Canning, said he could not serve under a pro-catholic.[1] Wellington and Peel, indeed, were suspected of encouraging a combination of anti-catholics against Canning. But Wellington emphatically denied this at the time, and his denial has been upheld by a recent authority.[2] Peel also repeatedly stressed that he was acting in isolation. Indeed, there is every reason to believe that their opposition to Canning was entirely passive. They had long experience of the discretion regarding the Catholic question which had been imposed by the 'open' system, and such discretion was quite incompatible with the intrigue of which they were accused. Considerable efforts were made to secure the appointment of a purely

---

7. A. G. Stapleton, *Political Life of Canning* (3 vols., London, 1831), iii. 585. See also Aspinall, *Canning*, xliv–xlv.

8. We know that he had a friend in the anti-catholic S. R. Lushington, one of the Secretaries to the Treasury. Lushington wrote to Sir William Knighton, who enjoyed the King's innermost confidence, that a ministry led by Canning on the same basis as Liverpool's Government was the best choice the King could make. 26 March 1827; *Geo. IV Letters*, iii. 207–10.

9. Mrs. Arbuthnot, ii, 88–89.

1. Aspinall, *Canning*, xxxvi–vii, xl.

2. See Aspinall, *Canning*, xxxix–xlii.

anti-catholic ministry, but these were confined to the extra-ministerial ultras, a body which for some time had been growing increasingly distinct from the ministerial anti-catholics. As one observer put it, the intrigues were carried on 'not by the heads, but subs, and persons out of office'.[3] The ultra combination was led by peers, with the support of Sir Thomas Lethbridge in the Commons. On 23 February Lord Kenyon, one of the ultra peers, reported to his son a conversation he had with Lethbridge, in which Kenyon had said:

... that if there should be a determination to form a Protestant Govt., & [if there were] difficulty in so doing I would not object to be in office for that purpose. I fear however the King has not firmness to do the one thing which might be necessary to secure that object, namely to dissolve Parlt. & appeal to the Nation distinctly on the Cathk. Question. I am convinced such an Appeal would be properly answered.[4]

The ultras set about trying to strengthen the royal firmness. On 13 March the Duke of Newcastle told Lord Colchester that he wished to form an association to support the King in forming an anti-catholic ministry; that he had been seeking the aid of Lords Mansfield, Salisbury, and Falmouth; and that Mansfield thought they could win the support of sixty peers.[5] Two days later Colchester wrote that Mansfield and Falmouth had spoken to him of the need to exclude Canning from the premiership by show-ing the King that a body of peers would support any other choice.[6] This seems to have been the aim of an interview which Newcastle had with the King on 24 March. An account of this audience, which lasted one and a half hours, survives in New-castle's papers.[7] From this a clear picture is obtained both of ultra policy and of the temporizing tactics which the King used to foil it. Very early in the conversation the King began to in-terrupt Newcastle, and thenceforth, the latter wrote, 'it was only occasionally that I could edge in my remarks & opinions'. The King launched into a long account of his anti-catholic principles: 'H.M. said that he had lived in habits of intimacy with Fox &

3. Lord Binning, quoted in Aspinall, *Canning*, xli.
4. Kenyon to the Hon. Lloyd Kenyon, 23 February 1827; Kenyon Papers.
5. Colchester's diary, 13 March 1827; op. cit., iii. 466.
6. Ibid., p. 467.
7. Newcastle MSS. The following summary and quotations are taken from this draft, written by Newcastle immediately after the audience.

other R.C. advocates but that he had always preserved the same profession & that if they could not turn him it was not to be expected that he could be turned now. His opinion was immutable.' At this point Newcastle began to speak of the staunch anti-catholic views of the ultra peers: 'I . . . said that it was our wish to see an administration formed on anti Rom. Cath. principles & that if it would be H.M.'s pleasure to form such an administration it would be certain of support & success.' The King, however, made the excuse that a premier could not be appointed until it was known for certain that Lord Liverpool would not recover from his illness. Newcastle said that delay could only be advantageous to the liberal politicians, and pressed the ultra desire for an anti-catholic ministry in the following terms:

We should be happy to act in concert with H.M. & assist his choice provided that it was directed by [the following rules]—that the Premier, all offices for Ireland & the influential majority of the Cabinet should be decidedly protestant. H.M. said 'I am placed in an awkward situation & cannot advise because it would seem like duplicity in me to plot against my ministers, but this I can assure you, you may rely upon it that I will not appoint a Rom. Cath. premier or others'. I replied 'I hope not doubtful Protestants but such as are staunch and unequivocal in their opinions'. 'That you may safely rely upon' said H.M.

A little later in the conversation the King raised the question of whom to appoint as premier. Newcastle was about to suggest Eldon, but the King forestalled him and made some unfavourable remarks implying that Eldon was *persona non grata*. George went on to praise Wellington, but this time Newcastle objected. The duke thought that Wellington was intent on preserving the 'open' system, and made it clear that this was not what the ultras wanted. He tried to persuade the King to make a firmer declaration in favour of an anti-catholic ministry. But he was protesting too much. The King was nettled:

H.M. seemed to think I was pushing him—he looked a little disturbed, & said, 'what more can I do?' I replied, 'nothing Sir can be more satisfactory than your Majesty's declaration & does Yr. M. authorize me to announce to those in whom I place confidence that such is your declaration?' He answered somewhat irresolutely, not from doubt but from not wishing to involve himself in difficulties with his Ministry thro' me, for he said 'your coming here ... will render me an object of suspicion with them & they will think that I am double dealing'. H.M. then said that except in the one point of R.C. [Catholic question] no set of men could agree better than the Ministers & that Canning did very well in his Foreign affairs. I said I regretted this for I thought their measures highly exceptionable and such as I could not concur in. H.M. replied 'I know little about other matters [but] on the Rom. Cath. question I am strong, that I do understand most perfectly'.

'The King', concludes Newcastle's account, 'then talked about the Duke of Rutland & gradually led me off the conversation.'[8] From the King's tone it appears that he was annoyed with the ultra intrusion and determined not to let his choice of ministers be ruled by it. The Hanoverian kings had considerable experience in resisting such attempts to 'force the closet'.

The interview was disappointing to the ultras, but they continued their efforts to obtain an anti-catholic government. In the Commons Sir Thomas Lethbridge gave notice of a motion calling on the King to appoint only anti-catholics. One observer described this as 'a struggle of the Tories who hate Canning & would do anything to get rid of him'.[9] A motion such as this, however, would probably have helped rather than hindered Canning's chances, for the King would have become still further exasperated with the ultras and more determined to resist their dictation. This seems to have been realized by some of Lethbridge's colleagues in the Commons, for they advised him to withdraw his motion.[1] Canning certainly understood the benefits of such a motion, for he sought to counteract the advice of Lethbridge's friends and urged him to bring his motion forward.[2] Lethbridge fell into the trap. He announced that he would introduce the motion after all. This was prevented, however, by the end of the

8. A week later, on 31 March, the King had a similar interview with the Duke of Rutland himself, whom he appeared to treat with just as little sincere attention as he had shown to Newcastle. Rutland's object, however, was different from Newcastle's: he was not a representative of the ultras, and he pressed the King to appoint as premier the Duke of Wellington, with whom Newcastle had expressed himself dissatisfied. For the interview, see Aspinall, *Canning*, pp. 43–44, 52–53.

9. Countess Cowper to the Hon. Frederick Lamb, 6 April 1827; Mabell, Countess of Airlie, *Lady Palmerston and her Times* (2 vols., London, 1922), i. 134.

1. Hansard, xvii. 280.

2. Ibid., 281–2.

ministerial hiatus: on 10 April the King asked Canning to prepare a plan for the reconstruction of the Government. This meant in effect that Canning was appointed premier.

The new premier was greeted with the resignation of six cabinet ministers, five of whom—Bathurst, Eldon, Peel, Wellington, and Westmorland—were anti-catholics, and one (Lord Melville) a pro-catholic. In addition, many minor officials resigned, and Croker assessed the full number of seceders at forty-one.[3] The reason given by the anti-catholics for secession was their difference with Canning over Catholic emancipation. Westmorland, for example, told Canning that it would require a premier of Liverpool's anti-catholic views to keep him in the Government.[4] Similarly, Goulburn wrote that even if Canning wanted to retain the 'open' system, his elevation to the premiership was bound to improve the prospects of emancipation.[5] It was suspected, however, that this reason for seceding was only a public façade, and that the seceders were really motivated by personal dislike or distrust of Canning. The Earl of Harrowby told his son that Wellington had intimated that 'the Catholic Question had nothing to do with his resignation—but that it was a personal objection to Canning. This is now the tone of the seceders.'[6] The seceders had perhaps altered their tone so that they might not lose the chance of returning to office in a neutral government, should Canning's ministry fail. For the ultras hoped that Canning would quickly be turned out and that they would then be able to dictate their own terms to the King. Lord Kenyon's daughter wrote to her aunt: 'It would be delightful to have [Canning] out again before Parliament meets, which they seem to think not impossible. All the Protestant party are in very high spirits, & think this will be the means of ridding us of Canning as he can never serve under Peel after this.'[7]

The secession presented Canning with enormous difficulties in the formation of a ministry. He knew, however, that he could

3. Aspinall, *Canning*, pp. xxxix and 127.
4. Ibid , p. 60.
5. Goulburn to William Gregory, 12 April 1827; Lady Gregory, *Mr. Gregory's Letter-Box*, pp. 228–9.
6. Harrowby to Viscount Sandon, April 1827; Harrowby Papers, third series, lxi, ff. 375–6.
7. The Hon. Margaret Kenyon to Miss A. Kenyon, 21 April 1827; Kenyon Papers.

rely on the staunch assistance of George IV. For the King was furious with the seceders and disliked the ultras' attempts to sway his decision. He was now saying that Newcastle had used an undignified tone in his presence.[8] Was the King's irritation so great that he would accept an entirely pro-catholic ministry? It seemed, in the first flush of his wrath, that it might be so. His resentment was so great, wrote the Marquess of Londonderry, that 'he swears he will give up the Catholic Question sooner than be separated from Canning'.[9] But the new premier must have realized that this was only a superficial reaction and that beneath it remained the old anti-catholic leanings, so closely associated with upholding the power of the Crown. For this reason, and for the sake of his own security in relation to parliament, it was essential that Canning should try to continue Liverpool's 'open' system. George IV, in his usual tortuous way, did his best to help him in this aim. The King proceeded to grant interviews in which he proclaimed his anti-catholic principles just as he had done in his conversation with Newcastle. On 13 April he saw the Marquess of Londonderry and said he was bound by his Coronation Oath to resist Catholic emancipation.[1] The following day he gave an audience of nearly six hours to the Archbishop of Canterbury and the Bishop of London. At this interview he was said to have avowed that he was a stronger anti-catholic than his father; that he would have a Cabinet of only nine, five of whom would be anti-catholics; and that the Lord Lieutenant, Chief Secretary, and Chancellor for Ireland must be anti-catholics.[2] Paradoxically, it appears that George IV was acting in this way not to ruin Canning's chances but to strengthen them. Londonderry gained the impression at his audience that the King was so far prepared to forget his anger with the seceders as to hint that he might take them back into his government.[3] To the Archbishop, too, the King said that he need not scruple to support the new administration. We know that the King was later anxious that Canning should strengthen his government

8. Minute of an interview between the King and the Marquess of Londonderry, 13 April 1827; WND, iii. 634.

9. Londonderry to Wellington, 18 April 1827; op. cit., iii. 649.

1. Londonderry's minute of the interview, 13 April 1827; op. cit., iii. 633.

2. Colonel Trench to Wellington, 18 April 1827 (op. cit., iii. 651); Harrowby to Canning, 16 April 1827 (E. J. Stapleton, Canning Corresp., ii. 299); G. G. Vernon to Lansdowne, 18 April 1827 (Aspinall, Canning, p. 112).

3. Londonderry to Wellington, 13 April 1827; op. cit., iii. 651.

by winning the powerful support of ultra peers.[4] It seems likely that the same motives were behind his remarks to Londonderry and the primate. By advertising his anti-catholic sentiments he hoped to obtain for Canning the support of the Church and perhaps to lure some of the seceders into the new government. If these aims succeeded he would at once strengthen his new ministry and ensure a continuation of the 'open' system. In both these ways royal dignity would be upheld. The King's choice of premier would stand, the seceders would sheepishly return to the fold, and George would not be harassed by a ministry committed to Catholic emancipation.

This policy, however, went astray. The seceders did not return, and in the new Cabinet there were only three anti-catholics against nine pro-catholics.[5] This was scarcely the balanced ministry which George IV desired. The King, moreover, had particularly wanted an anti-catholic Home Secretary, but one could not be found. George IV reconciled himself to these disappointments with 'the most perfect confidence and good humour'.[6] He was ready to relax his stipulations in order to preserve Canning's government and thereby his own pride. The next step necessary to strengthen the Government was the formation of an alliance with the whigs, in order to replace the tories who had defected. But in this matter most of the whigs were so amenable that the King had to yield scarcely any further ground.

The division of opinion between Grey and Brougham on the question of joining Canning's ministry was becoming increasingly irreconcilable. Grey and his followers refused to consider joining unless Canning promised to introduce Catholic relief, while Brougham was apparently ready to join on any terms. This division placed Lansdowne, who negotiated with Canning on behalf of the whigs, in a bad bargaining position. He could not seriously expect pledges to introduce Catholic emancipation, for Canning well knew that the 'moderate' whigs represented by Brougham were willing to join him without making any such

4. George IV to Canning, 1 May 1827; Aspinall and Smith, op. cit., p. 152.
5. The anti-catholics were Lord Bexley, Chancellor of the Duchy of Lancaster, the only anti-catholic minister in the previous Cabinet who did not resign; J. S. Copley, who became Lord Chancellor as Lord Lyndhurst; and the Marquess of Anglesey, the new Master-General of Ordnance, a temporary anti-catholic.
6. Canning to Wellesley, 22 May 1827; *Wellesley Papers*, ii. 159.

conditions. The premier was therefore able to insist, in an interview with Lansdowne on 19 April, that the Government position on the Catholic question should remain neutral. Lansdowne submitted to this. However, since he had been offered the post of Home Secretary, he asked that the Irish Lord Lieutenant and Chief Secretary, with whom he would be closely associated in the performance of his duties, should be of the same pro-catholic opinions as himself. This request Canning could not grant. The King was particularly insistent that the Irish Government should be mostly anti-catholic, and Canning had promised him this. It was on this point that the negotiations broke down.[7]

Lansdowne's rigidity was greeted by a storm of protest from a large number of whigs who were of Brougham's persuasion. These malcontents were not to be robbed of office by what they regarded as a mere quibble over the Irish Government, and they urged Lansdowne to re-open negotiations. Lansdowne gave way to their pressure, but still held out for a pro-catholic Chief Secretary. At first Canning could only repeat his inability to contravene the King's wishes in the matter. But it was impossible to find an anti-catholic to fill the post, and finally the pro-catholic William Lamb was appointed. Although the appointment was regarded as temporary, pending the discovery of a suitable anti-catholic and Lamb's own succession to the peerage, most of the 'moderate' whigs were satisfied with it as a basis for joining the ministry. On 27 April two of them, James Scarlett and the Duke of Devonshire, were given office. Lansdowne held to his scruples for the moment, but on 9 May he too yielded and entered the Cabinet without portfolio, while Carlisle and Tierney also took Cabinet office. In July, Lansdowne became Home Secretary and Carlisle took the Privy Seal.

The whigs' eagerness for office had enabled Canning to form his coalition without giving up his proviso that Catholic emancipation must remain an open question. The whigs made only a vague reservation that they might have to resign 'should circumstances occur connected with the construction of the Irish Government which would make them feel it contrary to their opinions and views of what is due to the tranquillity of Ireland

---

7. For this interview, see Canning to the Earl of Carlisle, 19 April 1827 (Aspinall, *Canning*, pp. 124-5), and Canning's memorandum of 22 April (ibid., p. 156).

to remain in office'.[8] Uncertain though this standpoint was, it was more than the whigs expressed on any other political issue. No objection was raised when Canning insisted that the new whig ministers must abandon any thought of advancing or even of supporting Parliamentary Reform, and that they should not raise the question of repealing the Test and Corporation Acts. Only those whigs led by Grey who had shunned an alliance with Canning still refused to compromise these principles.

Lansdowne insisted that he had not abandoned Catholic emancipation and was only awaiting a suitable time to urge it forward.[9] As matters stood at Canning's death, however, it appeared that many whigs had submitted to the 'open' system which they had previously so bitterly condemned. As the Grey whigs did not fail to rub in, many whigs who had attacked Canning and Plunket for subscribing to the system in 1822, now did exactly the same themselves. Indeed, the Catholic cause gained nothing from the replacement of an anti-catholic premier by a pro-catholic one, beyond a hypothetical improvement in future prospects. Ironically, the 'open' system now commanded a wider allegiance than ever before. The 'moderate' whigs had accepted it, and the anti-catholic seceders had not rejected it— they still favoured a neutral government, but not when led by Canning. Only two mutually hostile groups on either extreme of politics now opposed the system. These were the Grey whigs and the ultras. The latter had failed to establish an anti-catholic ministry, but they had not given up the intention. The seceders insisted, as before, that they would not join an organized opposition, but they occasionally supported the ultras when Canning was attacked. Anti-catholic policy was to challenge the Government to introduce a measure of emancipation. If the Government did this it would collide with the anti-catholic barrier of the Lords and the King; if it refused to do so it might lose the support of its whig allies.

Various anti-catholics made this challenge, and Canning had to be very careful in replying to their provocation. It was necessary to stress the obstacles in the way of Catholic emancipation, yet without giving any room for doubt that the premier's own pro-catholic principles were as firm as ever, and to hold out the

8. Devonshire to Canning, 9 May 1827; Aspinall, *Canning*, p. 219.
9. Lansdowne to Viscount Milton, 21 July 1827; Fitzwilliam MSS.

hope of a settlement in more convenient times. Canning exactly fulfilled these requirements in a speech in the Commons on 1 May.[1] Moreover, he was aided in repelling the ultras by the fact that one of their number, Lord Mansfield, aroused the anger of George IV. In a speech in the Lords on 2 May, Mansfield threatened to bring forward a motion which would reveal most explicitly the opinion of the Lords on the Catholic question. If this opinion were anti-catholic, as it was bound to be, Mansfield would move an address to the King asking for a specific anti-catholic declaration; and if the King made this declaration he could not, in Mansfield's view, retain Canning as his premier.[2] Once again, however, the ultras blundered. Mansfield did not content himself with announcing his policy but rashly castigated the King for allowing the present ministry to be formed. He said that George III would never have consented to a government with a large majority of pro-catholics and accused George IV of breaking his promise to the Archbishop of Canterbury that he would never do so.[3] Such outspokenness deeply offended the King, who regarded it as *a direct calumny upon my Protestant faith, & upon my honour*,[4] and he asked the primate to admonish the transgressor.[5]

Thus Canning and the King both helped to protect the Government against ultra attacks. Both, in fact, were equally anxious that the Government should succeed. It is questionable, however, how long this co-operation would have lasted. As time went on, Canning's ministry grew in strength. Some of the whigs who had remained aloof gradually declared their support, and it was expected that after the prorogation of Parliament in July there would be a further consolidation. As the number of Canning's whig allies increased, the more pressing became the question of whether they would persuade him to introduce a government measure of emancipation. Beyond this question was another. Would the King, faced with such a measure, still be so anxious to preserve Canning's ministry that he would submit to emancipation against his own inclination? The political

1. Hansard, xvii. 440–3.
2. Ibid., 471–2.
3. Ibid., 470.
4. The King to the Archbishop of Canterbury, 4 May 1827; *Geo. IV Letters*, iii. 228.
5. Ibid.

crisis to which these questions might have given rise was prevented by Canning's death on 8 August.

While Canning lived the King had relaxed his anti-catholic inclinations so that a premier in whom he had placed special confidence would have a chance of success. But in Goderich, Canning's successor, he had no such confidence. He made no secret of his desire to have more anti-catholics in the Government, and Goderich was in no position to put up much resistance. Besides being a weaker character than Canning, his general opinions were less liberal than his predecessor's, and he had less in common with the whig ministers whom he had inherited. One observer asked how Lansdowne could possibly co-operate with Goderich: 'they agree ... upon only one point, viz. R. Cath. emancipation, & I question whether Ld. G[oderich] is very anxious about carrying that.'[6]

Immediately after the change of premier there were rumours that the seceders might return and that ultras might be given Cabinet office, driving the whigs from the Government. One of these rumours was fulfilled when Wellington accepted an offer to resume his extra-ministerial post of Commander-in-Chief of the army. This, however, was no comfort to the ultras. They were dismayed that the duke cared so little for anti-catholic principles that he was willing to support the coalition government; for in their view his acceptance amounted to this, even though he did not return to the Cabinet. Lord Falmouth, one of the ultra peers, remonstrated verbally with him, saying that 'his act of unqualified acceptance would be a severe blow upon [anti-catholic] principles, that he could not actively & effectively uphold them inasmuch as he could not concert with his political friends'.[7] Falmouth proceeded to make the following remarks, which have an interesting relevance to Wellington's adoption of Catholic emancipation the following year:

I told him ... as my firm opinion, that if the Catholic question were brought forward & carried at any early period, to this act of his would that measure be mainly attributable—that I knew not how far

6. Lord Combermere, writing from India to Newcastle, 31 December 1827; Newcastle MSS.
7. Falmouth to Newcastle, 19 August 1827; op. cit.

we might yet be able to resist it successfully, but that if not I conscientiously believed it would be owing to the weight of his name having been, so far as it must be in the eyes of the country, attached to the new Government. He seemed a little struck with this last remark.[8]

Thus by returning to his old post Wellington had become further separated from the ultras over the Catholic question. His plans for a compromise settlement in 1825 had been unknown to them, but his unwillingness to participate in active opposition to Canning had dissatisfied them, and now with his virtual acquiescence in the coalition ministry he aroused grave suspicions regarding his anti-catholic integrity. The ultras feared, moreover, that his example might be followed by others. Falmouth wrote to Newcastle:

I have written to the Duke of Beaufort & others including Lord Eldon by whom this disaster [Wellington's behaviour] was but little expected. . . . The former I hope will remain unchanged, yet I cannot . . . speak confidently about him or others, & after this step taken by the D. of W. himself with his eyes fully open to its effect, it is indeed difficult to draw inferences as to the future by judging of any man from the past.[9]

But the political effects of Wellington's action were ambivalent. If it aroused the ultras' distrust, it also made the whig ministers feel less comfortable in their seats. And more formidable threats to their security lay ahead. The King determined that J. C. Herries, who was described by a leading whig as 'a bitter, active and insidious enemy of the Catholics',[1] should be given Canning's old post of Chancellor of the Exchequer. Moreover, Lansdown wanted to bring Lord Holland into the Cabinet, but this was rejected by the King. The disappointed whigs determined to resist Herries' appointment. The attack was led by Tierney, and at the end of August Herries was told that the whigs had decided to resign if he was appointed.[2] The whigs, however, were in an invidious position. They had taken office in explicit opposition to the seceders' and ultras' attempts to

8. Newcastle MSS.
9. 19 August 1827, cit.
    1. Lord Holland to Plunket, 23 August 1827; Plunket, ii. 252.
    2. Herries to his sister, 28 August 1827; E. Herries, *Memoirs of the Public Life of the Rt. Hon. J. C. Herries* (2 vols., London, 1880), i. 201–2.

'force the closet'; but now they were themselves threatening to leave office because they objected to a minister whom the King had chosen.[3] There was, moreover, a difference of opinion between them. Whigs like Brougham, who were anxious above all to preserve the coalition ministry, deprecated the ministers' threat to resign and advised them to acquiesce in Herries' appointment. The whigs remained in office. Lansdowne was mollified by the guarantee of a pro-catholic Chief Secretary for Ireland if Lamb were removed—the great point on which he had originally insisted when negotiating with Canning. There is some truth behind Goderich's statement at this time that the King sincerely wanted to continue Canning's system.[4] Certainly he had sound anti-catholic reasons for doing so. To keep the whig ministers was to keep the split in the whig party, and this was the likeliest chance of keeping the Catholic question quiet.

The whigs, by remaining in office after their bold talk of resigning, had made a humiliating submission. Their degradation was driven home when Herries' advancement was followed by further anti-catholic appointments. The new Irish Chancellor and the new Irish Solicitor-General were both anti-catholics. In the ecclesiastical field, moreover, the King insisted that vacant bishoprics should go to anti-catholics.[5] The more anti-catholic appointments were made, the more discontented both the Grey whigs and the Irish Catholics became with the coalition ministry. Whilst O'Connell declared himself thoroughly opposed to the Government and talked of new schemes of Irish Catholic combination,[6] there were rumours that the Grey whigs might ally with the seceders, or at least with a small anti-ministerial group of pro-catholic tories comprising Londonderry, Ellen-

3. Grey, who was still standing on the side-lines, described their difficulties thus: 'I can easily conceive that there might be objections to [Herries'] appointment by those, who justified their accession to the administration, upon the ground of its being necessary to keep out Ultra Tories & Anti-Catholicks, but with what face can they insist upon them after the absurd & anti-Whig clamour which they joined in & encouraged, against any attempt to control the King in the choice of his Ministers.' Grey to Fitzwilliam, 30 August 1827; Fitzwilliam MSS.

4. Goderich to Herries, 1 September 1827; Herries, i. 209.

5. This happened in the case of C. R. Sumner, whose translation to Winchester was engineered by the King. A similar case was the appointment of Dr. Copleston to Llandaff: it was previously ascertained that Copleston would give no more than theoretical support to Catholic relief.

6. Fitzpatrick, O'Connell, i. 151–2.

borough, and Sir Henry Hardinge.[7] The despised whig ministers tried to increase their influence by renewing their efforts to bring Lord Holland into office; and the King, realizing that some semblance of balance had to be preserved, promised to bring him in the following Easter.

Before this, however, Goderich's Government disintegrated through a quarrel between Herries and his whig and Canningite colleagues over the appointment of the whig Althorp as Chairman of the Committee of Finance. Lyndhurst urged the King to consider replacing Goderich with Wellington. On 9 January the duke was invited to form a government, and the coalition of 1827 came to an end. The likelihood of its improving the chances of carrying Catholic emancipation was never more than hypothetical; and in fact it did no more than continue the 'open' system, with more politicians acquiescing in it, willingly or unwillingly, than ever before. During its nine months of power the Catholic cause had made no tangible advance.

7. Lansdowne wrote to Huskisson on 14 December that he had heard from a reliable source that Grey and Bathurst, a leading seceder, had made definite plans for a coalition (Aspinall, *EHR*, xlii, p. 550); but a letter from Grey to Princess Lieven shows that this rumour was unfounded (Le-Strange, *Grey–Lieven Corresp.*, i. 93). Sir Henry Hardinge gave his plans for a junction with Grey in a letter to Londonderry, 11 December 1827 (Londonderry MSS.), but this project came to nothing.

CHAPTER VI

THE CRISIS OF 1828

AT the interview with Wellington at which he offered him
the premiership, George IV said that he approved of all
the ministers who had been in the Liverpool, Canning,
and Goderich governments, and that he was decidedly opposed only to having Lord Grey as a minister. He stipulated that
Catholic emancipation must not be made a government question,
and that he must have an anti-catholic Lord Chancellor in the
Home Government and an anti-catholic Lord Lieutenant and
Chancellor in the Irish Government. These conditions allowed
Wellington considerable freedom, and he used it to form a
ministry rather more liberal than Liverpool's. Both Wellington
and Peel, who returned to his office of Home Secretary, were
agreed that anything in the nature of an anti-catholic government was out of the question. Peel wrote to his old Oxford
tutor and confidant: 'I cannot advise the formation of an exclusively Protestant Government, still less the formation of an ultra
Government. My opinion is that in the first instance, a perfectly
sincere and honest attempt should be made to reunite the most
efficient members of Lord Liverpool's Cabinet. . . .'[1] In the following sentences Peel showed the extent to which he had come
to despise the ultras, who still regarded him as a leading anti-
catholic champion, and in this he spoke for Wellington too. The
ultras, he wrote, would naturally object to the proposed arrangements, and 'all parties but moderate & reflecting men will be in
some degree dissatisfied. Every Block head is for the complete
predominance of his own opinions and generally with a vehe-
mence proportionate to their impracticability.'[2]

The chief object of the duke and Peel was to reunite with the
Canningites, now led by Huskisson, and in order to do this they
were prepared to make generous allowance for the pro-catholic
feelings of that body. In his negotiations with Wellington,

1. Peel to Charles Lloyd, Bishop of Oxford, 15 January 1828; PP, 40343, ff.
104-5.
2. Ibid.

Huskisson wrote, the Duke had professed 'a great desire to avoid any thing ultra, and to retain, if possible, Mr. Canning's Friends, and further that, neither in the Cabinet, nor in the Construction of the local Govt. of Ireland, should he be disposed to give umbrage to my Catholick feelings'.[3] The satisfaction of Huskisson's pro-catholic proclivities amounted to the establishment of a predominantly pro-catholic government. Cabinet office was given to four Canningites—Charles Grant, Lord Dudley, Palmerston, and Huskisson himself. In addition, there were three other pro-catholics in the new ministry—Ellenborough, Melville, and Aberdeen—and the pro-catholics in the Cabinet were now in a majority of seven to six. As a guarantee of impartiality in the Irish Government the pro-catholic William Lamb was retained as Chief Secretary.

In order to form their coalition, both Wellington and Huskisson sacrificed their former associates—Wellington the more extreme anti-catholic seceders and Huskisson the whigs. Lansdowne considered Wellington's anti-catholic opinions an insuperable bar to a connexion with him, and as a body the 'moderate' whigs returned to opposition. Grey could now commend himself on his aloofness from the coalition of 1827. He had always foreseen, he wrote, that 'the court would get rid of our old friends, on the first opportunity that might offer, after having ruined their characters, & broken up the Whig Party irremediably'.[4] This, in Grey's view, meant 'an end to every hope & chance of carrying the Catholick Question'.[5] But Grey was concerned only with the rejection of the whigs, and forgot the rejection of the ultras. One of Wellington's methods of luring Huskisson into his ministry was to exclude Eldon, the *doyen* of the anti-catholic cause, and if this made the Government attractive to liberal opinion it made it unpleasing to the ultras. The Duke of Newcastle had wanted 'a sound, plain-dealing Protestant administration, devoid of all quackery and mysterious nonsense';[6] instead he was given a Cabinet with a majority of pro-catholics. The Duke of Cumberland was astonished at the exclusion and demanded an explanation. The

3. Huskisson to Harrowby, 16 January 1828; Harrowby Papers, first series, xv, ff. 201–2.
4. Grey to Fitzwilliam, 21 January 1828; Fitzwilliam MSS.
5. Ibid.
6. Newcastle to Colchester, 15 January 1828; Colchester, iii. 537–8.

thought cannot have been far from Wellington's mind that the
ultras might withdraw their support from his ministry altogether. But it was not his policy to let this happen. He hoped
to be able to move towards liberalism yet at the same time
retain the ultras' support, and he continued in this hope even
after he had adopted Catholic emancipation. He was faced, however, with an unattainable object, as was finally shown in the tory
split of 1829. Already, at the beginning of 1828, he was given
a sample of the difficulty. On 21 January he wrote to Newcastle,
hoping to retain his support for the Government:

I sincerely hope that this Ministry although not exactly in all its
parts such as Your Grace suggested, will conciliate your confidence,
than which nothing will tend more to its Stability and Efficiency. I
assure you that this reunion with the old Servants of the Crown in
Lord Liverpool's administration has been made without any sacrifice
of Principle on either side on any subject whatever.[7]

No reply was sent to this letter, and ten days later Wellington
wrote again:

I was very concerned not to receive from your Grace an answer to
the letter which I wrote to you as soon as the Administration was
formed; and still more concerned to learn from the purport of your
conversation with Mr. Arbuthnot this morning that this Administration did not possess your confidence. Nothing can be more unpleasant to me than that the friendly Relations between your Grace
and the Govt. should be suspended.[8]

It was noted at this time that 'the Duke of Newcastle amongst
others is gone out of town much disgusted';[9] and on 4 February
he wrote a last letter to Wellington saying that he could not give
the Government his confidence.[1] This was another step in the
alienation of Wellington from the ultras, which had begun with
his refusal to join an organized opposition to Canning and continued with his resumption of the military command.

Wellington may have partially alienated the ultras, but did
this mean that he was becoming more favourable to Catholic
emancipation? For several years the duke had shown that he
regarded the question from an empirical rather than a dogmatic

7. Newcastle MSS.
8. 1 February 1828; ibid.
9. Ellenborough's *Political Diary*, i. 18-19.
1. WND, iv. 257-8.

viewpoint. Such an attitude had been encouraged by his political situation as a discreet member of Liverpool's Cabinet, but its foundations lay in the essentially practical nature of Wellington's own character. This was noticed by *The Times* when prophesying the possible effects of the new ministry on the Catholic question:

> ... we cannot help thinking that the hopes of the Catholics must be improved, not by the transfer of pre-eminence from Mr. Canning to the Duke, but ... by the transition from Lord Liverpool to his Grace. The Catholics will not find, from the habits of military men in regard to religious subjects ... so fierce an enemy in the Duke of Wellington as they encountered in the Earl of Liverpool.[2]

Such anticipations can only have increased the suspicions of the ultras, and probably gave rise to a rumour which was afloat at this time that Wellington had declared himself a pro-catholic.[3] Had they seen some of the premier's private correspondence, the propagators of this rumour would have retailed it with more conviction and the ultras would have grown still further alarmed. Wellington was receiving communications from the Rev. Dr. Henry Phillpotts, later Bishop of Exeter and well known for his part in the Gorham Case. Phillpotts had become known as an anti-catholic pamphleteer but had changed his views and now wanted a compromise settlement of the question through Wellington. On 2 February Phillpotts sent documents to Wellington showing that Catholics were not debarred from taking oaths to maintain the civil privileges of the established Church.[4] On 25 March he sent a paper on Catholic concession, saying 'that your Grace may, in your own good time, be enabled to effect the settlement of this long agitated question, is not only my earnest wish but my fervent hope'.[5] We cannot, of course, assume that because Wellington received letters from Phillpotts he was in agreement with the views they contained. On the other hand, the very fact that he allowed the correspondence to continue suggests that he was not unwilling to consider favourably schemes of compromise such as he himself had drafted three years before.

2. 1 February, 1828.
3. Frances, Marchioness of Bute, asked Ralph Sneyd, 'can it be true that he has declared in favour of the Catholics? I cannot believe this' (26 January 1828; Sneyd MSS.).
4. WND, iv. 254–6.
5. Ibid., pp. 324–9.

But whatever effect Phillpotts' views may have had on Wellington, it was kept private for the time being. In public he appeared anxious to quash rumours of his increasing favour to the Catholic cause. When Lord Clifden asked him in the Lords whether he was inclined to concede emancipation, he denied any such intention. When Huskisson implied, in a by-election speech at Liverpool on 5 February, that Wellington had pledged himself to follow Canning's policy, the duke sharply denied in the Lords that such pledges had either been asked or given.[6] It appears from this that Wellington wanted to preserve an impression of strict neutrality in order to hold together the increasingly divergent wings of the tory party. He had coalesced with Huskisson in order to reconcile the pro-catholic tories, but would not yield so far to them as to make the ultras defect. This policy of balance does much to explain the apparent contradictions in Wellington's behaviour in the next few months.

In April Wellington submitted to the passage of a measure which gave a considerable moral boost to the Catholic cause—the repeal of the Test and Corporation Acts. The question of dissenters' disabilities was vastly different from Catholic emancipation, both in background and potential effects. The dissenters had no connexion with an extra-national power, nor did they subscribe to an intolerant ideology; their claims were not part of a burning nationalist problem, nor did they provoke serious fears that their emancipation might be the signal for democratic revolution. Freedom from these complications explains why the energies of religious reformers towards the end of the eighteenth century were largely absorbed in the cause of justice for dissenters, whereas Catholic emancipation was comparatively neglected.[7] But if the hazards of toleration were heavily weighted against the Catholics, the argument of present political necessity told heavily on their side. The dissenters had no Irish problem to back up their demands. Because of this difference the Catholic question had far outrun the dissenting question in importance. Most of the parliamentary advocates of civil liberty for dissenters

6. Hansard, xviii. 458.
7. The fact that the dissenters' appeal for freedom of conscience seemed directly at variance with the principles of the Catholic Church also explains why twenty M.P.s who were die-hard anti-catholics in 1829 supported the repeal of dissenters' disabilities a year earlier.

were primarily committed to Catholic emancipation. It was possible that their primary allegiance might prevent them giving whole-hearted support to the dissenters, for it was most unlikely that a majority of dissenters favoured Catholic emancipation. Many of the ministers of the older dissenting denominations had shown their pro-catholic sympathies, but their flocks had not done likewise; while the methodists, the most powerful and numerous of the sects, were noted for an anti-catholic bias which included minister and congregation alike. In 1827 Canning had stressed the dissenters' hostility to Catholic emancipation as an excuse for not considering their application for relief. In order to banish such suspicions, the dissenters acted in a way which showed that their relative position to the Catholics had been reversed since the later eighteenth century. Instead of the Catholics aping the dissenters in order to enjoy some crumbs of toleration, the dissenters had to sympathize with the Catholic cause and promise that, if relieved from their disabilities, they would work for Catholic emancipation thereafter. One nonconformist wrote to the whig Lord Milton:

... it should not be inferred from our silence ... that we are either indifferent or opposed to ... the Catholic claims. I for one most indignantly repel & resent the imputation ... I feel assured that every valid argument & principle which we urge to gain & secure our own rights, bears equally on theirs.[8]

Such avowals were often repeated in the Commons and elsewhere. On the other hand, the dissenters could scarcely hope to succeed if they relied only on the pro-catholic politicians. They had to make sure of the approval of a good number of anti-catholics. So we have the spectacle of the professions of support for Catholic emancipation made by certain dissenting M.P.s being explained away by other dissenting M.P.s.[9] This behaviour did not inspire confidence in dissenters' promises to support the Catholic cause in return for pro-catholic votes for their own cause. If most pro-catholics supported dissenters' relief, it was not for the sake of winning the votes of a few dissenting M.P.s but to establish the principle of breaking in upon the constitution. Such was the attitude of Grey;[1] and when the repeal was

8. Rev. Thomas Scales to Milton, February 1828; Fitzwilliam MSS.
9. e.g. Hansard, xviii. 96–97.
1. Ellenborough, i. 44.

debated in the Commons on 26 February the view was expressed that '. . . every step we make this night will be in favour of Ireland—every advance we make for the relief of dissenters will be so much gained in the great cause of Catholic emancipation. Break but once through the line of bigotry and prejudice, and the victory is our own.'[2] The Repeal Bill passed by a large majority in the Commons. The Government accepted the principle of the measure but insisted on the insertion of a clause protecting the privileges of the established Church. The Lords, bishops included, agreed to it, and the King reluctantly assented. Final innocuous protests were signed in the Lords' minutes, led by Eldon and including such names as Newcastle, Kenyon, Falmouth, and Mansfield, all of whom were leading ultras and afterwards played a large part in the opposition to Catholic relief.

The importance of the repeal of the Test and Corporation Acts can hardly be exaggerated. Exclusion of dissenters, although only a theoretical exclusion, was as much a part of the constitution as the actual exclusion of Catholics; once the first had fallen, the other was likely to follow. As a measure of religious toleration the repeal had special relevance for the Catholic question. 'It is really a gratifying thing', wrote Lord John Russell, 'to force the enemy to give up his first line, that none but churchmen are worthy to serve the state, & I trust we shall soon make him give up the second, that none but protestants are.'[3] Just as significant for Catholic emancipation was Wellington's acquiescence in the repeal, in contrast to his previous opposition. This showed his readiness to reverse his former standpoints when he thought the circumstances demanded it, and how little he was attached to principles of constitutional permanency. These characteristics were revealed still more effectively in the following year.

Meanwhile the parliamentary success of the dissenters' cause was followed by a victory in the Commons for the Catholic cause. The pro-catholics were encouraged by the large majority in favour of the dissenters, and they awaited the ultimate decision on the repeal before introducing their own motion on 8 May. Sir Francis Burdett then moved a resolution for a committee of the whole House to review the restrictive laws. Again the ques-

2. Hansard, xviii. 708–10.
3. Russell to Thomas Moore, 31 March 1828; quoted by Halévy, ii. 266.

tion of securities, that 'fertile topic of dispute', was not raised.[4] The recent relief of dissenters was now urged as an additional argument for Catholic emancipation. Sir James Mackintosh made much of the conciliatory attitude of the bishops in the former case:

It was now admitted that a test of belief was a most useless expedient for supporting an established church, and he hoped that the Right Rev. prelates, who had known such enlightened wisdom on the subject of the Test and Corporation Acts, would bring their minds to consider, with the same charitable feelings, the case of the Roman Catholics.[5]

In the division on 12 May the pro-catholics obtained a majority of six. This pro-catholic majority had more significance than previous majorities in the Commons, since it followed quickly on the heels of dissenters' relief. Wellington was so impressed that he made a minute examination of the M.P.s who had not voted and concluded that the Commons were definitely balanced in favour of emancipation. Perhaps this conclusion reinforced the letters of Dr. Phillpotts in persuading him to consider adopting Catholic relief. But his position was complicated by the need to hold his party together. The ultras' confidence in Wellington, already undermined by the composition of his ministry, had been further alienated by his consent to the relief of dissenters. At the end of May, however, this trend was brought to an abrupt halt. Two parliamentary seats were in the process of being removed from East Retford on the grounds of electoral corruption. They were to be given, not to manufacturing centres as the liberals wished, but to the hundred of Bassetlaw which was influenced by the ultra Newcastle. In protest against this measure Huskisson tendered his resignation, not expecting that it would be accepted. To his surprise, Wellington eagerly seized on the resignation and Huskisson had to go. His departure was followed by that of his friends—Grant, Dudley, Palmerston, and William Lamb. The Cabinet reshuffle which followed this virtual dismissal was not a revolutionary change, since no ultras were brought in and two pro-catholics, Sir George Murray and William Vesey Fitzgerald, replaced Huskisson and Charles Grant. Nevertheless, the anti-catholics regained their majority in the

4. Hansard, xix. 418.
5. Ibid., 558.

cabinet,[6] and the incident was regarded as an ultra triumph, not least by the ultras themselves. This was a belief which Wellington wished to foster. As an earnest of his intention to conciliate the ultras, he attended a dinner-meeting of the anti-catholic Pitt Club, where Eldon bibulously demanded 'one cheer more' for the toast of 'Protestant Ascendancy'.[7]

This policy may seem to be out of tune with Wellington's tentative moves towards Catholic relief, but a closer examination suggests that the former was done for the benefit of the latter. Wellington must have foreseen that adoption of Catholic relief would, unless handled with extreme delicacy, shatter the tory party. Anxious as he was to prevent this he may have thought that by dispensing with the Huskissonites he would regain enough of the ultras' confidence to win their neutrality, if not their support, for the measure which he contemplated. Certain uncanny prophecies of the departing Huskissonites support this interpretation. 'Now they have cleared the Cabinet of all of us,' said Huskisson, 'they will set about settling the question.'[8] Palmerston elaborated this comment: 'They may be disposed to do things, when they have the credit of doing them spontaneously, which they refused to do when it would have been supposed that we were urging them to do them.'[9]

These prophecies were soon fulfilled. It was decided that the Lords should discuss Burdett's resolution on 9 June. Before this, Wellington and Peel had a conversation, the date of which is unknown, which shows how far these ministers had progressed in their inclination to settle the Catholic question. Peel told the premier that his unpleasant situation of being in a minority in the Commons on Catholic emancipation, which had driven him to threaten resignation in 1825, was now revived and again led him to think of giving up office. This he felt the more compelled to do, since he believed a settlement of the question could no longer be withheld: he had become convinced of 'the embarrassment that must arise from the continuance of divided councils in the Cabinet', and of 'the necessity of maturely considering the whole state of Ireland'. His long commitment to the anti-catholic

6. The composition of the Cabinet was now 6:5 in favour of the anti-catholics.

7. *John Bull*, 2 June 1828.

8. W. T. McCullagh, *Memoirs of R. L. Sheil*, ii. 8.

9. Palmerston's journal, 7 June 1828; Bulwer, *Palmerston*, i. 282.

cause would not permit him personally to take a leading part in settling the question. But the duke was not so committed, and Peel wrote:

> I expressed . . . an earnest hope that in the approaching discussion in the Lords, the Duke of Wellington might deem it to be consistent with his sense of duty to take a course in debate which should not preclude him . . . from taking the whole state of Ireland into consideration during the recess, with the view of adjusting the Catholic question.[1]

Peels' liberal conduct of the Home Office since 1822 had aligned him politically with Huskisson rather than Eldon. He was still regarded as the leading anti-catholic in the Commons—a position emphasized by the fact that he represented the no-popery stronghold of Oxford University. But a survey of his career shows that he, like his chief, had little in common with the ultras, though the differences were not so strongly marked as in Wellington's case. His willingness to make concessions to the English Catholics in 1823, his discouragement of an ultra cabal in 1824 and his refusal to join one against Canning in 1827, his correspondence with Bishop Lloyd in January 1828, all exemplify his comparative moderation.[2] His conversation with Wellington now promised a complete rift with the ultras and was the first clear hint of his forthcoming conversion to the Catholic cause.

Wellington followed Peel's advice when he spoke in the Lords' debate on Burdett's resolution on 10 June. A few days earlier he had also consulted Ellenborough about his speech. The latter had advised extreme caution, and Wellington followed this counsel also, perhaps to excess. The duke's speech immediately followed a pro-catholic one by Wellesley, and the premier began by expressing concern that he differed from his brother; however, he would state his own opinions, 'hoping that, in the end, the views of my noble relation and myself will not be found to differ in reality from each other'.[3] The next part of the speech was based on advice given by Dr. Phillpotts, yet another of Wellington's counsellors, in a letter of 5 June. In this letter Phillpotts

---

1. Peel's *Memoirs*, i. 28.
2. Peel wrote: 'I entered into no cabals against those from whom I differed on the Catholic question. I contracted no political engagements with those with whom I concurred' (*Memoirs*, i. 9). The object of this statement was probably to emphasize his distinction from the ultras.
3. Hansard, xix. 1286–7.

attacked the persistent impression of many pro-catholics that the question should be settled by a concordat with the Pope. In Phillpotts' view the established Church could obtain much more effective securities through parliamentary legislation than through a concordat. The abandonment of a concordat, moreover, might win over many anti-catholics who disliked this means of settlement on strict Protestant principles.[4] Wellington exactly reproduced Phillpotts' argument:

I will say, that to enable the see of Rome to appoint the bishops to the dioceses in Ireland will be impossible under the present constitution of the country. ... What we must do must be done by legislation; and, although legislation has not affected this hitherto, I trust, if it shall be necessary, we shall do it fearlessly.[5]

The general tone of the speech, however, was extremely vague. What was it that we 'must do'? What sort of legislation might have to be carried out? Similarly tantalizing were Wellington's concluding words: 'If the public mind was now suffered to be ... tranquil—if the agitators of Ireland would only leave the public mind at rest—the people would become more satisfied, and I certainly think that it would then be possible to do something.'[6]

Words so favourable as these to a Catholic settlement had never before been uttered by an anti-catholic minister. Their significance, however, is only seen in the light of the policy which Wellington later adopted, and was clear at the time to no one but Wellington himself, Peel, and Phillpotts. The last-named wrote: 'It is impossible that such a speech should not largely contribute to prepare the minds of all for a settlement of the

4. WND, iv. 484–5.
5. Hansard, xix. 1291. Phillpotts' part in settling the Catholic question has so far not received fair treatment. Through his pamphlets of 1827 against Canning he had acquired a reputation as a violent ultra. When he supported Peel as a pro-catholic at the Oxford University by-election of 1829, he took the public by surprise and was long and virulently accused of being a turncoat. Later historians have accepted the view that he remained an anti-catholic until the last minute. Professor Aspinall, for example, has written: 'He vehemently opposed Catholic emancipation until the surrender of the Wellington Ministry in 1829' (Geo. IV Letters, iii. 336, n. 2). On the contrary, Phillpotts made clear in his voluminous correspondence with Wellington (WND, iv. and v.) that he had adopted the principle of emancipation, provided that it was accompanied by adequate securities; and, more important, his influence on Wellington's speech shows that he played a vital part in enabling the duke to hint at his intended policy.
6. Hansard, xix. 1292.

great question.'[7] Nothing of the kind happened. Wellington's speech was so obscure and ambiguous that most pro-catholics imagined it was merely another anti-catholic method of preserving the *status quo*. The ministers of the 'open' system had cried 'wolf' before, and the cry had proved meaningless. When uttered by Wellington it meant something at last, but no one heeded it. The public could not see the limitations imposed on all expressions by Wellington of his inclination to settle the Catholic question. He did not wish to lose the support of the ultras, he did not yet know whether the anti-catholic members of his Cabinet would profess conversion with him, nor had he obtained the King's permission to consider a settlement with his colleagues. Obscurity was necessary for all these reasons, and it effectively blanketed the undertones of the speech. The events immediately following the speech, moreover, seemed to reverse the favourable tone which might have been discovered in it. Wellington himself voted with the majority of forty-four, as large as ever, which threw out Burdett's resolution. Further, the allusions which the duke soon afterwards made to his speech seemed to support the cynical impression of most pro-catholics. At a Cabinet dinner he said that there was no one who desired a settlement more than he, but that he could not see how it was to be achieved.[8] On the surface, therefore, the Catholic question appeared to have made no tangible advance. Pro-catholic reactions were at best equivocal.[9] As for the ultras, Wellington's caution succeeded in keeping them free from alarm. When the ultra Lord Lowther, who had accepted a minor office, stood for re-election in Westmorland a few days after the speech, he announced his confidence in Wellington who, he said, was leading the Government back into the 'ancient ways' of the constitution.[1]

This was also the impression of the Irish Catholics, and they were enraged whereas the ultras were contented. Wellington's speech brought to a head the hostility which the Catholic Association had almost continuously shown to the ministry since its

7. Phillpotts to Wellington, 14 June 1828; WND, iv. 486.
8. Ellenborough, i. 143.
9. Grey was reported to have said after the speech that 'the Duke was bound to take [Catholic relief] up, and he expected some measure next year' (Ellenborough, i. 142); but Palmerston doubted any intention on Wellington's part to do so (Bulwer, i. 284).
1. *Leeds Intelligencer*, 19 June 1828.

appointment.[2] O'Connell had denounced the new ministry at mass-meetings in January, and the Association had resolved to oppose the election to parliament of every pro-ministerial candidate. O'Connell wanted to rescind this resolution when Wellington agreed to relieve the dissenters, but his proposal was defeated. The disappearance of the Huskissonites from the Cabinet was regarded by the Irish Catholics as an ultra triumph. The speech of 10 June was the last straw. Wellington's expressed desire that Catholic agitation should cease, holding out in compensation only vague and apparently meaningless hopes of relief, took on the appearance of a government threat of coercion. 'The Orange Party is elated with what they call a triumph', Lord Anglesey wrote, '[and] the Agitators are furious.'[3] The Catholic leaders gathered all their resources in a desperate attempt to rescue their cause from complete failure. An early opportunity came with a by-election in County Clare, and it was the Catholics' success in this which finally persuaded the Government that emancipation must be granted. Thus in its devious way Wellington's speech had a decisive effect on the removal of Catholic disabilities.

The Clare election took place because the pro-catholic William Vesey Fitzgerald, nominee of the landowners in the county, had replaced Charles Grant in the Cabinet and therefore had to stand for re-election. The Irish Catholics hoped to repeat their electoral triumphs of 1826 against the landlords. At first they sought only to return a Protestant pro-catholic who would be able to take his seat in parliament, like the members they had returned at the general election. However, invitations to two such people—Major Macnamara and Lord William Paget—were refused.[4] In desperation, only eight days before the poll, they

2. I owe this interpretation to Mr. M. G. Brock, of Corpus Christi College, Oxford.
3. Anglesey to Sir Arthur Paget, 20 June 1828; Sir Augustus Paget (ed.), *The Paget Papers* (2 vols., London, 1896), ii. 393.
4. It is not generally realized that Lord William Paget, son of Anglesey the pro-catholic Lord Lieutenant, was invited to stand. J. A. Reynolds, for instance, mentions only that Macnamara refused to stand (op. cit., p. 156). But letters written by Anglesey place the matter beyond doubt. He wrote to Lord Holland: 'O'Gorman Mahon who had been sent to Ennis, & who suddenly came back crestfallen at the defection of Macnamara, actually called upon Wm. Paget . . . to implore him to stand. William, of course, laughed in his face.' June 1828 (Seventh Marquess of Anglesey, *One-Leg*, p. 372). Anglesey also wrote to his brother Sir Charles Paget that Lord William had said he could not stand 'but by my sanction, and . . . he was sure I shd. object to that. The conduct of some of these People', he added, 'looks like imbecility.' 23 June 1828; *Paget Papers*, ii. 395.

decided on an entirely new departure: O'Connell, their Roman Catholic leader, would stand himself. Thus a Catholic, who if elected was prevented by law from taking his seat, was put up in opposition to a pro-catholic—and, in Fitzgerald, a consistent, vocal, and popular pro-catholic. The Catholics were openly setting at defiance the constitutional means which they had hitherto followed. They were trying to seize by force the concession which they had so long begged through parliamentary channels. Every effort was marshalled in the struggle: the Catholic Rent drew in a high subscription and the priests exhorted the forty-shilling freeholders to forsake the landlord interest and follow O'Connell. Victory was assured by this assiduous electioneering. On 5 July, the fifth day of the poll, Fitzgerald withdrew from a losing battle and O'Connell was returned by a majority of 1,075.

The Clare result was of tremendous importance, not so much for itself as for its potential effects. Never again could an Irish M.P. be given Cabinet office or a peerage without causing a by-election whose result might well repeat that of Clare. In a general election, moreover, it seemed that O'Connell's victory might be repeated many times by Roman Catholic candidates who when elected would be unable to take their seats. Debarred from the imperial parliament, they might well form their own unofficial Irish parliament—a natural development of that 'popish parliament' the Catholic Association—and perhaps even lay plans for dissolving the Union. The danger was reinforced by the immense popular support which O'Connell had received from the pauper forty-shilling freeholders. The Catholic Association had originally set out to use this popular force on behalf of one Protestant pro-catholic against another Protestant pro-catholic. In doing so the Irish Catholics had explicitly linked their own view of Catholic emancipation with popular democratic expression. This manifestation became much more significant when it was the Roman Catholic O'Connell who stood and triumphed. It now became possible that popular expression might turn into nationalist revolution if Catholic emancipation was much longer withheld.

None of the implications of the Clare result escaped the practical politician who was then premier, and it was this result which finally decided Wellington to adopt Catholic relief. It was not the first event to turn his thoughts in this direction, nor was it the first time that he was guided by considerations of empirical statesmanship rather than by theoretical views of religious and civil liberty. In 1825 he toyed with a Catholic settlement to keep out the whigs; in 1828 he adopted a Catholic settlement to prevent democratic upheaval, to preserve the Union, and to remove the threat to tory government. His main consideration was the restoration of order; Catholic emancipation was secondary to this end, an essential concession to render more palatable the firm measures which he envisaged. 'If I could believe', he afterwards confessed, 'that the Irish nobility and gentry would recover their lost influence, the just influence of property, without making these concessions, I would not stir.'[5] The problem exercised his mind between the Clare election and the dispersal of Parliament at the end of July. Mrs. Arbuthnot wrote that he was seeking 'a safe means of so far satisfying the friends of Catholic emancipation in England by setting that question upon fair & safe grounds, as to enable him at the same time to obtain from Parliament such powers as will be efficient for checking the progress of the *Agitators* & putting down the rebellion that seems hanging over our heads'.[6]

His proposed solution was set down in a memorandum to the King, dated 1 August.[7] Two possible remedies were suggested, but both had drawbacks unless accompanied by Catholic emancipation. The Catholic Association might be officially suppressed, but its leaders would continue to meet and would retain their influence over the people. The forty-shilling freeholders might be disfranchised, but they would retain their force as mobs. Only if Catholic emancipation were simultaneously granted were these measures likely to be effective. The concession must be seriously considered, since it was favoured by a majority of the Commons.[8] It was doubtful, Wellington admitted, whether even emancipation would satisfy Ireland. But if the Government adopted the measure it would at least win the support of the pro-catholics, and the Government would have this support

5. Wellington to Peel, 12 September 1828; WND, v. 43.
6. Mrs. Arbuthnot, ii. 198.
7. WND, iv. 565–70.
8. We have seen that Wellington had been making detailed calculations of pro-catholic strength in the Lower House after the division of 12 May. He now told the King that the actual pro-catholic majority was twenty to thirty, claiming that many pro-catholics had to be absent from the division on account of 'some local or personal influence' (WND, iv. 569).

should a civil contest with Ireland prove unavoidable. Wellington's letter accompanying this paper asked the King's permission to consider the question in confidence with Peel and Lyndhurst, the Lord Chancellor. He assured the King that no proposals would be submitted to the Cabinet before the royal opinion had been sought. 'Your Majesty will have the control over this subject in your hands till the last moment', Wellington wrote, 'at the same time that you will have done your government and the country the justice to have considered it fairly; and it will not be known that it is even under consideration.'[9] In these circumstances George IV readily permitted the discussions, stressing, however, that he was pledging himself to nothing.[1]

Wellington next sent a memorandum to Peel and Lyndhurst, advancing plans for Catholic emancipation accompanied by various securities.[2] Lyndhurst accepted the principle of concession, although differing from the duke over securities.[3] Peel returned two lengthy documents to the premier—a letter and a memorandum. The letter stated in full the reasons which had led him to accept the principle of settling the question. Again he said he would give full support to a final arrangement, but only as a private person out of office. He argued that, having formerly been so prominent an anti-catholic, he could not introduce a relief measure in the Commons without raising obstacles to its success—the scorn of his former anti-catholic associates and the distrust of the Catholics themselves. Peel's inclination to resign was kept up until January, but Wellington and his friends did not take it very seriously.[4] The accompanying memorandum showed that Peel wanted a more decisive emancipation than Wellington himself was prepared to grant at that stage. Wellington had suggested that the exclusion laws should not be repealed

---

9. WND, iv. 564–5.
1. The King to Wellington, 3 August 1828; ibid., 573.
2. Probably the paper dated 7 August 1828, which Wellington sent to the King on 16 November; WND, v. 254–68.
3. Ibid. Wellington must have known already that Lyndhurst was inclined to settle the question. Early in July Lyndhurst had told Ellenborough that 'we must try if we cannot set up the Duke during the vacation to endeavour to settle the Catholic question' (Ellenborough, i. 160); and Ellenborough wrote further, on 18 July, that Lyndhurst was very anxious to settle the question (ibid., 168).
4. Mrs. Arbuthnot thought Peel's letter proved that 'a little persuasion & flattery will induce him to remain in office & assist in managing the business thro' Parliament. For all that he said about quitting office was in a very doubtful way.' Journal, ii. 202.

but annually suspended, thus forcing annual indemnity on the Catholics—a yoke which the dissenters had just thrown off. Peel, on the other hand, was for a less blatant political inequality—he suggested that Catholics might be excluded from certain high offices, or that the number of Catholics in parliament might be restricted. Wellington had also proposed that the Irish county franchise should be limited to those paying at least £5 to the county rate; but Peel doubted the adequacy of this means as a test of property, and advised further investigations into the matter of property qualification. Lastly, Wellington had suggested that the Catholic clergy should be compelled to obtain a royal licence before performing their functions and should be paid by the State; Peel, however, thought that State payment of the Catholic clergy would arouse the hostility of the tax-payers and the jealousy of dissenters, while the royal licensing of priests would not necessarily ensure royal control over them. Peel thus showed himself inclined to full concession with a minimum of securities, and his view was finally to prevail against the more cautious plan of Wellington.[5]

During the autumn of 1828 the three appointed ministers continued to discuss plans for emancipation in desultory fashion, but no real progress could be made until the royal permission had been given for the question to be discussed in Cabinet. Anti-catholic thunderbolts from Cumberland in Germany, together with his own ill health, prevented the King from coming to a decision, and the year ended without the necessary permission being obtained. Consequently Wellington was compelled to keep his policy secret, and the prolonged silence was dangerous. Since its triumph at the Clare election the Catholic Association had continued to hold mass-meetings. The Association was becoming increasingly irritated because it thought that the Government had no intention of settling the problem.[6] The spread of Catholic demonstrations caused the Irish anti-catholics to adopt a similarly aggressive attitude and to organize a rival system of

5. The letter and memorandum are printed in Peel's *Memoirs*, i. 181 ff. Both are summarized in N. Gash, *Mr. Secretary Peel*, pp. 529–31.
6. 'The Government', said Sheil at an Association meeting, 'by allowing the Catholic question to convulse the country, and not at once interposing for its adjustment—by their strange procrastination, and almost imbecile indecision —by their fantastical irresolution and unaccountable infirmity of purpose, have caused the mind of Ireland to be infuriated.' McCullagh, *Sheil*, ii. 28.

Brunswick clubs both in Ireland and Britain.[7] In Ulster the rivalry became so fierce that a pitched battle was narrowly avoided between Orange and Catholic bands.

Two members of the Government, who were completely ignorant of Wellington's position, were convinced that the dangerous Irish situation could only be settled by Catholic emancipation. They made no secret of their opinion. One of these was George Dawson, a Secretary to the Treasury, who delivered a speech at Londonderry (the town he represented) announcing his conversion to the Catholic cause.[8] Not only had Dawson hitherto been a staunch and vocal anti-catholic, but he was the brother-in-law of Peel. Moreover, he secured the maximum publicity for his conversion by speaking on a most incongruous occasion—the anniversary of the siege of Derry, which was celebrated as an Orange victory.[9] Not surprisingly, therefore, his speech was widely assumed to represent a change of heart in government circles. The speech, wrote Spring-Rice to Brougham, 'tells sufficiently the intentions of ministers. . . . What may we not expect in Downing St. when such is the language at Derry?'[1] If the pro-catholics were delighted, the ultras were dismayed. Lord Chandos hoped that the speech had been mis-reported—'otherwise', he told Newcastle, 'I shall begin to fear that all is not well at Head Quarters'; and this led him to demand every exertion in support of the anti-catholic cause.[2] The ministers were deeply concerned at the reaction which Dawson's speech had aroused. Sir Henry Hardinge wrote that 'a more extraordinary piece of indiscretion never was committed';[3] while Ellenborough thought that it hurried on the Catholic question too quickly, for it would heighten antagonism in Ireland by raising the hopes of the Catholics and alarming their opponents.[4] Most embarrassed of all were Wellington and Peel. Ellenborough reported that the incident had 'thrown [Wellington] back with the King, and he is now no further advanced than he was a

7. The Brunswick movement in Britain is discussed in the next chapter.
8. The speech, delivered on 12 August, is printed in WND, iv. 604–10.
9. Dawson seems to have hinted at his conversion over a fortnight before the speech, according to information given in a letter from William Peel to Robert Peel, n.d., 1828; PP, 40397, f. 158.
    1. 20 August 1828; Brougham Papers.
    2. 18 August 1828; Newcastle MSS.
    3. Hardinge to Charles Arbuthnot, 3 September 1828; Aspinall, *Arbuthnot Correspondence*, p. 108.
    4. Ellenborough, i. 199–200.

week after he first opened the subject to his Majesty'.[5] George
IV was doubtless influenced by the Duke of Cumberland's letters,
which repeatedly claimed that Dawson was mad and demanded
that Eldon, 'whose Protestant principles are *decidedly* known',
should be restored to government office in order to 'knock up all
doubts where they exist'.[6] Fortunately for the Government, the
excitement soon died down. Anti-catholic newspapers were ready
to assume that reports of the speech had been exaggerated, and
Newcastle was told on 23 August that there was no foundation
for the inference that Peel and Wellington had changed their
views.[7] In the end it was not even thought necessary to remove
Dawson from office.

The Government suffered more prolonged embarrassment
through the activities of the Marquess of Anglesey, Lord
Lieutenant of Ireland. Anglesey had the same military training
and practical character as Wellington, and a brief stay in Ireland
had convinced him that only Catholic emancipation could solve
the problems of that country. Unlike Wellington, however, he
identified himself to a considerable degree with the Catholic
grievances, so that a swelling vein of sentiment was added to his
practical traits. 'He can scarcely speak of Ireland', wrote E. J.
Littleton, 'without rapture.'[8] He established bonds of sympathy
with the Catholic Association and became very popular in the
country. Unfortunately, Wellington could not intimate to
Anglesey his plan of emancipation because of his difficulties with
the King. Anglesey, therefore, was convinced that he had the
courage to adopt concession and that the premier had not.[9] He
repeatedly urged emancipation in his letters;[1] and when these,
owing to Wellington's predicament, had to be ignored, he be-

5. Ibid., 209.
6. *Geo. IV Letters*, iii. 438–9. The King passed on the suggestion to Wellington, who in a letter of 14 October showed himself determined to keep Eldon
out; WND, v. 134.
7. Alexander Cray Grant to Newcastle; Newcastle MSS.
8. Littleton to Harrowby, 30 October 1828; Harrowby Papers, first series, xv,
f. 229.
9. He wrote to his friend Lord Holland on 4 August 1828: 'I am disposed
to think the Duke of Wellington would willingly adopt the question, but that
he does not know how to set about it. I feel confident that I do, but he has not
the nerves to put himself into my hands, & to open his heart to me'; *One-Leg*,
pp. 204–5.
1. See the letters in Peel's *Memoirs*, i. 145–9, 163–5; also Anglesey to Wellington, 24 September 1828 (WND, v. 81–2); Anglesey to Sir Arthur Paget, 8
and 27 July 1828 (*Paget Papers*, pp. 395–8); Anglesey to Holland, 19 October
1828 (ibid., 400–3).

came increasingly indiscreet in his acts and correspondence. He confided his troubles to Palmerston, saying that he received no confidential information from either Wellington or Peel and had no idea of what they intended to do about the Catholic question. He asked Palmerston that if he could possibly learn the intentions of the Government, he would let him know. Such a request to a private gentleman was, Palmerston commented, a revealing instance of the lack of confidence between Anglesey and the premier.[2]

In a letter of 14 August Peel tried to soothe Anglesey by assuring him that the Government was considering every aspect of the Irish problem with a view to settling it. Still Anglesey was not satisfied. Wellington was soon protesting that Anglesey's whole public attitude was hostile to the Government, while Peel was receiving complaints from the Irish anti-catholics that Anglesey was partial to the Catholics. Among other incidents, Anglesey annoyed the Home Government in October by issuing a proclamation under his name alone, unaccompanied by the customary endorsement of Irish privy councillors; he annoyed them in November by refusing to find sufficient legal pretext for punishing two Catholic magistrates who had been guilty of partial conduct; and he annoyed them continually by granting audiences to the Catholic Association leaders. The King had wanted to recall Anglesey in August; but Wellington discouraged this, probably because he thought that Catholic turbulence would increase under a less popular Lord Lieutenant. During November and December, however, the accumulation of Anglesey's indiscretions and the increasing impatience of his letters persuaded Wellington that his recall could no longer be delayed. 'Lord Anglesey is gone mad,' Wellington told Lord Bathurst on 24 November; 'he is bit by a mad papist, or instigated by love of popularity.'[3] The recall was finally decided at a Cabinet meeting on 24 December.

Anglesey's dismissal was decided quite independently of another threat to Wellington's policy; in this, however, Anglesey was also involved and it was commonly but wrongly supposed that it led to his recall. In this matter Wellington himself must be charged with indiscretion. On 4 December Archbishop Curtis, Catholic Primate of Ireland and an old acquaintance of Welling-

2. Bulwer, *Palmerston*, i. 309–10.   3. WND, v. 280.

ton, wrote to the premier, mentioning the suspicion that it was intended to settle the Catholic question in the forthcoming parliamentary session. To this Wellington replied, in a letter not marked 'confidential':

. . . you do me justice in believing that I am sincerely anxious to witness a settlement of the Roman Catholic question. . . . But I confess that I see no prospect of such a settlement. . . . If we could bury [the question] in oblivion for a short time, and employ the time diligently in the consideration of its difficulties on all sides . . . I should not despair of seeing a satisfactory remedy.[4]

Doubtless Wellington had no intention in this letter of giving the Catholics more encouragement than they had already received. But it was sufficient to delight Curtis and was soon made known to several others; for on 22 December Curtis told the premier that

. . . as [the letter] was franked by yourself, the news was communicated from the post-office to the public before the letter reached my hands; so that I was obliged, in your Grace's defence and my own, to show its contents to a few chosen friends, for the multitude would otherwise have fabricated in its stead some foolish and perhaps mischievous nonsense of their own.[5]

Thus Curtis had some defence for advertising the letter, but it seems that his circulation of it was very wide. On 23 December it was published in the *Dublin Evening Post*. Anglesey thereupon wrote to Curtis, saying that he had now learnt Wellington's true sentiments for the first time.[6] In order to pacify the Irish Catholics, who were dismayed to hear rumours of his recall, Anglesey allowed this letter to be published. Some believed that this publication was the reason for Anglesey's recall. But the letter did not appear until 2 January, and as we have seen the

4. Wellington to Curtis, 11 December 1828; WND, v. 326.
5. Ibid, v. 352.
6. Anglesey to Curtis (*One-Leg*, p. 214). J. A. Reynolds says that Anglesey wrote this letter on 25 December 1828 (op. cit., p. 123). But the copy printed in *One-Leg* is dated 23 December; it was also given this date in contemporary newspapers. It is interesting to note that now he had realized Wellington's thoughts Anglesey was prepared to be as restrained and diplomatic as the duke could wish. He wrote: It is obviously most important, that the Duke of Wellington should be propitiated; that no obstacle, that can by possibility be avoided, should be thrown in his way; that all personal and offensive insinuations should be suppressed; and that ample allowance should be made for the difficulties of his situation' (op. cit., p. 214).

recall was determined on 24 December. The publication was, however, responsible for further instructions ordering Anglesey to leave Ireland without delay.[7]

Wellington's letter to Curtis did not cause much stir among the rival parties over the Catholic question. Some pro-catholics may have thought that Wellington was now certain to introduce Catholic emancipation into parliament.[8] But the wording of the letter was so obscure that the more judicious friends of emancipation could find no more definite encouragement in it than that afforded by Wellington's speech of 10 June. 'It seemed to me', said Grey, 'as much as possible the same as his speech in the House of Lords—an expression of his wish to settle the question, with a declaration of his inability to do so.'[9] The ultras for their part were not unduly alarmed. As *The Times* declared, if the Catholics were 'encouraged by his anxiety to witness a settlement', the Orangemen were 'assuaged by his hopelessness of effecting one'.[1] The fears which the letter had aroused were counter-balanced by the dismissal of the pro-catholic Anglesey. When Cumberland wrote expressing his dissatisfaction with the letter, Wellington sought to appease him by telling him the detailed circumstances which had compelled him to recall Anglesey.[2] Wellington was furious with Curtis for publishing the letter; and, although his wrath was not justified by the outcome, it is understandable in the circumstances. For the letter might have dangerously alarmed the ultras; and these, aggravated by the vociferousness of the Irish and puzzled by the Government's lengthy silence, had already been voicing their protests for some months.

7. Gash, p. 544.
8. T. Spring-Rice to Viscount Milton, 31 December 1828; Fitzwilliam MSS.
9. Grey to Holland, 9 January 1829; Grey MSS.
1. 3 January 1829.
2. Cumberland to the King, 10 January 1829 (*Geo. IV Letters*, iii. 452–3); Wellington to Cumberland, 14 January 1829 (WND, v. 442–3).

CHAPTER VII

THE ANTI-POPISH REACTION

ONE of the main objects of Wellington's policy in 1828 was to adopt Catholic relief without destroying tory unity. Owing, however, to the enforced secrecy and delay between July 1828 and the first parliamentary announcement of the Government's policy in February 1829, a tory split was foreshadowed. During the intervening months a widespread anti-catholic movement had developed, and the ultra peers had become so deeply committed to it that they were unable to follow the example of Wellington's conversion. The anti-catholic movement arose in Ireland, as a means of resisting the consolidation of Irish Catholic strength which followed the Clare election; and it had its counterpart in a British movement led by the ultra peers. Their object at first was to stimulate the ingrained anti-catholic feelings of the English masses as a counteraction to the demands of the Irish Catholics; later, when Wellington's intention to concede emancipation had been announced, the ultras sought to use anti-catholic sentiment to oppose the policy of the Government.

The first suggestions for anti-catholic combination took place in June. On 25 June Lord Kenyon wrote to Lord Colchester suggesting a meeting at the former's London house to consider the best means of organizing the expression of anti-catholic feeling.[1] The reaction which this proposal aroused suggests that some unorthodox method was contemplated, and it is clear even at this early stage that some ultras were frightened of taking any unconstitutional action. Colchester and four other ultra peers declined to attend the meeting, preferring to limit their opinions to the safer channel of parliamentary petitions.[2] The meeting, however, was apparently held, for on 4 July Colchester noted in his diary that 'another meeting' of ultra peers and

---

1. Colchester, iii. 574-5.
2. Colchester to Kenyon, 26 June 1828; Kenyon Papers.

commoners was held on that day.[3] At this gathering it was decided to establish a 'Protestant Club' to meet monthly during the parliamentary session; but when Eldon joined the club he had its name changed to the 'Brunswick Constitutional Club' in order to give the society a safer aspect.[4] Cumberland apparently took a leading part in the proceedings. 'The whole affair was started by Cumberland', wrote Princess Lieven; 'he boasted to me . . . that he had an organization which would defeat the Catholic Association.'[5] According to Cumberland's own account, the first 150 members of the club were to be peers and M.P.s, and when this number had been achieved the membership might be extended to other country gentlemen.[6] Cumberland soon returned to Germany; but, he told Kenyon, 'the moment anything should occur in Parliament that interests our Great Cause I shall not fail to be back on my post'.[7]

Thus the Brunswick movement was launched. Its name was taken from the dynasty which was, according to the ultras, peculiarly committed to Protestant Ascendancy through the circumstances of its accession to the throne; and its principles were those of other anti-catholic societies, the chief of which were the Orange Institution and the Pitt Clubs. Both these organizations had recently reiterated their anti-catholic standpoint. In 1825 the aims of the Orangemen had been reaffirmed by fresh regulations. These declared that no one who at any time had been a Catholic could be admitted to membership, except by special dispensation. In 1826 the Herefordshire Pitt Club had reaffirmed its no-popery principles by criticizing members who had supported a pro-catholic candidate for Hereford at the recent election.[8] The new association was not meant to

3. Colchester, iii. 578–9. This meeting was attended by the Dukes of Cumberland, Newcastle, and Gordon; the Marquess of Chandos (in the chair); the Earl of Longford, Lords Farnham and Hotham, and several commoners. *Birmingham Gazette*, 14 July 1828; *Liverpool Mercury*, 25 July 1828.

4. Colchester, iii. 582.

5. Princess Lieven to Countess Cowper, 24 September 1828. Lord Sudley (ed.), *Correspondence of Princess Lieven and Lord Palmerston, 1828–56* (London, 1943), p. 3. Mrs. Arbuthnot later said that Cumberland had organized the club (*Journal*, ii. 212).

6. Cumberland to Kenyon, 6 August 1828; Kenyon Papers. At the end of August the Marquess of Chandos, the secretary and treasurer of the club, agreed that the Hon. Lloyd Kenyon, who was not an M.P., should be admitted on payment of the subscription of two guineas; Chandos to Lord Kenyon, 27 August 1828 (ibid.).

7. Cumberland to Kenyon, 6 August 1828, cit.

8. *Birmingham Gazette*, 30 October 1826; *John Bull*, 6 November 1826.

replace these older societies but to run concurrently with them.[9] The membership of all three societies—Orange, Pitt, and Brunswick—appears to have overlapped. Cumberland was at the same time a Brunswick leader and Grand Master of the Orange Institution of Great Britain, while Kenyon was prominent simultaneously in the Orange, Pitt, and Brunswick movements.[1]

The Brunswick movement was naturally most successful in Ireland, where the Catholic menace was strongest. In September Anglesey told Peel that 'the Orangemen, or as I suppose I am now to call them, the Brunswickers, are rivalling the Association both in violence and in rent'.[2] Indeed, at the end of September it was reported that there was scarcely a town in Ireland without its Brunswick Club.[3] This was most gratifying to the ultras; but in Britain they were faced with a much more difficult task. The last important anti-catholic demonstration was the Gordon Riots, and the last general election in which no-popery feeling had been strong enough to influence many results was that of 1806. The 1826 election had shown that popular prejudice was still widespread but not sufficiently burning or well enough organized to have much effect. Since it was not challenged, as in Ireland, by an aggressive Catholic body, British no-popery remained quiescent. The Brunswickers, however, would have to stimulate no-popery if their movement was to succeed; and the Earl of Winchilsea now rose to prominence as an ultra leader through his determined efforts to stir up the English anti-catholics. 'I ... am determined to remain no longer quiet', he wrote to Lord Chandos at the end of August, 'but to exert, to the utmost, the humble talents & power which I possess, in rousing the dormant spirit of the Country, & awakening it to the perilous situation in which we now stand.'[4] Other ultra peers had the same intention. Chandos advised Kenyon that the best means of organizing popular expression would be a declaration, 'drawn up in firm & temperate language, calling on the Protestants to support the

9. The older societies continued to meet. In November the Halifax Orange Club met to declare its anti-catholic views (*Leeds Intelligencer*, 6 November 1828), and the Orange institution at Bolton held a procession, a church service, and a dinner (*Manchester Herald*, 13 November 1826).

1. In addition to these main associations there were various smaller anti-catholic societies, such as the Stockport Wellington Club and the Society for Promoting the Principles of the Reformation.

2. Peel *Memoirs*, i. 208.

3. *Spectator*, 27 September 1828.

4. 26 August 1828; Winchilsea Papers.

Constitution & signed by those in every parish, who are anxious for the good of their country'.[5] Lord Kenyon urged this scheme in four 'letters to the Protestants of Great Britain', which were widely published in the anti-catholic press. The first of these, dated 30 August, stated that the King would honour his Coronation Oath, which bound him to reject Catholic emancipation, provided that his subjects made clear that this was their wish. The letter then advanced what became an oft-repeated theme in ultra arguments—that the House of Commons, which had passed several Catholic relief bills in recent years, did not represent the anti-catholic sentiments of the people. The 'Protestants of the empire' must rely on their own efforts. 'Let every parish declare its sentiments', the appeal concluded; 'let them unite in a holy and constitutional declaration of their attachment to the Protestant Constitution of these realms as their dearest birthright.'[6]

On 18 September Newcastle issued a similar address endorsing Kenyon's appeal. Newcastle looked beyond parliament to the Government for the root of current evils. 'Nothing is to be expected from Parliament', he wrote, 'because nothing is to be done by the Government; nothing is to be done by the Government, because neutrality, conciliation, and modern liberality are still ruling the deliberations of the Cabinet.'[7] Newcastle was unwilling to blame this state of affairs specifically on Wellington, who 'may be the victim of a monstrous error'. Still, the duke had acquiesced in relief for dissenters, and his first parliamentary session as premier had been 'by far the most disastrous of any in the memory of man'. The ultras did not of course know that Wellington was already discussing a relief bill with his colleagues, but secrecy had made them suspicious.[8] In Newcastle's view, Wellington's failure to deal with the Irish problem was particularly inexplicable. The Catholic menace was growing, but 'who offers the slightest opposition to all this? No one.' Like Kenyon, Newcastle advised the anti-catholics to take their own action: 'They must unite in Protestant associations from one end of the

5. Chandos to Kenyon, 27 August 1828; Kenyon Papers.
6. *Standard*, 1 September 1828; *John Bull*, 8 September 1828.
7. *Standard*, 22 September 1828. Reprinted in Newcastle's *Thoughts in times past tested by subsequent events* (London, 1837), pp. 69–81.
8. The ministers, wrote Eldon, 'let us know nothing. For that Reason I believe they intend something.' Eldon to Lady Elizabeth Repton, 31 August 1828; Kenyon Papers.

country to the other, and as Parliament is not sitting, they should address their Protestant King.' Failure to do so might invite divine retribution: '... if we desert our God, will he not desert us? Will he not be avenged upon such a nation as this?'[9]

One method taken by the ultra peers to rouse anti-catholic feeling was the establishment of Brunswick Clubs throughout Britain on the model of the London club. Winchilsea took the initiative in founding a Brunswick Club in Kent, and Chandos did likewise in Buckinghamshire. These attempts, however, were weakened by doubts about constitutional propriety such as had already greeted the foundation of the central club. Winchilsea's effort in Kent brought many objections from peers in that county. Sometimes anti-catholic zeal overcame the constitutional conscience. Lord Guilford, for example, wrote to Winchilsea:

... altho' in ordinary times I certainly think political clubs unconstitutional, & that the regular mode for us to express our opinions is in Parliament, & for the community at large by petition; still as such associations of our Enemies are not suppress'd by law, we should not be upon equal terms with them were we not permitted to use their weapons in self defence, & upon this ground alone they are justifiable. I am therefore willing to lend my name to the County protestant Club which you propose to establish.[1]

But with others the aversion to 'club government' was complete. Lord Camden could not agree that 'Catholic intemperance should be met with Protestant intemperance', and thought that the matter was better left to Parliament.[2] Lord Bexley thought that the anti-catholics should wait until the Government had revealed its intentions before deciding what action to take.[3] Lord Stanhope feared that positive anti-catholic action would cause pro-catholic reaction:

There does not appear to exist in this or in any other County of England any popular feeling in behalf of the Catholics, but it would, I think, be excited through a necessary reaction by such measures as you have in contemplation, & for the Protestants in this Country

9. *Thoughts in times past,* pp. 77 f.
1. 24 August 1828; Winchilsea Papers.
2. Camden to Winchilsea, 31 August 1828; ibid.
3. Bexley to Winchilsea, 2 September 1828; ibid.

the wisest maxim appears to be *quieta non movere* & to avoid throwing any sparks which might lead to a mighty conflagration.[4]

Lord Romney, another Kentish peer, condemned the whole principle of political clubs:

The principle of a self constituted, permanent, political body I consider to be very objectionable. Different as the practice has been, the principle I consider to be uniformly bad, whether it originates a Whig Club, a Pitt Club, a Jacobin Club, a Corresponding Society, an Orange Lodge, a Catholic Association, a Brunswick Protestant Club.[5]

Winchilsea was not convinced. Surely, he asked Romney, a society which was formed to oppose unconstitutional societies could not be unconstitutional itself? He determined to persist with his plan. A meeting was held at Maidstone on 16 September in order to adopt some means for 'the public expression, on behalf of the inhabitants of the County of Kent, of their firm attachment to the constitution'.[6] The meeting was a great success: Winchilsea was supported by nearly all the speakers, including John Wells, M.P. for Maidstone, who said that he was ready to fight for Protestant Ascendancy 'up to his knees in blood'.[7] After this it was resolved to form a Brunswick Club whose membership should be open to all the 'noblemen and gentlemen' present.

The second provincial Brunswick Club was that founded in Buckinghamshire, through the initiative of Lord Chandos, at a meeting held at Aylesbury on 26 September. By the end of October there were said to be 1,200 members, but this claim is suspect since it was made by an anti-catholic newspaper.[8] Other early efforts to found Brunswick Clubs were made in different parts of the country. A resolution to form one at Leeds was said to have been carried by four hundred votes to four—though this again by the anti-catholic Press.[9] The *Spectator* had good reason to say, on 15 November, that 'the example of Kent had

4. Stanhope to Winchilsea, 3 September 1828; Winchilsea Papers.
5. Romney to Winchilsea, 7 September 1828; ibid.
6. *Standard*, 11 September 1828.
7. *The Times*, 18 September 1828.
8. *Leeds Intelligencer*, 2 October 1828. A glaring example of anti-catholic exaggeration is a report in the *Dublin Evening Mail* that only five or six opposed the Brunswick resolution in Leeds, out of a population of 240,000; the pro-catholic *Liverpool Mercury* pointed out (28 November 1828) that Leeds did not contain more than 100,000 inhabitants.
9. *Leeds Intelligencer*, 13 November 1828.

become epidemic'; a week later the same paper reported the existence of thirty-six Brunswick Clubs in Britain.

The Brunswickers continually insisted that their clubs were entirely defensive and constitutional. Their 'only constitutional object', a correspondent told Lord Kenyon, was to 'reveal the sense of the country on the Catholic question'.[1] The pro-catholics, however, refused to believe it. *The Times* advised the Irish Catholics to 'stand by the law alone' in order to enhance the righteousness of their cause against that of the Brunswickers. The same newspaper asked:

> ... what business has the majority of a great nation with confederacy of any description? The law administers itself—the Government enforces it. The *State* requires no support from clubs, composed of those in their individual character, who already, in their collective character, constitute the State. If clubs of such men exercise any power it is one which must overawe and supersede the Government—it becomes a revolutionary Government.[2]

The *Liverpool Mercury* compared the Brunswick Clubs with the Holy League in sixteenth-century France, and advised George IV not to become another Henry III.[3] This was also Lady Holland's view. The new association, she wrote, was 'formed much upon the intolerant & violent principles of the *League*; fortunately they have no *Guises*'.[4]

The pro-catholics had other objections to the clubs. To call them 'Brunswick Clubs' was, they asserted, most inappropriate. The house of Brunswick had come to the throne as upholders of religious liberty, not as attackers, and a more suitable name would be 'Stuart Clubs'.[5] The concentration of the clubs in rural areas and the predominance of landed gentry in their ranks produced the observation that British public opinion was now to be sought 'in the wealds of Kent, or round Dartmoor, or in Wales'.[6] Behind all these objections was simple contempt. Lord Althorp called the Brunswickers 'bigoted idiots'. In Ireland, he

1. John Hanmer to Kenyon, 30 November 1828; Kenyon Papers.
2. 16 October 1828.
3. 26 September 1828.
4. Sixth Earl of Ilchester (ed.), *Lady Holland to her Son* (London, 1946), pp. 88–89.
5. *The Times*, 19 September 1828.
6. *Spectator*, 22 November 1828.

declared, such associations might prove mischievous, but in England they could only be ridiculous.[7]

On several occasions the pro-catholics showed active opposition to the formation of Brunswick Clubs. This was certainly in evidence at Worcester, where an anti-catholic committee called a public meeting in November with the object of forming a Brunswick Club to serve the city and county. Pro-catholic opposition was expected by the promoters of the club, and in an effort to avoid it they had declared that only those who were favourably disposed to their intention would be allowed to speak. Despite this restriction, a noted Midlands pro-catholic named Richard Spooner began to address the meeting in the crown court of the Guildhall. Tumult followed; the chairman declared Spooner out of order, and after a show of hands against him he left the court. Amidst continued disturbance the Brunswick resolutions were carried and a hundred members were enrolled in the new club. Meanwhile, however, Spooner had retired to the balcony of the hall, and there he addressed a separate assembly consisting mainly of his own supporters. In a lengthy speech he accused the Brunswickers of having transformed the advertised 'public' meeting into a private one; they had thus pretended to give their club the general sanction of the inhabitants of Worcester when in fact it was 'only the meeting of a few respectable private gentlemen'. Spooner's assembly unanimously passed a resolution condemning this conduct and asserting that the formation of a Brunswick Club was uncalled for in any case. At the same time yet a third assembly had gathered in the *nisi prius* court of the Guildhall, presided over by a Mr. Foster of Evesham; at this meeting, too, resolutions were passed against a Brunswick Club. Thus three meetings on the subject of Brunswick Clubs were held simultaneously in the same building, one of them being in favour and the others against.[8]

While the pro-catholics actively opposed the clubs, the anti-catholics were far from united in their defence. Some of the staunchest anti-catholics only assented to them on sufferance. For example Lord Redesdale, a loyal upholder of Irish Protestant Ascendancy, wrote: 'I do not like clubs, nor do I like the leaders of the Brunswick Clubs in England, but I am convinced that

7. Althorp to Brougham, 30 September 1828; Althorp Papers.
8. *Birmingham Gazette*, 1 and 8 December 1828.

stout opposition to emancipation is our only safety.'[9] *John Bull* was against any non-parliamentary action; it insisted that anti-catholic feeling should be revealed not in clubs but in petitions to the legislature.[1] The anti-catholic *Leeds Intelligencer* endorsed this sentiment, and added the objection that if the Brunswick Clubs met too frequently they might become as powerful and dangerous as the Catholic Association.[2] Similar views were held by individual anti-catholics. Sir Thomas Lethbridge, M.P. for Somerset, said he could only join a Brunswick Club if he were not a Member of Parliament: 'I object to any fetters out of Parliament, *good or bad*.'[3] Lord Eldon, although he had joined the metropolitan club, was worried about some of the Brunswick tendencies: 'I cannot forbear to think', he wrote, 'that the strong language used in many of the clubs is most mischievous, and deters many from meeting to express in sober and temperate petitions their feelings.'[4] Such was the opinion of the *doyen* of the ultras. Behind other anti-catholic objections lay Wellington's personal influence, which in 1829 was strong enough to carry Catholic emancipation by handsome majorities. For example, Lord Hertford refused to join a Brunswick Club, and Croker told Wellington that this was because he was 'desirous to see quiet restored in Ireland at any price' and was 'ready to support *anything that your Grace may do*'.[5] This reason for not joining the Brunswickers was expressed more fully by the Duke of Northumberland, writing to Newcastle:

With respect to the Brunswick Club I have only to request that I am unable to comply with your wishes. To all similar applications, I have stated my unwillingness to take the Question out of the hands of the Duke of Wellington. Of his judgement & his justice I have the highest opinion, & I feel anxious to learn his view of the subject at the present crisis, before I allow my mind to come to any fixed determination.[6]

Thus, while some anti-catholics opposed the Brunswick Clubs on abstract constitutional grounds and others because they chal-

9. Redesdale to Colchester, 25 November 1828; Colchester, iii. 589.
1. 17 November 1828.
2. 6 November 1828.
3. *John Bull*, 30 March 1829.
4. Eldon to Lord Stowell, posted 28 November 1828; Twiss, *Eldon*, iii. 61.
5. Croker to Wellington, 29 September 1828; WND, v. 97.
6. 3 November 1828; Newcastle MSS.

lenged the competence of the Duke of Wellington, it was most unlikely that the movement would succeed. Indeed, the division in the anti-catholic ranks between Brunswickers and anti-Brunswickers must have given Wellington some indication of his own strength and of his opponents' weakness.

The Brunswick Clubs with their exclusive membership were the narrower manifestations of no-popery sentiment. Wider effects of the ultra calls to action were monster-meetings held in town and country. This form of assembly was derived from Wesleyan field-meetings; the Catholic Association had used it, and the ultras now did likewise. The first and most famous of these meetings was held on 24 October on Penenden Heath—two miles from Maidstone and a celebrated meeting-place since the Conquest—in response to a resolution of the Kent Brunswick Club. It was not to be a meeting of Brunswickers alone but a disputation between them and their opponents. Both Brunswickers and anti-Brunswickers wanted a large attendance. In one district, it was said, £20 was offered to anyone who would attend in the Brunswick interest.[7] Lord Holland wanted a large pro-catholic showing, since 'the tranquillity of the Empire may really depend on the result of that manoeuvre of the Kentish clodpolls and bigots'.[8] It was said that Wellington had asked the pro-catholic Lord Camden to attend the meeting, and the *Spectator* reported that Camden was forming a 'strong party' to oppose the Brunswickers.[9]

The meeting was attended not only by pro-catholic peers like Camden but by the radicals Cobbett and Hunt and the Irish Catholic demagogue R. L. Sheil. It is from Sheil's account that the following summary is largely taken.[1] It was universally agreed that there was a large concourse, but the stated number varied with the political views of the assessors.[2] The High Sheriff of Kent presided, and the pro- and anti-catholic bodies were

7. *Spectator*, 8 November 1828.
8. Holland to Lord John Russell, October 1828. Rollo Russell (ed.), *Early Correspondence of Lord John Russell*, i. 279.
9. 18 October 1828.
1. Sheil's sketch, dated November 1828, was first published in the *New Monthly Magazine* and reprinted in his *Sketches, Legal and Political* (ed. M. W. Savage; 2 vols., London, 1855), ii. 193–218.
2. Thus the ultras computed the attendance at 60,000 (Colchester, iii. 583) and the pro-catholics at 25,000 or 30,000 (*Spectator*, 1 November 1828).

marshalled respectively on his right and left. There were many local agricultural workers and inhabitants of Maidstone, but Sheil noted that numerous clergymen on the Brunswick side gave that section 'more of a clerical than an agricultural aspect'. Besides anglican clergy there were, under Lord Winchilsea's banners, many methodist ministers—easily recognizable, said Sheil, by their 'lugubrious and dismal expression'. After an anti-catholic petition had been read, Lords Camden and Darnley made pro-catholic speeches in succession—the former hinting, according to Sheil, that the Government intended some measure of Catholic relief. A speech by Winchilsea followed: his rhetorical force and stentorian voice indicated considerable demagogic ability. Among the remaining speakers, Sheil and Henry Hunt spoke unsuccessfully for the Catholics.[3] Cobbett inveighed against both sides.

When the 'question' was put to the vote, the Brunswickers obtained a large majority. 'The acclamations of the Brunswickers were reiterated', runs Sheil's extravagant account:

the whole body waved their hats, and lifted up their voices; the parsons shook hands with each other; the Methodists smiled with a look of ghastly satisfaction; and Lord Winchilsea, losing all decency and self-restraint, was thrown into convulsions of joy, and leaped, and shouted, and roared, in a state of almost insane exultation.[4]

The general impression was that the Brunswickers had won. Newcastle said that the people had shown 'magnanimous unanimity', and deduced from this that the Brunswickers enjoyed 'a support & protection superior to human means'.[5] Nevertheless, there had been enough 'emancipating' speeches to prevent the pro-catholics being downcast. The Irish Catholics were only too pleased that their claims had been discussed at an English public meeting, even if the result had been unfavourable.[6] The pro-catholics did not think that government policy would be influenced by the result. 'We are much calmed about Penenden

3. Of Hunt's speech, Sheil wrote: 'Whatever may be his sway with public assemblies on other occasions, he certainly showed few evidences of omnipotence upon this' (Sketches, p. 215). Sheil's own speech was so loudly and persistently interrupted that it could scarcely be heard.
4. Ibid., p. 216.
5. Newcastle to Kenyon, 28 October 1828; Kenyon Papers.
6. Resolution passed at a Catholic provincial meeting in Leinster on 29 October (Spectator, 8 November 1828).

Heath', wrote Countess Granville. 'It cannot have much influence as a precedent, or I think influence the minds of anyone.'[7] Lord Goderich dismissed the meeting more cavalierly as 'one of the most ridiculous proceedings ever known ... highly disapproved of by many very strong anti-catholics'.[8]

The ultras hoped that the Kent meeting would be emulated in other counties, but the example was slow to take effect. A proposed meeting in Lincolnshire had to be abandoned because its success was in doubt.[9] Cornwall was upbraided for 'supineness' in not calling a meeting.[1] It was said that the founding of a Brunswick Club in Lancashire would disturb county society too much, since the anti-catholics in that county were frequently thrown into contact with a large Catholic population.[2] 'Kent still remains alone', wrote Lord Harrowby two months after Penenden Heath.[3] When the example was repeated, the results were unimpressive. A county meeting in Cheshire in December, held to adopt anti-catholic resolutions, was said (by a pro-catholic paper) to have mustered only eight hundred people.[4] Cornwall at last bestirred itself in early January, and gatherings were held at several towns instead of a single meeting for the county. These meetings revealed that anti-catholic opinion was by no means overwhelming in Cornwall. At Bodmin and Lostwithiel anti-catholic motions passed by only 5:4; at Truro, an anti-catholic resolution was said to have been carried only because the ultra Lord Falmouth used his local influence; and at Launceston and Liskeard pro-catholics were excluded from the meetings— perhaps, as the *West Briton* said, because they could have mustered a formidable opposition.[5]

In January, too, there was held at Exeter the only county gathering comparable in weight to that of Kent. 'The thick headed Parsons & Squires of these parts', wrote the Hon. G. M. Fortescue, member of a prominent whig family, 'have got up

7. Countess Granville to the Duke of Devonshire, 6 November 1828. Hon. F. Leveson Gower (ed.), *Letters of Harriet, Countess Granville, 1810–45* (2 vols., London, 1894), ii. 33.
8. Goderich to E. J. Littleton, 28 October 1828; Hatherton Papers.
9. Sir Robert Heron, *Notes* (Grantham, 1851), pp. 174–5.
1. W. B. Elvins, *The Reform Movement and County Politics in Cornwall, 1809–52* (unpublished thesis), chapter V, pp. 2–3.
2. Lord Skelmersdale to Colchester, 3 December 1828; Colchester, iii. 589–90.
3. Harrowby to E. J. Littleton, 15 December 1828; Hatherton Papers.
4. *The Times*, 1 January 1829.
5. W. B. Elvins, op. cit., v. 3.

a Requisition, & we are now in for a County Meeting on the 16th.' Fortescue thought an anti-catholic resolution would surely be carried, for 'there is no County in England where a more deep rooted . . . bigotry on this Catholick question prevails with half the violence it does here'. However, he added, 'of the intellect, rank & Wealth of the Province we shall make a good muster & have an undoubted majority'.[6] His predictions were well fulfilled. Before an attendance assessed at 12,000,[7] two pro-catholic proposals were defeated and an anti-catholic petition was carried by what the anti-catholic press claimed as 20:1.[8] But the pro-catholics were not unduly depressed. The anti-catholics had attacked Sir Thomas Acland, the pro-catholic tory member for the county, and had threatened to oppose him at the next election; and this had helped to unite the Devonshire whigs and liberal tories against the ultras. 'The set that was made at Acland', wrote Fortescue, 'was to a degree disgraceful & I trust that the union of his party & ours which resulted from their conduct will secure him his seat.'[9] Fortescue was convinced, moreover, that anti-catholic feeling in Devonshire was considerably weaker than it had been: 'The Tories look on the decision so little in the light of a triumph', he wrote, 'that we shall not be troubled with any more County meetings of their calling.'[1] Lastly, the pro-catholics claimed—and it was by no means the only time—that the intelligence of their representatives compensated for their numerical inferiority. Lady Holland told her son that 'all the freeholders & persons of education & substance were on the liberal side'.[2]

Further anti-catholic county meetings were held in Wales and the March country before the Relief Bill was carried. Such a meeting in Anglesey challenged the political influence of the pro-catholic Paget family, and Lord Anglesey's name was fre-

6. Fortescue to Ralph Sneyd, 3 January 1829; Sneyd MSS.
7. *Royal Cornwall Gazette*, 24 January 1829.
8. *John Bull*, 26 January 1829.
9. Fortescue to Sneyd, 21 January 1829; Sneyd MSS. This incident was described more fully in another letter, from J. N. Fazackerley to E. J. Littleton: 'There existed an organized determination to prevent Acland from being heard till after the question had been put: against this [we] protested in vain, we were overpower'd by a mob headed & controul'd by a Parson named Lyte, a missionary friend of Ld. Farnham's recently imported from Ireland, & bringing with him the activity & zeal of the sister country.' 20 January 1829; Hatherton Papers.
1. Fortescue to Sneyd, 21 January 1829; Sneyd MSS.
2. 19 January 1829; *Lady Holland to her Son*, p. 94.

quently mentioned in the debate as an inducement to withdraw the anti-catholic address and petitions.[3] Similar meetings were held in Pembroke and Brecon during March, and April saw a final spate of them. The last were held in Anglesey and Caernarvonshire—'a last effort', announced a local newspaper, 'to support our sinking Constitution'.[4]

All these county meeting were held on the rural fringes of Britain, and this seems to justify a favourite pro-catholic accusation that the Brunswickers could find support only in the more remote areas. This picture, however, is not entirely correct. The Brunswick spirit was by no means absent in the recent urban growths; indeed, anti-catholic petitions in some towns obtained very many signatures.[5] But it was rather a long time before no-popery took effect in these areas, and it was faced with more strenuous pro-catholic opposition than in the counties. A fierce struggle took place at Leeds, where the rival parties were supported by each of the borough's two newspapers, the pro-catholic *Mercury* and the anti-catholic *Intelligencer*. The anti-catholics drew up a declaration and address, which were posted throughout the borough and attracted over a thousand signatures; the pro-catholics held their own meeting and drew up a rival address. On the initiative of the pro-catholics, who were hopeful of having their own views sanctioned by a large cross-section of the Leeds population, a public disputation was held in Cloth Hall Yard on 5 December. The chairman was John Marshall, M.P. for Yorkshire and a prominent local manufacturer, and the attendance was given as 16,000.[6] Speeches were made on both sides amidst uproar and confusion. A show of hands was then taken; but this was so indecisive that Marshall, who was anxious to make a pro-catholic decision but was pressed by the anti-catholics around him to decide otherwise, adjourned the meeting without reaching a verdict.[7] Other examples show that the anti-catholics did

---

3. Information on this meeting can be obtained from letters of January 1829 in the Plas Newydd Papers.

4. *North Wales Chronicle*, 9 April 1829.

5. Anti-catholic petitions at Birmingham were said to have received over 36,000 signatures (*Birmingham Gazette*, 9 March 1829); at Sheffield, an anti-catholic petition was said to have been signed by 15,000 in two days (*John Bull*, 2 March 1829). It is notable, however, that in London, the scene of the Gordon Riots fifty years before, there were no striking demonstrations of no-popery.

6. *Leeds Intelligencer*, 18 December 1828.

7. Op. cit., 11 December 1828.

not enjoy a monopoly of opinion in the larger towns. One of the
M.P.s for Leicester, Robert Otway Cave, actively encouraged
pro-catholic expression in that town. In 1826 Cave had been returned after pledging himself not to support Catholic relief. At
a public meeting in February 1829, he acknowledged this pledge
but said that the appearance of Brunswick Clubs now compelled
him to vote for emancipation; if his constituents still wished
him to remain neutral he would resign his seat. The crowd amply
showed, however, that they were willing to retain him as their
member even if he did support emancipation.[8] At Edinburgh a
combination of whigs and liberal tories revealed considerable
pro-catholic strength. Pro-catholic tories, including Sir Walter
Scott, decided to coalesce with the whigs in a parliamentary
petition and a public meeting. At this meeting, held in the
Assembly Rooms on 14 March, some of the most prominent
Edinburgh figures spoke on the pro-catholic side. The most powerful speech was that of Dr. Chalmers, the well-known theolo-
gian, who argued that only after emancipation would there be
much chance of converting the Catholics to Protestantism; and
very many intellectuals and professional men of Edinburgh supported the pro-catholic petition.[9] Numbers, however, defeated
intelligence, for whereas this petition received 8,000 signatures,
an anti-catholic petition received over 30,000.[1]

Most anglican clergy were active in drawing up anti-catholic
petitions, but there were the usual pro-catholic exceptions among
these clergy, notably Sydney Smith.[2] The methodists rivalled
the anglicans in expressing no-popery. There was a particularly
strong anti-catholic spirit amongst the Welsh calvinistic methodists. John Elias, one of their foremost preachers, excommuni-

8. *Nottingham Mercury*, 7 February 1829. This readiness, it appears, was
not based entirely on the wish for Catholic relief. A subsequent meeting revealed that a division existed between the anti-catholic corporation of the town
and a large number of citizens (op. cit., 28 February 1829). It seems likely
that a pro-catholic attitude was adopted because it symbolized opposition to
the power of the corporation.
   9. *Edinburgh Courant*, 23 March 1829.
   1. Henry Cockburn, *Memorials of his Time* (new ed., Edinburgh, 1909), p.
428.
   2. Sydney Smith preached a sermon at Bristol on 5 November, which he
described to E. J. Littleton as follows: 'I let off in the Minster no ordinary
collection of Squibs, Crackers, and *Roman* Candles. In short I gave . . . the
most Protestant Mayor and Corporation in England such a dose of toleration
as will last them for many a year.' 7 November 1828; Hatherton Papers.

cated the members of Jewin Street chapel, London, for daring to petition for Catholic relief; James Hughes, another of their leaders, was an anti-catholic propagandist; while the *North Wales Chronicle* asserted that the methodists of Wales were unanimously anti-catholic.[3] Leaders of the older nonconformist denominations, on the other hand, again supported Catholic emancipation, although they were rather lukewarm at first. The dissenting corporation of Nottingham unanimously voted a pro-catholic petition: they had a special interest in doing so as they were the sworn enemies of the Duke of Newcastle's influence in the area.[4] In January, the Committee of the Three Denominations (presbyterians, congregationalists, and baptists) passed a motion favouring emancipation, and organized petitions to support it amongst their congregations throughout the country. After the Relief Bill had passed, O'Connell thanked them for all their exertions at a meeting of the Protestant Society.

The pro-catholics tried other methods of resisting the Brunswickers. At Liverpool an attempt was made to collect a Catholic Rent: the town was divided into districts for the purpose, and several Protestants contributed.[5] O'Connell's declaration in favour of parliamentary reform at the Clare election and afterwards had won him the support of Henry Hunt and other radicals. Hunt championed Catholic relief on 21 July, at a meeting of the General Association of Friends of Civil and Religious Liberty;[6] and again in February, at a meeting at the Crown and Anchor Tavern in London, where his amendment to an anti-catholic petition was carried amidst uproar.[7] Further opportunities for pro-catholic expression were provided by the various whig clubs. At the eighth anniversary meeting of the Cheshire whig club in October, the speeches emphasized the growing signs that emancipation would be carried. Earl Grosvenor said that if Brunswick Clubs appeared in Cheshire the whigs would 'hold meeting for meeting . . . and take good care that if the

---

3. 27 November 1828; R. T. Jenkins, *Hanes Cymru yn y bedwaredd ganrif ar bymtheg* (*History of Wales in the Nineteenth Century*), Cardiff, 1933, pp. 65–66.

4. *Nottingham Review*, 20 February 1829.

5. *Spectator*, 11 October 1828.

6. There is a full report of this meeting, the first occasion when this association met in public, in Cobbett's *Pol. Reg.*, lxvi. 119–28, 155–60.

7. *Edinburgh Courant*, 21 February 1829.

Brunswick clubs disseminated poison, it should be accompanied by its proper antidote'.[8]

Such declarations were all very well, but not much encouragement was given to suggestions that the pro-catholics should unite in counter-associations. Lord John Russell wanted the establishment of a 'Committee for the promotion of Religious Liberty', but his fellow-whigs made strong objections reminiscent of those which anti-catholics had raised against the Brunswick Clubs. E. G. Stanley agreed that there should be greater unity in supporting Catholic emancipation, but suspected that the aims of the proposed committee might be too extreme for him;[9] and Lord Althorp thought the scheme would only arouse anti-catholic jealousy.[1] Similarly, when another proposal was made—supported by Lord John Russell, Lansdowne, Holland, E. G. Stanley, and Lord Grenville—that the pro-catholics should organize large petitioning meetings on the Brunswick model, Grey opposed it because he thought it would further provoke national anti-catholic feeling;[2] he said he had 'just the same constitutional objection to Catholic clubs which he had to Brunswick clubs . . . they would only embarrass the Government'.[3] The projects were therefore abandoned, and pro-catholics had to express their views without the aid of a system like the Brunswick Clubs. Such displays of pro-catholic opinion as there were showed that this opinion could not hope to compete with the Brunswickers' numerical weight. It was not because of the threat of pro-catholic opposition—still less the open manifestation of such opposition—that the Brunswick movement failed. It failed because of the apathy of the anti-catholics and because they preferred conservative paths to novel ones.

The ultras were particularly dissatisfied with the House of Commons and its persistent pro-catholic majorities, which belied

8. *Manchester Chronicle*, 18 October 1828. Another speaker warned the ultra Stockport Wellington Club 'not to denounce peremptorily Pitt and Fox, Canning and Castlereagh . . . as traitors and apostates from the Church of England, lest the Duke of Wellington should add his own illustrious name to that splendid catalogue' (*Liverpool Mercury*, 17 October 1828).

9. Stanley to Russell, 22 October 1828; *Early Corresp. of Ld. John Russell*, i. 282–3.

1. Althorp to Russell, 22 October 1828 (ibid., pp. 283–4).

2. Grey to Russell, 28 October 1828; S. Walpole, *Life of Lord John Russell*, i. 153–4.

3. Ellenborough, *Pol. Diary*, i. 266–7.

the mass opinion of those whom it was supposed to represent. The Brunswickers claimed that if this opinion were to be fully and accurately revealed, it would have to be done through extra-parliamentary channels. However, they did little to implement their designs. Brunswick Clubs and mass meetings were only token protests. When it came to putting these protests into effect, even the boldest Brunswickers declined to behave in a revolutionary way.

The movement took effect mainly in the tame and conventional process of petitioning parliament. Anti-catholic petitions were usually initiated in areas where Brunswick Clubs were established and public meetings held; the pro-catholics often attempted a counter-action by setting up their own petitions in the same districts. The established clergy played a particularly large part in encouraging anti-catholic petitions. The individual opinions of the bishops on the Catholic question again played an influential part. The anti-catholic Bishop of Bath and Wells self-confidently declared that anti-catholic petitions would come from 'almost every parish in his diocese';[4] but a pro-catholic petition came from the clergy of Henry Bathurst, Bishop of Norwich, a pro-catholic anomaly on an anti-catholic bench. The results of this petitioning rivalry were seen when the petitions were considered in parliament during February and March. Anti-catholic petitions were overwhelmingly in the majority. At the end of February 720 anti-catholic petitions had been presented, against only 220 pro-catholic ones; *John Bull*, which printed lists of the anti-catholic petitions, said at the end of March that the total number of such petitions was well over two thousand.[5] No less impressive was the number of signatures they contained. One from Glasgow, it was said, had 36,796 signatures; one from Bristol, 38,000; from Kent, 81,400; and from the Irish anti-catholics, 168,000.[6]

In spite of this patent numerical superiority, the pro-catholics in parliament constantly denied their opponents' claim that the country was overwhelmingly anti-catholic. They questioned the results of the Cornish meetings and mentioned the favourable meetings at Leicester, Leeds, and Edinburgh.[7] They also attacked

4. Hansard, xx. 134.
5. Op. cit., xx. 598; *John Bull*, 30 March 1829.
6. Op. cit., xx. 572, 1105–6, 1292; *John Bull*, 30 March 1829.
7. Op. cit., xx. 244, 358, 519–25, 613, 1458–64.

the validity of anti-catholic petitions, on the grounds that the subscribers to these petitions knew nothing of the political situation which made concession necessary, that they had the most exaggerated notions of the anti-Protestant threats which Catholic emancipation might produce, that the petitions were often signed by women, children, and illiterates, and that many people had been induced to sign them through the display of lurid anti-catholic placards.[8] All these objections, however, could do nothing to reduce the mass of anti-catholic petitions, and the pro-catholics laid themselves open to the charge of ineffective quibbling.[9]

Besides petitioning, the Brunswickers tried to influence parliament more directly by replacing pro-catholic M.P.s with anti-catholics. An attempt was made to remove Lord William Paget, M.P. for Caernarvon, on the grounds that he had voted pro-catholic. In May 1828 the anti-catholic burgesses arranged a meeting to consider Lord William's conduct, and they were joined by the parliamentary reformers in the borough, who wanted to overthrow the Marquess of Anglesey's influence. The meeting carried a resolution calling on Lord William to resign. His Lordship, however, returned an uncompromising refusal, saying that the meeting did not represent the opinions of a majority of his constituents and denying that he had given any pledge to vote anti-catholic.[1] The matter revived in October, when Lord William presided at a dinner given by Lord Anglesey to the Caernarvon burgesses. The latter, led by the radical Dr. Owen Roberts, challenged Lord William to drink a toast to 'Protestant Ascendancy'. Lord William did so, and then said he had drunk it according to his own interpretation of the phrase. This did not satisfy the burgesses, who made clear that their

8. Hansard, xx., 245–6, 579, 645–6, 904–5. J. S. Upton, a tutor at Cambridge, wrote to Viscount Milton: 'I wish the placards and copies of the scrawls on the walls were regularly forwarded from every place from which an anti-Catholic petition comes. It would then only be necessary to read them, nothing need be said against the petition, to show what feelings the promoters of the petition endeavoured to infuse into the breasts of their neighbours.' 13 March 1829; Fitzwilliam MSS.

9. 'It seemed almost impossible to satisfy these hon. members', said Sir Robert Inglis, an anti-catholic member. 'If petitions were adopted by vast multitudes of the people, they were represented as the offspring of a riotous and ignorant rabble; and if they proceeded from more secret meetings, they were designated "hole and corner" petitions.' Hansard, xx. 704.

1. Letter from Lord William Paget to the burgesses; written in Dublin, 29 May, and published in the North Wales Chronicle, 12 June 1828.

view of 'Protestant Ascendancy' meant the continued exclusion of Catholics from constitutional benefits, and wished Lord William to commit himself to this opinion. Thereupon Lord William declared:

> Now, gentlemen, you have thrown off the mask—you have shown me that, in your minds, Protestant Ascendancy can alone be upheld by trampling on the rights and liberties and happiness of our Roman Catholic fellow-countrymen, and it is with this meaning you will have me join your toast. Never! I hurl back with indignation the treacherous insult you thus offer me. ... I would rather die than regain your confidence and popularity by subscribing to your toast in the odious sense you have affixed to it. ... So long ... as I shall have the honour to be your representative, I must and will, upon all the vital questions, be unfettered.[2]

Pro-catholics were delighted with Lord William's courage, but anti-catholic hostility was by no means lessened. It was now said that 'his Lordship's return at any succeeding Election can only be calculated upon in the Event of there being *no* Candidate to oppose him'.[3] Anglesey was told that his only hope of keeping the representation of Caernarvon in the family was to advance an anti-catholic candidate: '*whoever the candidate may be* . . . one qualification will be indispensable; namely, that his opinion on the *great*, and *unfortunate* question . . . should coincide with that of his Constituents'.[4] Anglesey, however, had no intention of yielding. 'We often hear', he wrote, 'of the independence of Electors, but I humbly conceive that the independence of the Elected is not less material . . . when a person is returned to serve in Parliament, he is not a mere local Member —he becomes the Representative of the People of the Empire'.[5]

Thus the constituents of Caernarvon were unable to defeat the Anglesey influence, and Lord William Paget retained his seat. An M.P. was more likely to be displaced when his views on the Catholic question conflicted not with those of his constituents but with those of his parliamentary patron. In the 1826

2. *Manchester Gazette*, 11 October 1828.
3. R. A. Poole, a supporter of the Paget influence, to John Sanderson, Anglesey's chief agent, 6 October 1828; Plas Newydd Papers.
4. F. Goddard to Anglesey, 26 February 1829; ibid.
5. Anglesey to Richard Garnons, 2 March 1829; ibid.

election it had not always been insisted that a member should reflect the opinion of his patron on this topic; but as the Catholic crisis heightened, the patron became more desirous of filling his seats with nominees whose views coincided with his own. An attempt by a pro-catholic patron to do this, however, was liable to be obstructed by anti-catholic constituents. At Tiverton, where influence was held by the pro-catholic Lord Harrowby, the corporation refused to accept the proposed replacement of an anti-catholic with a pro-catholic.[6] Anti-catholic patrons were more successful. At Marlborough, where the anti-catholic Marquess of Ailesbury held the nomination, the members—both of whom were pro-catholics—resigned and were replaced with anti-catholics.[7] There was a similar replacement at Newark, which was under the influence of the ultra Newcastle. One of the members, Sir William Clinton, Lieutenant-General of the Ordnance, came out in support of the Government's relief measure. This was incompatible with the pledge of hostility to the Catholic claims under which he had been returned, and he resigned the seat under pressure from Newcastle.[8] The duke's candidate in the ensuing by-election was M. T. Sadler, one of the few talented anti-catholics.[9] Sadler was successful against pro-catholic opposition. His opponent, Sergeant Wilde, protested that his proposer and seconder had both been turned out of their homes by Newcastle;[1] while the *Nottingham Mercury* denied that anti-catholic feeling was predominant in Newark and said that the result was solely due to Newcastle's corruption.[2] The argument was continued the next year when a petition against the election was presented to parliament; Sadler insisted that he had collected a majority of uninfluenced votes, and the petition failed.[3]

More excitement was aroused by the defeat of Peel at Oxford

6. Harrowby wanted his pro-catholic son, the Hon. Granville Ryder, to succeed his anti-catholic brother, the Hon. Richard Ryder. Hon. G. Ryder to Lord Ebrington, 29 December 1827; Harrowby Papers.
7. Lord Brudenell was succeeded by W. J. Bankes, and Earl Bruce was succeeded by T. H. S. B. Estcourt.
8. Ellenborough, i. 355.
9. Sadler had made a celebrated speech at a meeting of the Leeds Pitt Club on 28 May (*Leeds Intelligencer*, 5 June 1828). He had also written a book entitled *Ireland: Its Evils and their Remedies* (2 vols., London, 1828), which insisted that the only satisfactory cures for Ireland were economic and social rather than religious or political.
1. *Nottingham Journal*, 7 March 1829.
2. 14 March 1829.
3. Hansard, xxii. 1077 ff.

University, though this was due to the fame of the defeated rather than the length of his fall, since the anti-catholics won only a pyrrhic victory. Oxford was still impregnated with the high tory spirit: in February 1829 the usual anti-catholic petition was carried by a large majority in Convocation.[4] Peel regarded himself as the elected representative of this spirit; consequently, when he had decided to remain in office and initiate the Government's policy in the Commons, he determined to resign his seat. He made his decision known a few days before the Government conversion was announced in Parliament.[5] His Oxford friends, however, insisted that he should stand for reelection, and eventually he agreed.[6] The anti-catholic candidate was Sir Robert Inglis, who had made a lengthy anti-catholic speech in the last parliamentary debate. The election was regarded as a crucial one. The *Morning Journal* said that the ascendancy of the Church of England depended 'more upon the issue of the approaching contest at Oxford than upon the decision of the House of Commons itself'.[7] An anti-catholic victory was by no means universally expected, in spite of Oxford's reputation. John Henry Newman, then Fellow of Oriel, said he thought the 'Peelites' would succeed.[8] Indeed, Peel was supported by majorities in seven colleges, by a London committee of non-resident members of the university, and by many London lawyers who thereby upheld their alleged divergence from the established clergy over the Catholic question.[9] He was also supported by the Irish Catholic leaders, but according to John Cam Hobhouse this endangered his chances of winning.[1] Inglis, on the other hand, was supported—ironically enough, for he was a staunch evangelical—by most of the future leaders of the Oxford movement. At this time Newman came under the in-

4. Peel's *Memoirs*, i. 317.
5. Peel to the Vice-Chancellor of Oxford University, 4 February 1829 (*Memoirs*, i. 312–15).
6. See N. Gash, *Mr. Secretary Peel*, pp. 546 ff.
7. Among the extracts of the election, in the Bodleian Library.
8. Newman to his sister Harriet, 17 February 1829. Anne Mozley (ed)., *Letters and Correspondence of John Henry Newman during his Life in the English Church* (2 vols., London, 1891), i. 200–1.
9. Bishop Lloyd to Peel, 12 February 1829; PP, 40343, ff. 362–3.
1. Hobhouse wrote: 'O'Connell was fool enough to canvass for Peel, and O'Gorman Mahon, the Irish delegate, actually came down to Oxford in one of Peel's coaches. Luckily he was not discovered, or he would have lost Peel many votes and perhaps his own life.' Diary of J. C. Hobhouse, 28 February 1829; Lord Broughton, *Recollections*, iii. 306.

fluence of the anti-catholic Keble, and the latter issued a series of questions to the electors, suggesting that Peel's conversion was unjustifiable.[2] Hurrell Froude and Robert Wilberforce were also for Inglis; only Pusey supported Peel.[3] The bulk of Inglis's support, however, came from the non-resident parsons.[4]

The poll started on 26 February in a scene of wild uproar which was 'equal to anything that ever occurred in Covent Garden'.[5] Inglis finally won by 755 votes to 609. 'The odium theologicum has done it', wrote J. C. Hobhouse's cousin; 'the outlying Parsons are strong, Church against State. One of them told me just now, they could fight as well as vote, if necessary.'[6] Inglis wrote that he valued the result 'as recording deliberately the opinions of the most intellectual and most ardent body in England on the Roman Catholic Question'.[7] However, so narrow a majority, particularly in view of Oxford's reputation, seemed more of a victory for Peel and the Government than for Inglis and the ultras. Peel was now pleased that he had stood and proud of the support he had received. His numerical minority was counterbalanced by an overwhelming majority of talent. Statistics of this election completely endorse the pro-catholics' claim that they were superior in ability to their opponents. Dr. Whately of Oriel wrote to Peel:

The majority is not quite five to four ... & it is hardly invidious to say that the minority wh. is so near a numerical half, is notoriously & palpably much more than half in everything else ... of nineteen professors who voted, we had *thirteen*; & ... of forty members of parliament, thirty eight! After this, few will talk of the sense of the University being against you.[8]

2. In the extracts concerning the election.
3. H. P. Liddon, *Life of Pusey*, i. 198 f.
4. Lord Donoughmore found on looking through the Oxford Calendar that at least five-sixths of the voters were clergymen, resident and non-resident. Donoughmore to Sir Robert Wilson, 3 March 1829; Sir Robert Wilson Papers, Add. Mss. 30126, f. 144.
5. J. B. Hobhouse to J. C. Hobhouse, 27 February 1829; Broughton Papers, Add. Mss 36465, ff. 80–81.
6. H. Hobhouse to J. C. Hobhouse, 27 February 1829 (ibid., f. 76). Ellenborough wrote that 'the violence of the parsons was beyond belief, and far beyond decency; they made faces at and abused each other'. *Pol. Diary*, i. 366.
7. Inglis to the chairman of his committee, 2 March 1829; extracts, no. 119.
8. 1 March 1829; PP, 40399, ff. 11–12. In addition to the figures mentioned by Whately, Peel was supported by twice as many First Class men as Inglis, and by twenty-four out of twenty-eight prizemen.

Peel was immediately elected for the pocket borough of Westbury, where the proprietor, Sir Manasseh Lopez, retired in his
favour. Lopez's action was so unpopular with the local inhabitants that they threw stones at his windows.[9]

The by-election successes were no doubt a temporary encouragement to the anti-catholics, but they did nothing to stop
the progress of the Catholic question. Once the ministers had
announced their policy, nothing could stem the flow of conversions in parliament. The ultras, however, fought desperately
throughout the final parliamentary struggle. Winchilsea renewed
the Brunswickers' appeals to the people; his new exhortation was
similar to the original ones of Newcastle and Kenyon, though
shorter and more resounding: 'Let the voice of Protestantism
be heard from one end of the Empire to the other. Let the sound
of it echo from hill to hill, from vale to vale. Let the tables of
the Houses of Parliament groan under the weight of your Petitions; and let your Prayers reach the foot of the Throne.'[1] There
was large-scale anti-catholic activity in Ireland. A Protestant
meeting took place in Dublin on 20 February, and a general
meeting of the Brunswick Constitutional Club of Ireland was
contemplated.[2] But in England the enthusiasm for popular meetings was exhausted, and the only fresh onslaught came from
the ultra Press. 'The anti-catholic press is furious', noted J. C.
Hobhouse, 'and abuses Wellington and Peel in good set terms.'[3]
The most unrestrained attacks came from the *Birmingham
Monthly Argus*, whose March and April numbers were full of
anti-ministerial venom. The ministers were accused of 'fear,
treachery, mental imbecility, producing cowardice, political in-
capacity, a want of wisdom, of fortitude, and of a firm and conscientious adherence to protestant principles; a desire of fame,
and a thirst for popularity . . .'[4] Peel, as the leading apostate,
received the most opprobrium: 'No acts of his future life—no
services however valuable—no personal sacrifices however great
—no canting, no whining, no sanctimonious deceit, can ever

9. This transaction is described by W. G. Hoskins and H. P. R. Finberg,
Devonshire Studies (London, 1952), pp. 414–17.
1. *John Bull*, 16 February 1829.
2. Ibid., 16 and 23 February 1829.
3. Broughton, *Recollections*, iii. 305.
4. *Birmingham Monthly Argus*, 1 March 1829.

wash away the damned spot. He stands before the public the victim of his own mean ambition—the slave of his own avarice.'[5] Such, however, was not the tone of all anti-catholic newspapers; *John Bull*, for one, castigated 'the violences which have disgraced the press'.[6]

The ultras lost hope of defeating Catholic emancipation in a House of Commons which was so far out of sympathy with the anti-catholic majority of the nation. Their final hope was that the King might be persuaded to reject the bill.[7] George IV, however, gave his assent to the measure, and with this the whole no-popery movement ended in failure. The failure was not predetermined. Contemporary observations show that anti-catholic prejudice was still widespread and deep-rooted in British society; [8] this is underlined by the popularity of the anti-catholic movement and the overwhelming number of anti-catholic petitions. It is equally clear, on the other hand, that the ardent no-popery of the Gordon Riots had been transformed into sullen impassivity. It is impossible to say whether this torpid prejudice could have been turned into a movement which could effectively prevent the Government carrying emancipation. Certainly the Brunswick leaders were not the men to do it. They were defeated not so much by pro-catholic opposition as by their own inherent conservatism, which prevented them from taking measures that might appear unconstitutional. The establishment of clubs seemed to question the competence of the King's government, and many anti-catholics had disliked this from the start. Moreover, the whole Brunswick movement was based on the presumption that the anti-catholic views of the nation were not represented by a predominantly pro-catholic Commons. Only a radical reform of parliament could correct this situation. But the Brunswick leaders were not the men to imitate Cobbett and Hunt in stimulating an active popular reform movement. Winchilsea may have shown on Penenden Heath a demagogic ability which would have told well at a monster-meeting of the Catholic Association. But this was quite untypical of most ultra leaders. New-

5. Ibid.
6. 16 March 1829.
7. Their efforts in this direction are dealt with in the following chapter.
8. For example, see W. E. Gladstone's account of the opinions of college servants at Oxford. Morley, *Gladstone* (1903 ed.), i. 53–54.

castle, for example, with his belief in a rigid social hierarchy and vested interest in an exclusive parliamentary system, could hardly lead a movement for parliamentary reform. Largely because of this, the potential role of the Brunswick movement as a rival to the unreformed parliament was not fulfilled.

CHAPTER VIII

THE PASSAGE OF CATHOLIC EMANCIPATION

THE weakness of the Brunswick movement was amply demonstrated in the long run, but it was not obvious in the early stages, and considerable concern was caused to the Government. The delay in introducing Catholic emancipation, which had been forcibly imposed on Wellington, provided the ultras with a lengthy opportunity to marshal popular anti-catholic feeling in an effective manner. Until their failure to do so became manifest, it seemed possible that they might succeed in destroying Wellington's whole plan. Brougham wrote in November that an attempt to settle the question would be too late 'if the country is allowed to be inflamed for 2 or 3 months by *No Popery*'.[1] Mrs. Arbuthnot thought that the early success of the movement showed that the duke had not been secretive enough in his intentions. She wrote:

[Wellington] is *very cross* with the Brunswickers & the success they have, & I wrote to beg him to remember that they really have good grounds for alarm, and that his enemies industriously circulate the notion that he means to yield to the Catholics. In fact, I do not think the Duke has managed very adroitly. I think he shd have *seemed* more Protestant & he would have carried his point more easily.[2]

Such alarms were exaggerated. The Duke of Newcastle, it is true, had grave doubts about Wellington which he did not hesitate to express. But this was by no means true of all the ultras. Winchilsea went out of his way to assure Wellington that, notwithstanding his part in the Kent Brunswick Club and the Penenden Heath meeting, he had 'not been actuated by any feeling of distrust towards your Grace & the Government'.[3] Brougham, moreover, wrote as follows about the Brunswickers: 'Nothing can be more clear than that a large proportion of those who are active in such fooleries ... do *not believe* the Govt. to be averse to them

1. Brougham to Grey, 5 November 1828; Brougham Papers.
2. *Journal*, ii. 219.
3. Winchilsea to Wellington, 1 November 1828; Winchilsea Papers.

and who can say that they are averse, if they give no intimation of their dislike.'[4]

Various incidents during the hiatus seemed, when regarded as hints of the Government's intentions, to cancel each other out. In October Peel visited several manufacturing towns in Lancashire. He repeatedly refused to be drawn into making a declaration of anti-catholic principles, although persistent efforts were made to persuade him to do so.[5] It was hopefully suggested in some pro-catholic papers that Peel's silence indicated the Government's intention to emancipate.[6] However, there was no obvious concern among the anti-catholics over Peel's attitude, which in any case could be construed merely as a discreet observance of the official neutrality of the Government.[7] George Dawson's speech at Londonderry and Wellington's letter to Archbishop Curtis caused only temporary alarm among the ultras, while the recall of Anglesey convinced some that Wellington had actually aligned himself with this group. 'No Catholic question & no liberal treatment of the Catholics, is the tardy decision of the Duke', wrote Palmerston imperceptively.[8] 'What a melancholy picture Wellington will make in history', echoed Lord Donoughmore, '. . . a fellow who regards his future fame so little, that in the 19th Century he has the folly to place himself at the head of a faction of Bigots!'[9] A more prescient view was expressed by Lord Durham:

It is quite Evident . . . that the tone of the Ultra Tories is much higher, & therefore more offensive, than before Anglesey's dismissal —but, if I mistake not, without much reason. The violent coercive measures which would alone satisfy them, will not I think be proposed by the D. of Wellington, who will therefore be just where he was, as far as their confidence goes, & much worse off, in respect of the feelings & proceedings of the liberals.[1]

4. Brougham to Grey, 5 November 1828; Brougham Papers.
5. *Manchester Chronicle*, 11 October 1828.
6. *The Times*, 11 October 1828; *Spectator*, 11 October 1828.
7. Wellington himself used this argument of neutrality to avoid committing himself to the Brunswick cause. *Standard*, 13 November 1828. Wellington to Lord Rolle, 8 November 1828 (WND, v. 228–9).
8. Palmerston to the Hon. William Temple, 7 January 1829; Bulwer, *Palmerston*, i. 323.
9. Donoughmore to Sir Robert Wilson, 20 January 1829; Sir Robert Wilson Papers, Add. Mss. 30126, f. 118.
1. Durham to Brougham, 19 January 1829; Brougham Papers.

Continued uncertainty about Wellington's Catholic policy was shown in speculations as to who would fill the vacant offices of Lord Privy Seal and Lord Lieutenant of Ireland.[2] The former was kept vacant until June, but the latter was filled by the Duke of Northumberland soon after Anglesey's recall. Northumberland pleased the anti-catholics by his former allegiance to their cause and the pro-catholics by his current attitude. He told Wellington that he had hitherto opposed any concession to the Catholics 'when such concession was sought by persons unauthorized by the crown to make such a proposition'; but, he added, 'I confess that I shall rejoice to see a settlement of this question originating with your Grace, as Prime Minister, in the House of Lords'.[3]

Whether Wellington would be able to obtain such a settlement was still problematical. He had recently made two unsuccessful efforts to win over the opinion of ecclesiastical leaders for his plan. The second attempt was made in January when he discussed the matter with the Archbishop of Canterbury and the Bishops of London and Durham. All three declared their decided hostility to concession.[4] This seemed a major reverse for Wellington, for it was possible that it would encourage the King to put up an insuperable resistance. Perhaps it was because of this turn of events that Peel now withdrew his threat of resignation and undertook to remain in office.[5] His decision was contained in a letter written to Wellington on 12 January, but Wellington had considered it likely for some weeks before.[6] Peel announced his change of course at a Cabinet meeting on the 17th. The decision cannot have failed to strengthen immeasurably Wellington's determination to overcome the resistance of ecclesiastics, ultra leaders, and the King. Cabinet solidarity immediately made itself felt, and George IV gave way before it. On 15 January he gave separate interviews to the six Cabinet ministers who had hitherto been anti-catholics,[7] and being confronted with their unanimous demand he permitted the Cabinet to take into consideration the whole state of Ireland. In this way George ex-

2. In September 1828 Lord Ellenborough had been transferred from the Privy Seal to the Board of Control.
3. Northumberland to Wellington, 18 January 1829; WND, v. 453.
4. WND, v. 324–5.
5. This view is advanced by N. Gash, *Mr. Secretary Peel*, p. 546.
6. Gash, pp. 548–50.
7. Wellington, Lyndhurst, Bathurst, Peel, Goulburn, and Herries.

tended to the Cabinet the permission he had given to Wellington, Peel, and Lyndhurst the preceding August. But he was just as careful as at that time to insist that under no circumstances was he pledged to accept any advice which might be offered.

Parliament was scheduled to meet on 5 February, and at least the broad lines of a Catholic settlement had to be decided before then. The Cabinet set to work on 18 January. In over a week of intensive preparation the basic principles were laid down, but many of the details had to be postponed for future settlement. It was decided that the Roman Catholics should have civil equality with the exception of certain offices, but it was not yet settled what these exceptions were to be. It was decided that the Irish pauper freeholders should be disfranchised in order to reduce Catholic electoral influence, but the details were passed on to committees and to future cabinet discussion. It was decided that the Catholic Association should be suppressed, but the technicalities were left to the legal officers. Disfranchisement and suppression of the Association were to be the two securities of the Government measure. But much of the long history of Catholic emancipation had been concerned with other and more controversial securities, namely various forms of control over the Catholic clergy. These were revived and considered at length in the cabinet discussions, but the various possibilities were eliminated one by one. Wellington was adamantly opposed to a concordat with the Pope, as he had declared in his speech of the preceding June. On the other hand, he favoured systems of State licensing and State payment of Catholic priests, but these suggestions were opposed by almost all his colleagues. This matter also was left for future discussion, but it was already clear that the question of clerical securities which had generated so much heat in the past was likely to make no appearance in the final settlement. For this the chief responsibility lay with Peel.[8]

Before the end of the month a draft of the general proposals for a Catholic settlement, which were to be announced in the King's Speech at the opening of Parliament, was produced and submitted to the King. George assented, but with obvious reluctance, and he feigned surprise at the scope of the Cabinet's inten-

8. The Cabinet discussions may be followed in Ellenborough, i. 297–324. A summary, concentrating especially on Peel's role, is given in Gash, pp. 552–5.

tions.[9] The completed speech was read at a council meeting on 2 February, and the King then made a mischievous suggestion, as Ellenborough described:

The speech, after expressing the confidence of the King that Parliament would give him power to put down the Association, proceeded thus: 'His Majesty recommends that when this essential object shall have been accomplished, you should take into your deliberate consideration the whole condition of Ireland, and that you should review the laws which impose civil disabilities on His Majesty's Roman Catholic subjects.' The King said: 'The whole condition of Ireland includes the Catholic question, and I see no reason why that part of the paragraph should not be omitted.' The Duke said: 'Your Majesty has Roman Catholic subjects in other parts of your dominions besides Ireland.' The King acquiesced, and at the end of the speech he expressed himself quite satisfied with it.[1]

Three days before Parliament was to meet, the ministerial plan was thus complete. How far were those outside the Cabinet aware of it? The whigs were quite ignorant of the Government's intentions. On 24 January Althorp wrote that the whigs' policy should be to persuade Wellington that he must carry Catholic emancipation unless he wished to be harassed by a powerful Opposition.[2] At the same time Thomas Spring-Rice wrote that he thought Wellington wanted to carry the question, but that he 'believed the real obstacle to be Mr. Peel & his friends, who are said to declare that any approach to concession will be the signal for their resignation'.[3] Suspicion of the true situation was stronger among the ultra leaders, and in addition to their Brunswick efforts they encouraged the Duke of Cumberland to come to England in order to strengthen the anti-catholic resistance of the King.[4] The Government, however, hoped to weaken the

9. When Wellington said that Catholics were to be excluded from judicial offices connected with the Church, the King said, 'What, do you mean a Catholic to hold any judicial office? To be a Judge of the King's Bench?' Again, when the premier mentioned parliamentary seats, he said, 'Damn it . . . you mean to let them into Parliament?' Ellenborough, i. 325.
1. Ellenborough, i. 332.
2. Althorp to Milton, 24 January 1829; Fitzwilliam MSS.
3. Spring-Rice to Milton, 26 January 1829; ibid. Lord Grey also thought that Wellington was disposed to settle the question; Grey to Howick, 1 February 1829 (Grey MSS.).
4. 'I have every reason to believe', wrote Lord Farnham to Cumberland, 'that every engine is set on foot to gain the Consent, in a certain quarter, which your Royal Highness alone can prevent.' G. M. Willis, Life of Ernest Augustus, Duke of Cumberland and King of Hanover (London, 1954), p. 174.

ultras by winning the support of many of those who had previously voted anti-catholic. In early January Joseph Planta (a Secretary to the Treasury) calculated that the ministers would carry a large majority with them in the Commons.[5] In addition to those anti-catholics who would be prepared to change their vote out of reverence for the ministers, there were others who were alienated by the extremism of the Brunswick movement. A test of the attitude of the less extreme anti-catholics came when Peel asked Viscount Clive, who had hitherto been consistently anti-catholic, to move the address in the Commons in answer to the King's Speech. After consulting his father and brother, who had also been anti-catholics, Clive accepted, 'feeling that the time is arrived when some legislative measure is indispensable, entertaining also a sincere conviction that to no two Persons I can with more safety rely for submitting to Parliament measures likely to secure a safe & satisfactory adjustment of this Question than to the Duke of Wellington & yourself'.[6] Ellenborough noted that certain anti-catholic members of the Government below Cabinet rank were pleased at the prospect of a settlement.[7] However, no general attempt could be made to commit the Government supporters to Catholic emancipation before Parliament met, for secrecy about the ministers' intentions was nominally preserved to the end. 'It is a bad arrangement this,' Ellenborough thought, 'or rather a bad want of arrangement which leaves none at liberty to speak.'[8]

The first open intimation of ministerial policy was made to government supporters in the House of Commons at a dinner on 4 February, the eve of the new session. The session was opened the following afternoon. E. J. Littleton, who was present, wrote in his diary:

The known intention of the Govt. to recommend the repeal of the Penal Laws affecting the R. Catholics had drawn together a larger assemblage than usual in the H. of Commons. But there was no more mob about the Doors in Palace Yard than always attends on the same occasion: probably not a thousand people. The crushing

5. Lists enclosed in Planta to Peel, 3 January 1829; PP, 40398, ff. 33–49.
6. Viscount Clive to Peel, 30 January 1829; PP, 40398, ff. 105–6.
7. Ellenborough, i. 328.
8. Ibid., 331.

of the members following the Speaker from the H. of Co[mmons]
to Bar of the H. of Lords was terrible.[9]

In the Lords there were not a great many present.[1] The Lord
Chancellor read the King's Speech which, in accordance with
the decisions reached at the planning stage, demanded that the
Catholic Association should be suppressed and that the reason
for agitation—the exclusion laws—should be repealed. It was
emphasized, however, that it was necessary to safeguard the permanent security of the Protestant establishment, which 'it is the
duty and the determination of his Majesty to preserve inviolate'.
Finally the assembled peers and Commons were warned to discuss the problem, which had been the subject of such heated
controversy in the past, with moderation and good temper.[2]

The announcement naturally absorbed the greatest attention
in the debates on the Addresses in answer to the Speech. In the
Lords the Marquess of Salisbury moved the Address in an embarrassed and barely audible manner, saying that he would never
agree to Catholic relief unless it were accompanied by the fullest
securities.[3] Ultra hostility to the policy was shown in speeches
by Newcastle, Winchilsea, Eldon, Farnham, and Redesdale, and
pro-catholic sentiments were expressed by an equal number of
peers. In the Commons the Address was moved by Clive and
seconded by Viscount Corry, who like Salisbury was surprised
at the announcement and made reservations as to his support.[4]
Ultra speeches were made by Henry Bankes, Sir Robert Inglis,
the Marquess of Chandos, and General Gascoyne (member for
Liverpool). Gascoyne said that the Government's policy would
open the flood-gates to all manner of reforms: 'The hon. gentlemen around him need no longer despair of obtaining universal
suffrage and parliamentary reform: they had nothing to do but
to get up an association, and straight the alarmed minister would
come down to the House with a proposal to grant all they

9. 5 February 1829; Hatherton Papers.
1. Ellenborough, i. 336.
2. Hansard, xx. 4–5. In reading this speech Lyndhurst enhanced his reputation for duplicity. 'The cunning Chancellor', noted E. J. Littleton, 'who is well
known to be anything but a Bigot, affected to read that part of the Royal
Speech which referred to the Catholic Question with intense feeling—he almost
cried—lest he should be suspected of having given way easily.' Diary, 5 February 1829; Hatherton Papers.
3. Op. cit., xx. 9; Ellenborough, i. 337.
4. Op. cit., xx. 48–58.

wanted.'[5] However, there were speeches in support of the announcement which already hinted at conversions that would thin the anti-catholic ranks. Sir Joseph Yorke, member for Reigate, said that although hitherto anti-catholic he was now 'ready to go heart and hand with ministers, in any measure that they might bring forward for securing the tranquillity of Ireland'.[6] The main speech was a self-justification by Peel, giving the history of and reasons for his conversion.[7] The whig members, wrote J. C. Hobhouse, 'could not help smiling to hear from his mouth arguments which he had so often opposed'.[8]

Wellington was not very pleased with the general reception given to the King's Speech. The whigs, he wrote, were disposed to stir up opposition;[9] and according to Ellenborough they were 'very sulky. They see the measure brought forward by those they cannot bear, and they know the carrying of it will destroy their party, by leaving it no bond of union.'[1] Wellington also complained that it was now the practice to say that nobody was informed of his intentions, 'that all are taken by surprise; that I acted with duplicity &c, &c.'[2] A few, no doubt, concealed prior knowledge and suspicions, but there were many whose surprise was real enough. 'What has happened to bring the King or the Duke round since the letter to Abp. Curtis?' asked Viscount Sandon; 'what sufficed to justify so notorious & sudden change of opinion & conduct I cannot conceive.'[3] Similarly, the Earl of Donoughmore wrote to Grey that, particularly after the recall of Anglesey, 'I was led to imagine that the D. of Wellington, if he

5. Hansard, xx. 96.
6. Op. cit., xx. 58–59.
7. Ibid., 72–87.
8. Broughton, Recollections, iii. 302. Lord Donoughmore wrote to Sir Robert Wilson: 'I hate Peel! However I acknowledge that he has made a very plausible defence for himself . . . I should not have had sufficient courage to have acted as he has done. I never had confidence enough in myself or rather impudence enough to vote on different sides of the same question'; 9 February 1829 (Sir A. Wilson Papers, Add. MSS. 30126 f. 128).
9. Wellington to the Earl of Westmorland, 7 February 1829; WND, v. 488–9.
1. Ellenborough, i. 337. Brougham was a notable exception: Charles Arbuthnot wrote that he made a speech lauding Wellington and Peel to the skies, '& observed that with this measure on the one hand & the rigid economy now practising on the other, the Government could have nothing to apprehend'. Arbuthnot to Peel, 10 February 1829; PP, 40340, f. 211.
2. Wellington to the Marquess of Camden, 6 February 1829; WND, v. 488.
3. Sandon to the Countess of Harrowby, 5 February 1829; Harrowby Papers, third series, lxii. 98.

attempted to legislate at all would legislate against the Catholics rather than in their favour'.[4]

The greatest interest lay in the attitude of the anti-catholic tories, for whether or not Catholic emancipation would pass seemed to depend on the number of conversions among this group. E. J. Littleton described their dilemma:

All the High Church Tories, Peers, Bishops, & M.P.s in a quandary —some facing about at the Duke's Command and without hesitation, though with evident shame—others pretending to be squeamish . . . only waiting for time to come round decently, others more bigoted & therefore more honest. We Liberals are dying with Laughter at the just confusion & shame, to which . . . Selfishness & Intolerance are at length put.[5]

While the Cabinet was united in its policy of emancipation, the Government as a whole was still divided, and the ministers were concerned at the attitude of anti-catholic placemen. Lord Beresford, Master-General of the Ordnance, finally acquiesced in Wellington's policy; but George Bankes, Chief Secretary to the Board of Control, preferred to resign rather than expose himself to the necessity of opposing the policy as an individual from within the Government.[6] Wellington expostulated that if Bankes resigned other ultra placemen would follow him, and Ellenborough advised him to wait and see how far he would be compelled to oppose.[7] Bankes must have decided to postpone his withdrawal, for the matter slept until the Relief Bill had passed. However, it was soon clear that the Cabinet would have to contend with the opposition of two other placemen, Sir Charles Wetherell and Viscount Lowther. Peel, moreover, failed to win the support of certain personal friends for emancipation. Lord Hotham promised to avoid any violent hostility, but felt he must oppose the Government all the same;[8] and efforts to win over the anti-catholic Bishop Jebb of Limerick were completely unavailing.[9]

Such obstructions, however, were no doubt partially out-

4. 21 February 1829; Grey MSS.
5. Diary, 6 February 1829; Hatherton Papers.
6. George Bankes to Peel, 6 February 1829; PP, 40398, ff. 146–7.
7. Ellenborough, i. 338–9.
8. Hotham to Peel, 8 February 1829; PP, 40398, ff. 202–3.
9. See the correspondence in Peel's *Memoirs*, i. 358–63.

weighed by the notable conversion of Sir Thomas Lethbridge, M.P. for Somerset and hitherto an active ultra. Lethbridge was among those who had not suspected the Cabinet's intentions, for he had volunteered to second the Commons' Address in innocent ignorance of the contents of the speech. 'I have been surprised beyond all former example', he wrote to Peel.[1] But this did not prevent him from executing a swift rotation. In the same letter he stressed his utmost confidence in Peel's judgement; honour and duty would compel him to demand full security for the Protestant establishment, but beyond this he undertook to do everything possible to smooth the course of emancipation.[2]

Lethbridge said he was ready to act in this way in order to protect the country from the terrible fate of losing the existing government. How far would this fear persuade the anti-catholics in general to support Wellington's policy? Wellington wanted to keep together all shades of tories, except the Huskissonites, in order to avoid having to form another coalition. Sooner than be at the mercy of whigs and Huskissonites, he said, he would throw up office.[3] The Brunswick leaders clearly showed that they at any rate would entertain no compromise;[4] but it was possible that anti-catholic peers who were not so deeply implicated in the ultra cause might be more amenable. The Duke of Rutland was one possibility; the Earl of Lonsdale was another. Wellington sent explanatory letters to both, declaring that 'if this government is not supported by those highly respected individuals and parties in this country who are the main pillars of the monarchy, it is time that I should take my leave'.[5] Lonsdale replied that he was a strong supporter of the Government but suggested that his anti-catholic feelings might prove stronger still.[6] Rutland's reply was even less encouraging;[7] but Mrs. Arbuthnot was sure that his admiration for Wellington would prevent any violent opposition on his part.[8] Nearly all the bishops were apparently firm anti-catholics, but on this point the Hon. Granville Ryder wrote

1. 8 February 1829; PP, 40398, f. 206.
2. Ibid.
3. Mrs. Arbuthnot, ii. 238–9.
4. See above, p. 154.
5. Wellington to Rutland, 7 February 1829; WND, v. 492.
6. Lonsdale to Wellington, 8 February 1829; op. cit., v. 494–5. Lonsdale voted against the second reading of the Catholic Bill in the Lords, but abstained on the third.
7. Rutland to Wellington, 8 February 1829; op. cit., v. 493–4.
8. Mrs. Arbuthnot, ii. 239.

to his brother, Viscount Sandon: 'The leading Bishops . . . who look to no higher preferment, have expressed hostility to the concession of the claims—but it is not uncharitable to suppose that with many, if better motives have no influence, the prospect of a translation will at least secure neutrality.'[9] Ellenborough summarized optimistically the position of the anti-catholic tories: 'Some time must be allowed to enable our people to come round. It has been a great shock to them. Most, however, begin to confess the Government could not have acted otherwise.'[1]

If the prospects were reasonably favourable for a pro-catholic majority in parliament, it was still possible that the King might be persuaded to withdraw his assent to the Government's policy. The ultras' chief hope was that the Duke of Cumberland would take York's place as an anti-catholic power behind the throne. Cumberland suffered a great disadvantage—the unpopularity arising from the scandals which were attached, probably wrongly, to his name. His ultra friends attributed this to radical spleen. 'It is a sad pity he is so dreadfully unpopular', wrote Lord Kenyon, '[but] those who are on the right side have never fair play at all.'[2] It was also fortunate for the ministers that Cumberland was in Germany, and Wellington did his best to keep him there. He persuaded the King to write to his brother, advising him not to exacerbate matters by appearing in England, and also wrote himself. Wellington's letter, written on 2 February, informed Cumberland of the Government's conversion; it advised him, particularly in view of the possibility that he might one day be Regent or even King, not to become the leader of a faction in the State.[3] Both letters were sent to Germany by the hand of Sir William Knighton.

The ultras, however, had forestalled them. By 2 February Cumberland had received letters which made him decide to leave immediately for England. He departed within the next few

---

9. 14 February 1829; Harrowby Papers, third series, lxii. 104–5.
1. Ellenborough, i. 340.
2. Kenyon to his aunt, 22 February 1829; Kenyon Papers. The pro-catholics welcomed Cumberland's reputation as a stroke of political luck. Agar Ellis wrote that the current scandal over Captain Garth was 'politically speaking . . . a good thing, as Cumberland with the aid of his Brunswick Clubs was becoming popular in the country'. Ellis to Ralph Sneyd, 29 January 1829; Sneyd MSS.
3. Cumberland would become Regent in the case of the minority of the Princess Victoria, and King in the case of her death.

days, missing Knighton on the road.[4] By 12 February he was at
Brussels, where he learnt the Government's full intentions for the
first time. On the 15th he arrived at Windsor, and his sudden
appearance put the King in a panic. According to Cumberland's
account, George IV immediately protested that he did not know
that Wellington's plans included Catholic emancipation and
said that he could never consent to such a measure.[5] On the same
day Cumberland attended a dinner given by Wellington and
received a completely contradictory impression. Undaunted,
however, he resolved to continue fighting on 'the straight line'.[6]
He began to attack concession in the Lords, becoming embroiled
on 23 February in an undignified quarrel in that House with
his pro-catholic brothers Clarence and Sussex.[7] His determination was soon to help precipitate the most dangerous crisis in
the last stage of Catholic emancipation.

Meanwhile, the proposed Catholic settlement continued to be
debated in parliament and discussed in Cabinet. In parliament
the way was obstructed by lengthy discussion of the anti-catholic
petitions and attacks on the apostate ministers.[8] However, during February there was pushed through a bill to suppress the
Catholic Association, an essential part of the Government's plan.
When Peel introduced the motion on 10 February, whigs and
Huskissonites reluctantly accepted it because it was thought a
necessary accompaniment to Catholic relief;[9] while the ultras
could not refuse to support a measure which crushed the hated
Association, even if it was designed to assist emancipation. The
bill passed both Houses without a division.

Recollections of the quarrel over the 'wings' in 1825 promised
greater difficulties with the other security, the disfranchisement
of the Irish forty-shilling freeholders. All the Cabinet, except
Fitzgerald, were fearful of the measure. Ellenborough was afraid
that, by carrying disfranchisement concurrently with Catholic

4. Willis, *Cumberland*, p. 174; Ellenborough, i. 345–6; Brook Taylor to
Henry Wynn, 18 February 1829 (Williams Wynn MSS.).
5. Cumberland's memoir, 15 and 17 February 1829; Willis, pp. 176–7, 179.
6. Cumberland to the Duchess of Cumberland, 18 February 1829 (Willis,
p. 178).
7. Ellenborough commented that the three royal dukes all seemed insane;
Pol. Diary, i. 357–8.
8. See above, pp. 148–9.
9. Hansard, xx. 200 ff. Burdett had said that he would 'gulp the measure,
for the sake of carrying the great question'; Broughton, *Recollections*, iii. 303.

relief, a new grievance might be opened at the same time that the old one was abolished.[1] Nevertheless, the measure was decided on and a county freehold qualification of £10 was adopted.[2] Nearly all opposition vanished. It had been expected that O'Connell would be bound to uphold the rights of the forty-shilling free-holders, through whose support he had obtained his victory in County Clare. When the point arose, however, neither he nor the other Catholic leaders were ready to show more than nominal resistance. In the Commons the bill was opposed by an odd assortment consisting of Irish pro-catholics, Huskisson and Pal-merston, and the ultra Henry Bankes. The last-named thus showed that hatred of emancipation had brought out a belated regard for the elective rights of Irish peasants which the ultras had so strongly condemned in the past. The second reading passed by 223 votes to seventeen; the minority included five pro-catholic tories, two anti-catholic whigs, five ultras, and four pro-catholic whigs (three of whom were Irish). Joseph Hume had never seen such a heterogeneous collection voting together.[3] In the Lords there was another minority of seventeen on 6 April, when the second reading was debated. In this debate the bill was opposed by two ultras, Winchilsea and the Duke of Richmond, on the ground that it infringed elective rights. Winchilsea's speech on this occasion was one indication that certain ultras, being exasperated by the pro-catholic majorities of the un-reformed parliament, were becoming favourable to parliamentary reform.[4] Such were the strange political contortions produced by the Catholic crisis.

But this is to anticipate. The Government's main concern was with the central relief measure. Towards the end of February Cabinet discussions showed that any additional securities, clerical or otherwise, would only arouse needless turmoil and that it was better to introduce a plain bill which would enjoy a smoother passage. Just as this was being settled, however, the King was preparing to make a last resistance which kept the ministers on

1. Ellenborough, i. 347–8.
2. A £20 qualification had been suggested, but the ministers were advised that this would withdraw political influence from the landlords and give it to the inhabitants of large towns, where a £20 freehold was of far less value than in the country. F. R. Bonham to Peel, March 1829 (PP, 40399, f. 22).
3. Hansard, xx. 1478.
4. Ibid., 424.

tenterhooks until 5 March, the very day when their scheme was scheduled to be introduced in the Commons.

Responsibility for this is usually attributed to Cumberland, whose single-minded determination is said to have imposed on his brother's irresolution. It is no doubt true that George IV was suffering from mental as well as physical decomposition during his last phase of life. But even if only a few shreds of his true character remained, such an explanation for his attitude would be insufficient. George's character, although machiavellian, was not without its peculiar strength. So far in his political career he had not been obviously weak or easy to influence. In 1812 he had shown himself independent of the whigs, in 1827 of the ultras. He easily dominated weak politicians such as Goderich; and he himself was certainly not dominated by, but rather worked in conjunction with, strong politicians such as Canning. He exercised his ingenuity in playing off one political group against another, rather than allying with either; while in a crisis he would prefer to reconcile both sides as far as possible rather than uphold the rightness of one and thereby arouse the hatred of the other. The emancipation crisis gave full rein to these characteristics and to George's histrionic ability. Bathurst thought he was quite capable of feigning madness in order to resist emancipation.[5] It was unnecessary to go to such lengths, but Protestant Ascendancy was a prized remnant of royal power and its imminent relinquishment presented him with a formidable *crise de conscience*. However, George IV was primarily a politician; no doubt he fully understood the necessity for granting emancipation, and more practical reasons must be found for his final resistance. They are perhaps to be found in the political situation. George IV was anxious to retain his current ministry, since the only other likely to stand was one containing whigs and radicals. But Wellington's ministry might well be jeopardized by the split in the tory party which would come if the ultras proved irreconcilable. It seemed beyond hope that the ultras would retain any personal faith in Wellington, but might they not be persuaded to remain loyal to the King and to whichever ministry had the King's confidence? This might be achieved if the ultras could be convinced that George retained his abhorrence of Catholic emancipation to the end,

5. Ellenborough, i. 381.

and only consented to it under great pressure from Wellington and in order to keep out the whigs. In view of this possible object in the King's mind the ultra machinations of Cumberland seem only an incidental factor in the final crisis. This was also a very useful factor, for Cumberland might persuade his fellow-ultras that the King's resistance was sincere.

This possible explanation helps to clarify the theatrical caprice of the King's attitude towards his ministers at the end of February and the beginning of March—a caprice which it is difficult to believe was due entirely to the King's physical state. Wellington saw the King at Windsor on 25 February and found that he was apparently about to revoke his assent to emancipation. The premier arranged another interview for 27 February, at which he was determined to obtain permission to state in parliament either that the King approved the proposed measures or that he would dismiss his government.[6] On the 27th Wellington saw Cumberland for an hour and the King for five hours. The former denied that he had interfered to change his brother's mind.[7] The King lengthily expounded his father's opinions and the binding nature of the Coronation Oath. But when Wellington urged him to form an ultra government, he 'shed tears, said the Duke was the only Minister he cd or wd have in whom he had any confidence, and ended by giving way'.[8] George also permitted Wellington to write in his name to the Lords of the Household, requesting their support in the forthcoming debates.[9] As soon as the premier had departed, the King assured Cumberland that he 'had not given up one point'.[1] Nevertheless, Wellington was now confident that even if Cumberland persisted in interfering he was capable of counteracting the influence. Wellington was anxious to get Cumberland out of the country. But a letter from Cumberland and a personal interview on 28 February discouraged this hope. On 1 March the King asked Lyndhurst to take a letter to Cumberland, asking him to leave. But this letter showed the King's tactics to the full. It said that he had not made up his mind on the Catholic question, and that he might require Cumberland's assistance in the future. Lyndhurst refused to take the letter.[2] This, together with a discouraging interview

6. Mrs. Arbuthnot, ii. 243–4.   7. Willis, pp. 185–6.
8. Mrs. Arbuthnot, ii. 246.   9. Ellenborough, i. 366; WND, v. 513.
1. Willis, p. 186.   2. Ellenborough, i. 369.

which Wellington had with the King on 2 March, amounted to another royal volte-face. The Cabinet decided that they could proceed no further unless they obtained a written statement that the King endorsed their policy.

The final melodramatic episode commenced with a five-hour interview between the King, Wellington, Peel, and Lyndhurst on 4 March. On the King's side it was lubricated with tears, alcohol, and capricious objections. He claimed not to have realized that a Catholic relief measure would entail an alteration in the Oath of Supremacy, and said he must withdraw his assent for this reason. The ministers replied that they had no alternative but to resign, and they returned to London in the evening with the impression that they had been dismissed. Much of what Wellington had worked for over the past seven months seemed to have been shattered within an inch of success. His one hope was that another ministry could not be found and that the King would have to reappoint him. But even so the task of emancipation was likely to be much more difficult than before. 'We may possibly come in again in about ten days', wrote Ellenborough, 'but under what different circumstances—the King having declared his dissent, and having made an appeal to the people.'[3] But this never happened. Under pressure, it was said, from Knighton and Lady Conyngham, the King immediately recanted and informed Wellington that he had decided to consent to the bill.[4] A hasty exchange of notes at midnight put the matter beyond further reversal.[5] This final turn of fortune in the small hours assured the ministers that they would face the Commons later that day not with an announcement of resignation but with a plan of emancipation.

Crowds queued outside the House of Commons all day, hoping to hear the momentous debate from the gallery. When doors opened at 6 p.m. all available seats were occupied within two minutes. Peel commenced the debate by moving for a committee of the whole House to consider the exclusion laws. In a masterly speech of four hours' duration he analysed the necessity for emancipation and described in detail the Government's measure.[6]

3. Ellenborough, i. 377.
4. The King to Wellington, 4 March 1829; WND, v. 518.
5. WND, v. 518 f. See Gash, op. cit., pp. 569–70.
6. Admirably summarized in Gash, pp. 570–5.

This proposed that Catholics should be admitted to parliament without restriction; that the exceptions to offices opened to Catholics should be those of Regent, Lord Chancellor both of England and Ireland, Lord Lieutenant of Ireland, and various minor posts.[7] O'Connell thought the scheme 'very good; frank, direct, complete; no veto, no control, no payment of the clergy'.[8] Several speeches followed, mainly against the measure; the debate was then adjourned until the following day, when the crucial division took place. The Government obtained a majority of 188. Fifty-eight Government supporters were new pro-catholic converts;[9] but the anti-catholic minority of 160 was a good deal larger than expected. In his January calculations Planta had estimated that only 119 members would vote against concession if it were introduced by the Government, with thirty-three 'doubtful'.[1] Out of Planta's 'doubtfuls', only fourteen opposed the measure.[2] On the other hand, the minority included no fewer than forty-nine of those whom Planta had said would vote with the Government. The result was therefore rather disappointing. Nevertheless, the Government had secured more than adequate support.

The Relief Bill was introduced and given its first reading on 10 March. The second reading was moved on 17 March, and the debate again lasted two days. For the first time, Lord Holland thought, the debate was 'in favour of No Popery'.[3] Effective speeches by Sir Edward Knatchbull and M. T. Sadler, the new member for Newark, indicated that the ultras were resolved to go down fighting. Sadler said that the Commons had no right to decide the question without making a fresh appeal to the people: 'I know how dear this sacred, this deserted cause is, to the hearts and to the understandings of Englishmen. The principle may be indeed weak in this House, but abroad it marches in all its wonted might, headed . . . by the intelligence, the reli-

7. The minor exceptions embraced offices attached to Church establishments, ecclesiastical courts, universities, public schools, and schools of ecclesiastical foundation.
8. O'Connell to James Sugrue, 6 March 1829; Fitzpatrick, *O'Connell*, i. 174.
9. Two whigs were also among these converts. A few whigs, however, including Henry Bright (Bristol) and William Dickinson (Somerset), opposed emancipation to the end.
1. PP, 40398, ff. 33–49.
2. Planta's list of 'doubtfuls' was a very odd one: it included such decided pro-catholics as George Tierney, James Scarlett, and Charles Brownlow.
3. Holland to Brougham, 18 March 1829; Brougham Papers.

gion, the loyalty of the country.'[4] The pro-catholic majority in the division was only 180, but the loss of eight votes from the total of 6 March was because of absences rather than reconversions.[5]

This debate brought to a head the question of whether members of the Government who opposed the bill should be dismissed. The three chief ministerial opponents were Wetherell, Lowther, and George Bankes. The problem had been under discussion since January. The whigs wanted to see them dismissed, since they thought Wellington would be forced to fill their places with members of the Opposition.[6] But this was just what Wellington wanted to avoid. True to his consistent policy, he said that, once the bill had passed, he wished 'to reunite the whole Tory Party & wd not bring any Whigs in'.[7] Several placemen, including Lowther and Lord O'Neill, voted against Wellington on 6 March, and both offered their resignations in consequence. Wellington, however, did not want to accept them, lest he might thereby weaken his chances of conciliating the ultras. Wetherell, however, made such a violent attack on his colleagues on 18 March that the duke had perforce to remove him. Wetherell's denunciation presented in unrestrained terms the feelings of many ultras:

He dared [the ministers] to attack him. He had no speech to eat up. He had no apostacy to explain. He had no paltry subterfuge to resort to. He had not to say that a thing was black one day and white another. . . . He would rather remain as he was, the humble member for Plympton, than be guilty of such apostacy—such contradiction—such unexplainable conversion—such miserable, such contemptible apostacy.[8]

Wetherell was thereupon turned out, for other reasons besides his abuse;[9] but Lowther and Bankes were permitted to keep their places and eventually decided to remain.

4. Hansard, xx. 1168.
5. According to the lists in Hansard, only one member voted pro-catholic on 6 March and anti-catholic on 18 March. This was J. E. Dowdeswell, member for Tewkesbury.
6. Donoughmore to Sir Robert Wilson, 10 March 1829; Sir R. Wilson Papers, Add. MSS. 30126, ff. 147–8.
7. Mrs. Arbuthnot, ii. 251.
8. Hansard, xx. 1263–4.
9. One charge against him was that he had betrayed official confidence by mentioning the time when Peel first communicated to him the intentions of government (Ellenborough, i. 400–1).

Meanwhile, the ultras had been making further appeals to the King. 'Don't let us suffer ourselves to be dismayed', Lord Wodehouse wrote misguidedly to Kenyon. '. . . Thank God we have a Protestant King who will not shrink from doing his Duty to his Subjects.'[1] Anxious as he was to retain their attachment, George IV received various ultra peers and told them that he was being forced against his will to accept emancipation. He saw Newcastle for two hours on an uncertain date, Mansfield for two hours on 26 March, and Eldon for four hours on the 28th.[2] Lord Kenyon presented some anti-catholic addresses, and a deputation of Irish Protestant bishops came to petition the King to veto the bill. At this time there were also various meetings of ultra peers, whose purpose was doubtless to discuss plans for resistance.[3] Cumberland planned to get 20,000 Londoners to march to Windsor and petition the King; but Wellington was ready to clamp down on any such demonstration and said he 'wd send the Duke of Cumberland to the Tower as soon as look at him'.[4] Newcastle was deputed to present the petition to the King in person, and it was feared that many people would accompany him to Windsor. Wellington, however, persuaded the King with some difficulty to order Newcastle to present his petition through the normal channel of the Home Secretary.[5] The ultras had to give way. Their defeat had already been symbolized by the famous duel between Wellington and Winchilsea, arising out of a slanderous attack on the duke by the latter, in which Winchilsea retired from the field without firing at his antagonist.[6]

Various ultra amendments were defeated at the committee stage of the Relief Bill, and Peel moved the third reading on 30 March. The ultra cause was again presented in speeches by Wetherell, Inglis, and Sadler, but the last-named naïvely spoiled

1. 15 March 1829; Kenyon Papers.
2. Ellenborough, i. 389–90, 394–5, 410; Mrs. Arbuthnot, ii. 258.
3. Lord Kenyon's diary, 27 and 30 March 1829 (Kenyon Papers); Ellenborough, i. 410.
4. Mrs. Arbuthnot, ii. 254.
5. Ellenborough, i. 413–14.
6. Winchilsea's attack was made in a letter withdrawing his name from the list of subscribers to King's College, London. He said that Wellington, in supporting the foundation of this anglican college, had stepped out of his usual course for once to advocate morality and religion; and he accused the duke of doing so only as a blind, beneath which he could continue his insidious design of establishing popery. The duel took place in Battersea Fields on 21 March. Ellenborough, i. 395–6, 402–4; Mrs. Arbuthnot, ii. 257.

a powerful effort by saying that he argued the question 'perhaps with more of my heart in it than my understanding'.[7] In the last Catholic division in the Commons the Government majority was 178. But the greatest parliamentary trial was still to be faced in the Lords. In February Lord Colchester had predicted that Wellington would obtain a majority of only four in the Upper House.[8] At this early stage it had been feared that the bishops in particular would prove obstinate. In a protracted correspondence Wellington had no success whatever in shaking the anti-catholic views of Thomas Burgess, Bishop of Salisbury.[9] However, the Government had been encouraged by a letter to the King from C. R. Sumner, Bishop of Winchester, giving the measure his full support.[1] The Archbishop of Canterbury, moreover, had resisted pressure from the ultras to urge their views on the King, although he himself remained unconverted.[2] Meanwhile the Government had been making strenuous efforts to obtain the votes of peers. In February a king's messenger was sent to Italy to collect proxies;[3] and by March Wellington was counting on a substantial majority.[4]

On 31 March Wellington moved the first reading in the Lords and proposed that the second reading should take place on 2 April. The ultras demanded a longer delay, but the proposal was agreed to. On the 2nd, Wellington explained the provisions of the bill, and the ensuing debate lasted three days. The main attack came from the clerics. They were supported by Lords Falmouth and Mansfield, both of whom thought it necessary to deny that their anti-catholic zeal had made them parliamentary reformers.[5] The most effective pro-catholic speeches were made on 4 April by Grey and Plunket. 'The whole day has been

7. Hansard, xx. 1623.
8. Colchester, iii. 599.
9. WND, v. 509–31.
1. 9 March 1829; *Geo. IV Letters*, iii. 455.
2. Kenyon wrote in his diary on 24 March that he had been at Lambeth 'trying to persuade Archbp. to confirm the King in his duty as to Coronation Oath. Archbp. personally very kind, but very sneaking sophistical and cowardly'; Kenyon Papers.
3. Buckingham's *Private Diary*, iii. 93.
4. Ellenborough, i. 383.
5. Mansfield stated that 'in theory the opinion of the people should be ascertained by the votes of their representatives, representing as they do the wealth and intelligence of the country. . . . I have never been, and notwithstanding the example of so many conversions, I believe [never] shall be, an advocate for Parliamentary Reform'; Hansard, xxi. 246–7.

most triumphant', wrote the Bishop of Oxford; 'L. Grey magnificent and Plunket equally so. L. Eldon's [speech] in my judgement a total and most spectacular failure.'[6] The House divided that day, and to the delighted surprise of the pro-catholics the Government had a majority of 105.[7] Ellenborough said it would quieten the agitation in England and tranquillize Ireland. To the ultras, on the other hand, it was 'a most calamitous division for the Protestant Church and Constitution'.[8]

The sense of spectacular victory was sustained in the remaining debates. In committee various ultra amendments were withdrawn or negatived, and on 10 April the third reading was carried by a majority of 104. Over thirty ultra peers thereupon entered their protests in the Lords' journals. But these were the protests of beaten men. The final blow had been the fact that ten members of the episcopal bench, the core of the Protestant establishment, had voted for the bill. 'God grant His protection to the Church in its deserted state', wrote Kenyon.[9]

The royal assent, however, had still to be given. The ultras had striven to prevent it until the last moment. Cumberland wrote the King a last unsuccessful exhortation, and various ultra bishops and lay peers went to Windsor with petitions.[1] The notion was revived of a procession of Londoners to Windsor; it was to take place on 10 April, preceded by a public meeting in Hyde Park. Wellington repeated his former determined tactics. He warned the King that such a proceeding was illegal and urged him to accept petitions only through a formal channel such as the Home Secretary.[2] Peel went to Windsor to repeat this advice in person. The day before the meeting it was thought necessary to lock all the gates of Hyde Park,[3] but Ellenborough thought the scheme would be a failure: 'There is no agitation in London', he wrote; 'no feeling, no excitement.'[4] A failure it was. The bearers of the petition to Windsor filled only four carriages;

6. Dr. Charles Lloyd to Peel, dated 'Saturday night' (i.e. 4 April 1829); PP, 40343, f. 398.
7. 'The general notion', wrote J. C. Hobhouse, 'was that there would be [a majority of] no more than between 70 and 80'; Broughton, *Recollections*, iii. 316–17.
8. Kenyon's diary, 4 April 1829; Kenyon Papers.
9. Op. cit., 10 April 1829.
1. Willis, pp. 193–4; Ellenborough, ii. 9.
2. Wellington to the King, 9 April 1829; WND, v. 577–8.
3. Charlotte, Lady Williams Wynn to Henry W. Wynn, 9 April 1829; Williams Wynn MSS.
4. Ellenborough, ii. 9.

they were told to present their petition through the Home Secretary, and dispersed quietly. In this sad fashion the no-popery movement petered out. After the last successful division in the Lords, which occurred the same day, there were no further assaults on the royal position. On the 13th, George IV assented to the bill.[5]

Thus ended a problem which had been a leading controversial issue for thirty years and one of particular intensity in the past decade. Plunket's success in 1821 came after eight years of unrelieved defeats. Although a false start, it none the less heralded eight years of better fortune for the cause of emancipation. Ultimate success, however, cannot be traced beyond the founding of the Catholic Association in 1823. This body provided a heightened consciousness of the danger from Ireland which was largely responsible for the startling advance of the Catholic question in 1825. Its electoral success, first seen in the elections of 1826, presented such formidable implications in 1828 that the Government was persuaded to adopt emancipation, and with this the 'open' system came to an end. Fear of Irish demagogy, possible revolution, and the break-up of the Union— these were the reasons for the Government's response. The Government's solution was no less practically political than its motives. Relief was only granted along with disfranchisement; vetos, concordats, and state salaries were jettisoned in order to secure the maximum support. It was an entirely secular settlement; tolerant conviction played no part in the Government's purpose. On the other hand, intolerant conviction was not strong enough to defeat this purpose. The ultras were helpless. They failed both to impose their demands on the King and to arouse effectively the popular anti-catholic prejudice. Nevertheless, though beaten, the ultras would not accept defeat. Despite all Wellington's efforts, Catholic emancipation was only achieved at the price of his government's stability. In its disintegration the ultras were to take their revenge.

5. He was said to have played his temporizing game to the end. John Cam Hobhouse wrote on 24 June that three days before he assented he swore that nothing would induce him to do so; Broughton, iii. 323.

CHAPTER IX

THE DECLINE OF WELLINGTON'S GOVERNMENT

THE passage of Catholic emancipation produced various reactions of relief which were the stronger because the period
of tension had been so long. The Catholics rejoiced in
their new privileges; long-standing pro-catholics were delighted
that they had lived to see their cause won. Others, both pro- and
anti-catholics, were only too thankful that so persistent a cause
of disunion was at length laid to rest. Charles Wynn wrote to the
anti-catholic Southey:

At length we have a prospect of release from the Catholic Question
and though our opinions upon it may be as wide as the two poles yet
there is the tertium quid in which we may equally agree and that
is in enjoying relief from the controversy which worn down as it
was *threadbare*, every thing valuable or brilliant long ago brushed
off, was become no longer supportable.[1]

But a controversy which had become so bitter in its closing
stages could not be expected to disappear without trace. It had
indeed caused a political situation which eventually destroyed
Wellington's Government. The ultras were alienated from the
Government, but Wellington had no intention of replacing their
support by allying with the whigs. He had to thank the latter
publicly for their help in carrying the Relief Bill, but did so
with visible reluctance and showed that he did not wish to turn
that temporary accord into a firm partnership.[2] Nor did he wish
to return to the position before May 1828 and recall the Huskissonites. His policy for a year had been to retain the support of
the ultras; and this policy had not been changed by his collisions,
sometimes most violent, with the ultras in recent weeks. He was
anxious, for example, that ultra ministers who had threatened

---

1. 7 April 1829; Williams Wynn MSS.
2. Princess Lieven to Count Benckendorff, 14 April 1829; L. G. Robinson,
Letters of Princess Lieven, p. 193.

resignation should keep their places.[3] Necessity compelled him to give office to certain pro-catholics, but he was inclined to ally only with the Marquess of Londonderry's group of pro-catholic ultras,[4] and with the 'high' whigs led by Grey. Lord Rosslyn, Grey's friend, was given the vacant office of Privy Seal; James Scarlett, a protégé of Earl Fitzwilliam, was made Attorney-General. But there was no indication that the Government would receive consistent whig support in return, even from Grey. The latter told Fitzwilliam that he stood 'precisely as before, well disposed towards the Government which has carried the Catholick Question, but entirely unconnected with it, & at liberty to act upon particular measures that may arise, according to my sense of public duty'.[5]

The tragedy of the situation was that while Wellington did not engage the whig party in his support, ultra hostility to him did not cease, so that his government fell between two stools. It would be a long time before the ultras recovered from the destruction of what they regarded as an indispensable part of their sacred constitution. 'The world seems altered in every way', wrote Lord Kenyon's aunt; 'it seems that seasons, People, & principles, are so altered that I can hardly believe that I am still in poor old England.' [6] 'As to the duke of Wellington', she wrote in another letter, 'he does deserve hanging.' [7] The Birmingham Monthly Argus continued to abuse the apostates, calling Peel and Lyndhurst traitors and the duke a puffed-up dictator. 'Our's [sic] is the PEOPLE'S CAUSE', it announced in December 1829; 'OUR PARTY IS THE COUNTRY—OUR rallying point is LOYALTY and PATRIOTISM—TRUTH and ORTHODOXY—honest TORYISM and honest PROTESTANTISM.' The fact that certain ultras remained attached to the Government did not mean that their following was conciliated. Brougham wrote that in Westmorland all the Lowther supporters were furiously against the Government, 'with Lord Lowther holding one of the best places under it'.[8]

3. Mrs. Arbuthnot, ii. 260. George Bankes, after seeking Cumberland's advice, decided to retain office; Lord Lowther and John Beckett also remained.
4. Viscount Castlereagh, Londonderry's son, was appointed to a vacant Lordship of the Admiralty in preference to two liberal tories, Viscount Sandon and John Stuart-Wortley; Mrs. Arbuthnot, ii. 282.
5. Grey to Fitzwilliam, 30 June 1829; Fitzwilliam MSS.
6. Miss A. Kenyon to Lord Kenyon, 3 May 1829; Kenyon Papers.
7. Miss A. Kenyon to Lord Kenyon, 28 April 1829; ibid.
8. Brougham to Grey, 8 October 1829; Brougham Papers.

The ultras continued to meet and lick their wounds;[9] they were anxious to remain combined in order to preserve their strength in case they enjoyed a better turn of fortune. 'Let us not despair', Falmouth told Newcastle. 'Many things not half so improbable as recent events were before they happened may now occur to restore [to] our principles their now weakened preponderance, & we must tell our Country friends above all things to *keep together*.'[1] Soon the ultras were trying to revive some of their old projects. The fact that this was necessary suggests that the Brunswick Clubs were no longer functioning, and indeed there is no further trace of them. Kenyon proposed that a Protestant Club should be established to uphold anti-catholic principles. Winchilsea said he would gladly join such a society;[2] Thomas Burgess, Bishop of Salisbury, was equally encouraging, but disliked the word 'club' and wanted 'union' added to the title.[3]

More significantly, it was rumoured that the ultra peers were thinking of trying to form a government. Lord Mansfield was reported to have said that, at the next Pitt Club dinner in May, 'we shall make such a display of Protestant force as will enable the King to take us as his Ministers';[4] and Cumberland was said to be busy forming a new government.[5] It was important to the ultras that Cumberland should remain in the country, for they hoped he would provide a powerful link with the King. A rumour that he was to leave for Germany produced an anxious appeal to remain from Sir Richard Vyvyan, ultra member for Cornwall: if Cumberland went, he said, there would be no avenue open between the ultras and the throne, and Wellington's influence over the King would be unchallenged.[6] Cumberland replied that he was prepared to make any personal sacrifice to save the country: 'what has been done cannot be undone, but I still am of Opinion that if *we* Tories will hold firm and strong together, there is still a hope of rescuing the Country.'[7] He

9. Kenyon wrote in his diary on 18 April 1829: 'Duke of Newcastle, Lds Farnham & Falmouth with me abt. Protestant cause' (Kenyon Papers).
1. 20 April 1829; Newcastle MSS.
2. Winchilsea to Kenyon, 24 April 1829; Kenyon Papers.
3. Burgess to Kenyon, 25 April 1829; ibid.
4. Ellenborough, ii. 34.
5. Mrs. Arbuthnot, ii. 270.
6. Vyvyan to Cumberland, 13 July 1829; Vyvyan MSS. Part of this letter is quoted in Knatchbull-Hugessen, *Kentish Family* (London, 1960), pp. 178–9.
7. Cumberland to Vyvyan, 16 July 1829; Vyvyan MSS.

added that he would certainly remain in the country if his friends thought this would be of use to their 'sacred Cause'.[8]

Vyvyan had assumed a leading position in the new ultra movement. During the parliamentary recess he continued to correspond with Cumberland and other ultras about the possibility of forming an ultra government.[9] Should the new government be entirely new, or would the ultras perhaps consider coalescing with some members of Wellington's ministry? Cumberland replied:

... if a proposition is made to the [Wellingtonian] Tories, it must be perfectly understood not that we strengthen the present Government, but that it is to be *dissolved* & broke up and a *new one formed* keeping in perhaps some of the present members who may be the least objectionable; but there are certain members that it is utterly impossible for any of us Tories to unite with without degrading ourselves.[1]

Surely, Vyvyan asked in reply, Cumberland would not include Wellington himself among these 'least objectionable' ministers?[2] In a letter to Newcastle, Vyvyan stressed the impossibility of ever trusting Wellington again:

... after what has been effected by the Duke of Wellington have we not just grounds for expecting that he will stoop to any manœuvre for the purpose of compassing his ends? When I reflect upon his system of policy and his avowed contempt for public opinion, I must own I dread anything like a coalition between him and the [ultra] Tory party even were he alone in a cabinet without one personal supporter.[3]

Cumberland, however, said in answer to Vyvyan that many people thought the presence of Wellington would be essential to an ultra government, if only because his opposition would be a tremendous embarrassment. If this was the opinion of most ultras, Cumberland continued, he would not oppose it provided there was an ultra majority in the Cabinet and ultra principles

8. Vyvyan MSS.
9. These letters are in the Vyvyan MSS. Some of them are summarized in Knatchbull-Hugessen, op. cit., pp. 179 f.
1. Cumberland to Vyvyan, 17 August 1829; Vyvyan MSS.
2. Vyvyan to Cumberland, 22 August 1829; ibid.
3. Vyvyan to Newcastle, 25 August 1829; ibid.

prevailed.[4] Vyvyan, however, disagreed about Wellington's power as an opponent and retained his opinion that the duke should be excluded.[5] The most critical and objective of the participants in this intrigue was Sir Edward Knatchbull, M.P. for Kent. In a letter of 26 August Knatchbull drew Vyvyan's attention to several obstacles in the path of an ultra ministry. Cumberland, chronically unpopular as he was, provided a leading disadvantage.[6] Knatchbull also thought that various people whom Vyvyan had suggested, would be unlikely to join such a government. Lord Chandos was firmly attached to Wellington; Lord Aberdeen and Vesey Fitzgerald, whom Vyvyan had apparently included, were unlikely to leave the duke; and Sadler '[though] with great talents and great information will never be a minister'. In addition there would be a lack of dependable subordinates to fill the non-cabinet offices; the King's support would be uncertain, and Irish hostility to such a government would present a great problem.[7] Knatchbull also disagreed with Vyvyan in that he favoured the inclusion of Wellington.[8] There is even evidence that he was in communication with the premier at this time.[9]

Meanwhile, Vyvyan busied himself with calculations as to the number of supporters the ultras were likely to find in the Commons. An undated memorandum in his hand[1] listed thirty-five tories 'strongly opposed to the present government', including such names as Inglis, Colonel Sibthorp, Sadler, and Wetherell;[2] and eighty-nine possible ultras, 'who voted in favour of the 3rd reading [of the Relief Bill] but whose sentiments are unknown'. On the other hand there were twenty-two 'present government connections who will be hostile to a new one', and 234 general

4. Cumberland to Vyvyan, 25 August 1829; ibid. In a subsequent letter, Cumberland said that he did not envisage retaining Wellington as premier, but would offer him his former post of Commander-in-Chief. Cumberland to Vyvyan, 2 September 1829; ibid.
5. Vyvyan to Cumberland, 8 September 1829; ibid.
6. 'We must have a Government composed of men whose Moral & Religious character is beyond exception', he wrote again in November. Knatchbull to Vyvyan, 15 November 1829; ibid.
7. Knatchbull to Vyvyan, 26 August 1829; Knatchbull-Hugessen, pp. 183-4.
8. Knatchbull to Vyvyan, 4 September 1829; ibid., p. 185.
9. J. Planta to Wellington, 8 September 1829; ibid., p. 189.
1. Vyvyan MSS.
2. It was presumably to these that Ellenborough was referring when he wrote in his diary that 'in the House of Commons there is a small Ultra party, not fifty'. Ellenborough, ii. 44.

supporters of the Government, including seventeen 'Huskissons'. In view of these figures it behoved the ultras to strengthen their numbers, and they sought to do this by making overtures to certain discontented Huskissonites and whigs. Brougham's reputation for political inconstancy made him a possible recruit, and it was conceivable that he might be lured by an offer of the Woolsack in a new government. 'Of all men amongst the Whigs', wrote Vyvyan, 'he seems to me the most assailable, provided the offer be large enough.'[3]

There is no evidence that an approach was actually made to Brougham. There is considerable documentation, however, for an approach made to Palmerston. It was unlikely, Vyvyan thought, that the latter could rise very quickly as a follower of Huskisson.[4] 'I mean to try to get Palmerston', he wrote on 7 September, 'but I shall be very careful how I do it.'[5] He broached the matter to Palmerston at the Travellers' Club.[6] During the conversation Palmerston observed that Wellington seemed to be regaining the alliance of the ultras and was in a hopeful position for the 1830 parliamentary session. Vyvyan sharply contradicted him: 'the Tories were more adverse than ever . . . the Duke of Wellington was more tottering than ever, and . . . even in a fortnight or three weeks a new Government might be formed'. He went on to enquire how far Palmerston was bound to Huskisson, for with his economic schemes Huskisson frightened the country gentlemen who provided support for the ultras. Palmerston said that he was in harmony with Huskisson on such matters. Vyvyan then asked whether he would allow his name to be suggested to the King as Secretary for the Colonies and Leader of the Commons in a new government. Palmerston firmly declined. Despite these discouragements Vyvyan went on to discuss the composition of the projected government:

Lord Mansfield would of course be the head. Eldon would be a member. Brougham . . . must be got out of the House of Commons, as he would be too formidable an antagonist, and why should he not make an excellent Chancellor? . . . [Vesey] Fitzgerald is a quick, clever

3. Vyvyan to Knatchbull, 31 August 1829; Vyvyan MSS.
4. Ibid.
5. Knatchbull-Hugessen, p. 179.
6. The interview was described in detail by Palmerston to his brother-in-law, Laurence Sulivan, in a letter dated 7 October, printed in the Marquess of Lorne, *Palmerston*, pp. 56–62. The following summary and quotations are taken from the letter.

fellow and would be most useful. . . . Young Stanley he praised as a man that should be obtained. . . . Herries he commended as a man full of the most useful knowledge. Huskisson he mentioned in connection with the Chancellorship of the Exchequer. Robert Grant would make an admirable Speaker. . . . The Duke of Newcastle lauded generally for his good sense and understanding, and Sir E. Knatchbull pointed out as Secretary to the Home Department.

Palmerston gathered from this that the cabal had realized the impossibility of forming a government of ultras alone, and that the next step was to reinforce the ultras with 'a few young men of the Liberal parties who shall not be able to set up as objectors to any course proposed'.

In all this there is certainly no indication that Palmerston sympathized with Vyvyan's aims, but rather the reverse. Yet Vyvyan, in relating the conversation to Cumberland, claimed not only sympathy but positive commitment. 'By detaching Lord P. from the Huskisson party', he wrote, 'we have dislocated the strength of that party and gained a most valuable auxiliary, a good speaker, a man of business, & if necessary a competent leader in the house of Commons.' [7]

Although the ultras needed the support of individual Huskissonites and whigs, they were not prepared to adopt whig principles, which act alone might have made a whig-ultra coalition possible. This is seen from the fate which befell the Marquess of Blandford's motion for parliamentary reform, which he introduced in the Commons on 2 June 1829. The underlying reason for the motion was Blandford's desire to prevent the accumulation of Catholic power in the House. As soon as Catholic members entered the Commons, he argued, they would form a party which the Catholics of Great Britain and Ireland would regard as their only true representatives. The system of borough ownership would allow them to gain strength.[8] This system, therefore, must be altered. Blandford moved two resolutions for the extinction of rotten boroughs. His motion was seconded by an ultra, O'Neill, and supported in speeches by Joseph Hume and John

7. Vyvyan to Cumberland, 22 October 1829; Vyvyan MSS.
8. 'Seats in this House will be bought up by the agents of this wealthy, powerful, and enterprising body, and thus to their county strength in Ireland will be added their burgage tenure strength in this country.' Hansard, xxi. 1674.

Cam Hobhouse. The latter, however, made it clear that he did not support Blandford's anti-catholic motives:

If . . . the adoption of parliamentary reform would be calculated to make that House less inclined to the great principles of civil and religious liberty, he would rather that the House should remain as it was at present constituted, than that such a change should be effected in its character. He uniformly advocated parliamentary reform, because it was calculated to produce a quite different result.[9]

It was left to the radical dissenter William Smith (member for Norwich) to demonstrate the incongruity of such a motion: 'One effect he was happy to find had been produced by the Roman Catholic Relief Bill—an effect which its best friends had not anticipated: it appeared to have transformed a number of the highest Tories in the land to something very nearly resembling radical reformers.'[1] As a body, however, the ultras did not support Blandford. Most of them were as unprepared to go to the length of adopting parliamentary reform as they had already shown during the debates on the Relief Bill. The motion obtained only forty votes, nearly all whig.

Because of their small numbers and, perhaps, their fear of being drawn into radical policies such as Blandford's, the ultras lost their aggression as the parliamentary recess went on. Talk of a new government gradually subsided. In November, Vyvyan wrote to Eldon about the weakening of the ultras: 'the object of the Protestants is to strike an immediate blow, if that were possible, as that would put an end to the gradual defections from their ranks.'[2] Lord Rolle, he continued, had deserted them, promising his support to the Government in return for a chancery living for a nominee of his, and this was only one of many instances where the Government had contrived to obviate opposition. 'An unpatriotic egotism', he concluded, might make it impossible to obtain a majority against the ministers.[3] The ultras, moreover, were divided over the possibility of making a parliamentary attack. Vyvyan believed in an 'immediate blow', but Knatchbull thought that 'there is no distinct & definite object that can justify us in taking such a course'.[4]

9. Hansard, xxi. 1685.   1. Ibid., 1688.
2. Vyvyan to Eldon, 30 November 1829; Vyvyan MSS.
3. Op. cit.
4. Knatchbull to Vyvyan, 15 November 1829; op. cit.

After November no further letters concerning the ultra combination have come to light. Meanwhile, there were certain indications that anti-catholic revenge was becoming a dead topic. In November preparations were in progress at Maidstone for a dinner in honour of Knatchbull, 'as a mark of approbation of his consistent support of Protestant principles'.[5] But several former anti-catholics declined to attend on the grounds that outworn antagonism would be needlessly revived.[6]

If the ultras were not unduly menacing to Wellington on the eve of the new parliamentary session, this very fact made it unlikely that the whigs would commit themselves to support the Government. Brougham wrote that Wellington seemed to be relying 'on our dislike of the D. of Cumberland'; but, he added, it would be impossible to carry on the Government in the Commons 'on that bottom alone'.[7] Many whigs, indeed, were prepared to vote with the ultras against the Government. When parliament met on 4 February 1830 Knatchbull moved an amendment to the King's Speech. He was supported by ultras, whigs, and Huskissonites, and was defeated by only fifty-three votes. The Government owed its victory to the support of twenty-eight whigs. This exemplified its instability. Charles Arbuthnot summarized the position in a letter to Peel:

The Ultra-Tories will never . . . give us Vote [sic] . . . The Canning Party will only support us when they feel they have been previously committed to our line of conduct. The Whigs are behaving most shabbily . . . with compliments in their mouths they will try to destroy us because they see that they are not to be taken in in a body.[8]

Ellenborough thought that a junction with the whigs was imperative to prevent their joining the ultras against the Government.[9] But Wellington was still determined to do without them.[1] He was apparently relying, as Brougham put it, 'upon the placable & place-loving nature of Tories making them forget

5. Knatchbull-Hugessen, pp. 176–7.
6. Several letters in the Winchilsea Papers give this opinion. Winchilsea played a large part in organizing the dinner.
7. Brougham to Grey, 10 January 1830; Brougham's *Life and Times*, iii. 19.
8. 16 February 1830; PP, 40340, f. 218.
9. Ellenborough, ii. 183.
1. Mrs. Arbuthnot, ii. 342.

& forgive the Cath[olic] Question'.[2] Meanwhile, ultra M.P.s either abstained from divisions in the Commons or joined the whigs in opposing the Government.[3]

The death of George IV in June made a general election necessary. It took place in July and August. Wellington hoped that the results would strengthen the Government, but they turned out to be more satisfactory to the whigs. The Government was notably unsuccessful in the counties and 'open' boroughs. A liberal victory in Devonshire, formerly the theatre of a vast Brunswick meeting, was particularly satisfying.[4] The election showed how ultra force was slackening. There was no sign of combination among the ultra candidates, and there are only a few examples to show that the Catholic question survived to play a part in the British contests. The *Birmingham Monthly Argus* warned the electors of Warwickshire not to vote for Frank Lawley, who was said to have been converted to Catholic emancipation since the 1826 election.[5] There was a no-popery election at Evesham, where A. Raphael was said to have been defeated because he was a pro-catholic.[6] The question also overshadowed the election at Caernarvon, where the anti-Paget party procured the unopposed return of the anti-catholic William Ormsby Gore.[7] There is little doubt that the Government suffered in the elections. Very few ministerialists succeeded in contests, and by attacking the Huskissonite candidates the Government helped to drive them into the whig camp. Gains in 'open' constituencies, moreover, helped to raise whig morale. As a result, Wellington's position was even more uncertain than before.

The opinion spread that the duke would have to take in some liberal elements. In the autumn he at last tried to do so, but

2. Brougham to Grey, 6 April 1830; Brougham Papers.
3. The ultras who were inclined to vote against the Government were a core of ten or fifteen comprising such men as Henry Bankes, the Marquess of Blandford, Thomas Duncombe, Viscount Encombe, T. B. Fyler, Sir Robert Inglis, Sir Edward Knatchbull, T. P. Macqueen, M. T. Sadler, Colonel Sibthorp, W. H. Trant, the Earl of Uxbridge, Sir Richard Vyvyan, and Sir Charles Wetherell.
4. 'It is a great sign of the times', wrote Viscount Sandon, 'that such an event shd. happen in the most Tory County in England.' Sandon to E. J. Littleton, 19 August 1830; Hatherton Papers.
5. July 1830.
6. *The Times*, 9 August 1830.
7. Llewelyn Jones, *An Edition of the Correspondence of the First Marquess of Anglesey relating to the General Elections of 1830, 1831 and 1832* (unpublished thesis), p. xxxii. Ormsby Gore was narrowly defeated in 1831, in an election in which the Catholic controversy still persisted.

ill-fortune accompanied his attempts. It is believed that he was
about to suggest a coalition to Huskisson at the chance meeting
on the railway line where the latter was killed. In October he
invited Palmerston to join him, but the whig party was a more
powerful attraction to the Huskissonite remnants, and Palmerston would only consider joining the Government if certain
whigs were also asked to do so.[8] It was thought, moreover, that
Wellington made these approaches but half-heartedly. He was
still set on reconciling the ultras. If the upsurge of democracy,
encouraged by the revolution in France, made such a reconciliation likely,[9] it also seemed that the growth of the parliamentary
reform movement would destroy all possibility of the whigs
joining the Government. Despite the insinuation that Wellington might adopt parliamentary reform just as he had adopted
Catholic emancipation, the duke never considered such a policy.
His firm declaration against it in the Lords on 2 November
caused the final alienation of the whigs. The latter now sought
an early chance to overthrow the Government. The opportunity
came on 15 November, with a division on Sir Henry Parnell's
motion to refer the Civil List to a select committee. Wellington
was defeated by a majority of twenty-nine, and thereupon resigned.

His defeat was directly affected by the tory split over Catholic
emancipation. The majority, most of which was whig, included
fifteen members whom Joseph Planta, in a recent review of the
House of Commons, had labelled 'violent ultras';[1] if these had
voted the other way, the Government would have had a majority
of one. Many of the thirty-seven members whom Planta had
classed as 'moderate ultras' also voted against the Government.
Ultra individuals and newspapers were alike delighted at Wellington's fall. 'Thank God', sighed Lord Kenyon.[2]

Having reached this extreme of hostility, the relations of the
ultras and the Wellingtonian tories rapidly mended. They re-
combined to resist parliamentary reform. This junction was
rendered easier because, though the Catholic crisis had driven
both groups towards the whigs, neither had actually allied with

8. Mrs. Arbuthnot, i. 395–6.
9. As Grey suggested to Princess Lieven, 6 October 1830; Le Strange, *Grey-Lieven Correspondence*, ii. 101–2.
1. Dated 21 September 1830; PP, 40401, ff. 181 ff.
2. Diary, 18 November 1830; Kenyon Papers.

them. Wellington could not do without whig support to carry his Relief Bill, but had stubbornly insisted on doing without it ever since. Some of the ultras, as a reaction against the unreformed parliament which had passed emancipation, had temporarily toyed with parliamentary reform. But they had varied in their enthusiasm for it. Blandford went to the length of introducing parliamentary motions on it; Winchilsea was attached to it for a while; and the Duke of Richmond actually joined Grey's Government. As a body, however, the ultras never seriously considered adopting so revolutionary a policy. It was as antagonistic to their principles of constitutional permanency as was Catholic emancipation itself; it was, moreover, a direct threat to their own parliamentary proprietorship. Although their differences over Catholic emancipation were never forgotten, the Wellingtonian and ultra wings of the tory party made up their quarrel and remained united against the whigs and the outcast Huskissonites, who were left to form the new government and to carry the next great reform.

EPILOGUE

CATHOLIC emancipation was one of the closing acts of the unreformed parliament. It was urged by a pro-catholic Commons against the wishes of a largely anti-catholic populace, and thus it epitomized that separation of parliament from people which was execrated by radical reformers. In this way it may seem a retrograde step, out of tune with the reforming spirit of the age. If viewed less closely, however, it appears as part of a progressive trend, the second of three great steps towards constitutional liberty, following the relief of dissenters and followed by the Reform Act. Having been encouraged by the relief of dissenters, the Catholic emancipation movement in its turn encouraged parliamentary reform by providing an example of successful agitation. In 1827 and 1828 parliamentary reformers recommended that associations should be founded with a national subscription like the Catholic Rent. The Irish example was urged at radical meetings in 1829 and was finally imitated in the Birmingham Political Union founded in December that year.[1] In a speech of November 1830 Grey predicted that the later movement would enjoy the same success as the earlier.[2] The example of organized agitation later spread to other reforming bodies such as the Chartists, the Anti-Corn Law League, and the later movements for parliamentary reform.

Catholic emancipation also affected the growth of democracy in other ways. It was a stage in the declining power of the Crown and a victory for the Commons against the Lords. It foreshadowed the later struggles between the Houses which culminated in the Parliament Act of 1911. In the realm of party, Catholic emancipation heralded the progressive liberalization of the tories. The split of 1829 was followed by another in 1846, and in some respects the circumstances were remarkably similar. Peel in 1846, like Wellington and Peel in 1829, was compelled by the alarming condition of Ireland to adopt a remedy which he had previously rejected. There was a difference, however. Whereas the dissentient tories in 1829 were a minority of the

1. J. A. Reynolds, p. 173.　　2. Hansard, third series, i. 31 f.

party, in 1846 they were the bulk, and it was the small band of
Peelites who were driven into the wilderness. In this respect,
therefore, the split of 1829 should rather be compared with
other crises when a tory fragment fought to the last ditch against
a liberal innovation. It was a recurring characteristic of tory
leaders to yield to causes which they had formerly opposed—
Disraeli in 1867 no less than Peel in 1846 and Wellington in
1829.

The effect of Catholic emancipation on liberal progress justi-
fies, perhaps, the vague idealistic hopes which the more radical
pro-catholics placed in their cause. On the other hand, concession
had been expected to achieve a more specific object, namely the
end of Irish discontent, and all such hopes were disappointed.
Catholic emancipation was delayed so long that discontented agitation had become an Irish habit. Emancipation removed only
one of the Irish grievances, and even this only partially, for
Protestant electoral influence remained and even increased after
the Relief Bill had been passed. Because of O'Connell's policy of
using all possible grievances in his agitation, the emancipation
campaign helped to open up a whole series of other problems.
The basic struggle was not one of Catholic against anti-catholic
but of Irish against English. The fundamental discontents of
Ireland were economic, social, and plain nationalist. As the anti-
catholics had asserted, Catholic emancipation could no nothing
to alleviate these grievances. Throughout the nineteenth century,
indeed, the fundamental discontents gathered momentum.
Catholic emancipation had only exacerbated the problem: it
held out an example of popular combination which charac-
terized subsequent agitation until national independence was
finally achieved.

Thus, some anti-catholic arguments which the pro-catholics
had treated as exaggerated and desperate ramblings were confirmed by later events. Some pro-catholics blamed this on the
delay in passing emancipation.[3] 'As a political measure, it has
hitherto been a signal failure', said Bishop C. R. Sumner about
the Relief Bill fifteen years after its passage. He continued:

It has not restored tranquillity to the country—it has not lightened
the difficulty in the councils of the state—it has not contributed to

3. See Melbourne's remarks, above, p. 19.

the safety of the branch of our church in Ireland—it has not opened up the way to converts from Popery . . . if I could have read that measure by the light of the fifteen years which have elapsed since its enactment, I could not have given, in 1845, the vote I gave in 1829.[4]

Subsequent events alarmed those politicians who had supported emancipation on the understanding that the position of the Established Church would not be infringed. In 1869 Lord Ellenborough, the last survivor of the Cabinet which had adopted emancipation, wrote a speech against the bill to disestablish the Church of Ireland.[5] The ultras, of course, were only too ready to blame uncongenial later developments on the Acts of 1828 and 1829, which they held responsible for starting a continuous encroachment on the constitution and the privileges of the landed classes. When the Corn Law was repealed Cumberland said that 'England's downfall began in 1829'.[6] Thus the anti-catholics felt that their cause was vindicated by subsequent developments, and many pro-catholics were disappointed that emancipation did not provide a more permanent settlement. However, this is no satisfactory argument against the passage of Catholic emancipation. The ministers who adopted that measure were faced with a gnawing problem of over thirty years' standing which finally threatened to cause civil war in Ireland. A practical solution was urgently needed. Whether it would ensure a permanent settlement of the Anglo-Irish conflict, or provide only a temporary respite, was hardly relevant to the circumstances of the time.

Catholic emancipation was one of the great liberal achievements of English statesmanship, but it was more of a practical expedient than an act of altruism. It was achieved, it is true, without any fervent opposition from the masses. This means, however, only that popular anti-catholic feeling was dormant, not that it was dead. Popular outcry which led to the Ecclesiastical Titles Bill in 1851 shows that no-popery continued to charac-

4. G. H. Sumner, *Life of C. R. Sumner, Bishop of Winchester* (London, 1876), p. 163, n. Some of the champions of parliamentary reform felt similar regret when it seemed that the Act of 1832 might lead to democratic extremes.
5. Ellenborough, i. 357, n.
6. Cumberland (then King of Hanover) to his chaplain, the Rev. D. C. Delafosse, 3 January 1846; H. van Thal, *Life of Ernest Augustus* (London, 1936), p. 304.

terize public opinion for many years. Though in a much diluted form, it persists at the present day.[7] Catholic emancipation as passed in 1829 was neither the product of toleration nor did it have any tangible effect on the promotion of toleration. It was, quite simply, an act of practical politics.

7. For example, in the Orange-Catholic feuds among the inhabitants of Liverpool. Such quarrels, however, appear to be of only token significance.

THE GENERAL ELECTION OF 1826

(a) *Changes for and against Catholic emancipation*

	Pro-catholic gain	Anti-catholic gain
Contested seats: Changes for	13	
Changes against		18
Uncontested seats: Changes for	24	
Changes against		30
Extra members		2
	37	50
Net anti-catholic gain	13	

(b) *Ages of the new M.P.s compared with their opinions*

	Pro-catholic	Anti-catholic
Those born before 1780	13	11
between 1780 and 1790	16	22
between 1790 and 1800	20	19
in or after 1800	18	22
	67	73

BIBLIOGRAPHY

(i) Primary Sources

A. MANUSCRIPTS

1. British Museum Additional Manuscripts

The most useful volumes for Catholic emancipation appear in brackets.

Broughton Papers 36455–83 (36461–5)

Huskisson Papers 38734–70 (38743, 38747–8)

Liverpool Papers 38190–38489 (38290, 38300–1, 38371)

Peel Papers 40181–40617 (40305–7, 40311, 40319–20, 40322, 40328–33, 40340, 40342–3, 40370, 40373–7, 40397–9, 40401)
    The most important manuscript source for the subject. Valuable selections are published in Peel's *Memoirs* (see below) and less valuable ones in C. S. Parker, *Sir Robert Peel* (see below).

Correspondence of Lord John Russell (38080)

Wellesley Papers 37274–37318 (37297–8, 37310)

Sir Robert Wilson Papers 30095–30144 (30123–4, 30126)

2. The Bodleian Library

Sir Francis Burdett Papers, in the Burdett–Coutts collection
    Disappointing on the Catholic question, but contains a few interesting letters.

Bishop Burgess Papers
    Correspondence of the ultra Thomas Burgess, Bishop of Salisbury. A few letters of interest.

3. Other public repositories

Brougham Papers, University College, London

Fitzwilliam Papers, Northamptonshire Record Office

Grey Papers, Durham University

Hatherton Papers, Staffordshire Record Office
    Correspondence and diary of E. J. Littleton.

Newcastle Papers, Nottingham University
    Correspondence and memoranda, etc., of the fourth Duke of Newcastle.

Plas Newydd Papers, University College of North Wales, Bangor
    Papers of the first Marquess of Anglesey. Much useful material on parliamentary elections in North Wales.

Sneyd Papers, University of Keele
  Correspondence of Ralph Sneyd (a pro-catholic tory) and of the
  first and second Earls of Clare.
Vyvyan Papers, Cornwall Record Office
  Correspondence of Sir Richard Vyvyan with other leading ultras.
Williams Wynn Papers, National Library of Wales
  Correspondence of Charles and Henry Williams Wynn, members
  of the Grenville connexion. Includes correspondence between
  Charles Wynn and the ultra poet Southey.
Winchilsea Papers, in the Finch-Hatton collection, Northamp-
tonshire Record Office

4. *Private Collections*
Harrowby Papers, Sandon Hall, Stafford
Kenyon Papers, Gredington, Flint
  Correspondence and diary of the Second Lord Kenyon.

B. PRINTED MATERIALS

1. *Newspapers and periodicals*

(A) NATIONAL
  Annual Register
  Blackwood's Magazine. *Ultra*
  Cobbett's Political Register. *Pro-catholic*
  Courier. *Government*
  Eclectic Review. *Nonconformist interdenominational. Pro-
    catholic*
  Edinburgh Review. *Pro-catholic*
  John Bull. *Anti-catholic*
  Morning Chronicle. *Pro-catholic*
  Quarterly Review. *Anti-catholic*
  Spectator. *Pro-catholic*
  Standard. *Ultra*
  The Times. *Pro-catholic*

(B) PROVINCIAL
  Birmingham : Chronicle
               Gazette
               Journal. *Commenced 1825. Ultra, 1828–30*
               Monthly Argus. *Commenced October 1828;
                 monthly from January 1829. Violent ultra*

Cornwall:	Royal Cornwall Gazette. *Anti-catholic*
	West Briton. *Pro-catholic*
Edinburgh:	Courant. *Pro-catholic*
Leeds:	Intelligencer. *Ultra*
	Mercury. *Pro-catholic*
Lichfield:	Mercury. *Pro-catholic*
Liverpool:	Mercury. *Pro-catholic*
Manchester:	Chronicle. *Ultra*
	Herald. *Ultra*
	Guardian. *Pro-catholic*
	Mercury. *Ultra*
	Gazette
North Wales:	Chronicle. *Anti-catholic*
	Gazette. *Anti-catholic*
Nottingham:	Journal. *Ultra: Duke of Newcastle's interest*
	Mercury
	Review. 1825–9. *Pro-catholic*
Preston:	Chronicle. *Pro-catholic*
	Pilot. Commenced 1825. *Anti-catholic*
	Sentinel. *Anti-catholic*
Staffordshire:	Advertiser. *Pro-catholic*
	Pottery Mercury
Warwick:	Advertiser

2. *Parliamentary Reports and Debates*

(A) REPORTS

Report of the Committee of the House of Commons on the nature and extent of the disturbances in the districts of Ireland ... in three parts (London, 1824).

Report of the Committee of the House of Lords on the same subject (London, 1824).

Reports of Committees of the Houses of Lords and Commons on the same subject (London, 1825).

(B) DEBATES

Hansard's *Parliamentary Debates*, second series, vols. iv–xxv, 1821–30.

The Catholic question absorbs a great deal of these volumes, and almost the whole of vol. xx (February–March 1829). Hansard was not always accurate at this period. Its reports may be compared with those in the press, in various collections of speeches by individuals, and in the *Mirror of Parliament* which commenced in 1828.

3. *Pamphlets*

No attempt has been made to cover the voluminous mass of pamphlets concerning Catholic emancipation which were published in the years 1820–30. The following, however, were politically effective or interesting.

Lawless, John: *An Address to the Catholics of Ireland . . . on Sir F. Burdett's Bill of Emancipation* (London, 1825).

Newcastle, Fourth Duke of: *Thoughts in Times Past tested by subsequent Events* (London, 1837).
Republication of several pamphlets written in the 1820s.

Phillpotts, Henry: *A letter to the Rt. Hon. G. Canning, on the bill of 1825 . . .* (London, 1826).

——: *A short letter to the right hon. George Canning on the present position of the Roman Catholic question* (London, 1827).

——: *A letter to an English Layman on the Coronation Oath* (London, 1828).

4. *Election Literature*

Historical Sketches of the Coventry Election, in June 1826 . . . by an Observer (Coventry, 1826).

The Poll for two members of Parliament to represent the city of Lincoln . . . June 1826 . . . with all the speeches , , , etc, (Lincoln, 1826)

Extracts from the literature of the Oxfordshire election, 1826, in the Bodleian Library.
A few relevant addresses, etc.

Extracts from the literature of the Oxford University by-election, February 1829, in the Bodleian Library.

Collection of literature on the Preston election, 1826, in the Lancashire Record Office.
A few extracts of interest.

W. A. Abram: Sketches in the Local History of Preston (5 vols.); in the Harris Public Library, Preston.

This is a collection of newspaper extracts from numbers of the *Preston Guardian* of 1880 and 1881. It contains much useful information on the Preston election of 1820, and on other elections in the borough.

5. Other Contemporary Works

Butler, Charles: *Historical Memoirs respecting the English, Irish and Scottish Catholics* (4 vols., London, 1819–21).

Sadler, M. T.: *Ireland: Its Evils and their Remedies* (London, 1828).

Smith, Rev. Sydney: *Works* (complete in 1 vol., London, 1850). Contains several of Smith's pro-catholic articles and addresses.

Southey, R.: *The Book of the Church* (2 vols., London, 1824).

Wyse, T.: *Historical Sketch of the Catholic Association of Ireland* (2 vols., London, 1829).

6. Later Works containing contemporary speeches, memoirs, and correspondence

The headings are the names of the subjects.

ALTHORP

le Marchant, Sir Dennis: *Memoir of Viscount Althorp* (London, 1876).

ANGLESEY

Anglesey, Seventh Marquess of: *One-Leg* (London, 1961).
This life of the First Marquess of Anglesey contains useful correspondence from the Paget Papers.

Jones, Llewelyn: 'An Edition of the Correspondence of the First Marquess of Anglesey relating to the General Elections of 1830, 1831 and 1832' (unpublished M.A. thesis, Liverpool University).
Some of the letters contain references to Catholic emancipation as it persisted as an issue in Caernarvon politics in 1830 and 1831.

Paget, Sir Augustus (ed.): *The Paget Papers, 1794–1807*; with appendices covering the years 1808–29 (2 vols., London, 1896).

ARBUTHNOT, CHAS.

Aspinall, A. (ed.): *Correspondence of Charles Arbuthnot*. Camden Society, third series, lxv (London, 1941).

ARBUTHNOT, MRS.

Bamford, F., and the Duke of Wellington (eds.): *The Journal of Mrs. Arbuthnot, 1820–32* (2 vols., London, 1950).

BARNARD

Powell, A. (ed.): *The Barnard Letters, 1778–1884* (London, 1928).

BATHURST, THIRD EARL

Bickley, F. (ed.): *Report of the Historical Manuscripts Commission on the Manuscripts of Earl Bathurst* (London, 1923).

BATHURST, HENRY, BISHOP OF NORWICH

Thistlethwayte, Mrs.: *Memoirs and Correspondence of Dr. Henry Bathurst* (London, 1853).

BENTHAM

Bowring, J. (ed.): *Works of Jeremy Bentham* (11 vols., Edinburgh, 1843).
Contains correspondence between O'Connell and Bentham.

BLOMFIELD, C. J., BISHOP OF LONDON

Blomfield, A.: *A Memoir of Charles James Blomfield* (2 vols., London, 1863).

BROUGHAM

Aspinall, A.: *Lord Brougham and the Whig Party* (Manchester, 1927).

Brougham, W. (ed.): *The Life and Times of Henry, Lord Brougham: written by himself* (3 vols., Edinburgh, 1871).
Contains much important correspondence; but the transcripts are notably inaccurate and should be read in conjuction with Aspinall, A.: 'Lord Brougham's "Life and Times"', *EHR*, lix (1944), pp. 87–112.

BUCKINGHAM

Buckingham, First Duke of: *Private Diary* (3 vols., London, 1862).

Buckingham, Second Duke of (ed.): *Memoirs of the Court of England, during the Regency, 1811–20* (2 vols., London, 1856).

——: *Memoirs of the Court of George IV* (2 vols., London, 1859).

BURDETT

Patterson, M. W.: *Sir Francis Burdett and his Times* (2 vols., London, 1931).
Contains several useful letters from the Burdett Papers. Other letters of Burdett are in the original four-volume typescript of this work, in the Bodleian Library. The published work is an abridgement of the typescript.

BURGESS

Harford, J. S.: *The Life of Thomas Burgess, late Bishop of Salisbury* (London, 1840).

BURGHERSH

Weigall, Rachel (ed.): *Correspondence of Lord Burghersh, 1808–40* (London, 1912).

CAMPBELL

Hardcastle, Mrs.: *Life of John, Lord Campbell* (2 vols., London, 1881).

CANNING

Aspinall, A. (ed.): *The Formation of Canning's Ministry, February to August 1827.* Camden Society, third series, lix (London, 1937).

Bagot, Josceline: *George Canning and his Friends* (2 vols., London, 1909).

Stapleton, A. G.: *The Political Life of the Rt. Hon. George Canning, 1822–27* (3 vols., London, 1831).

Stapleton, E. J. (ed.): *Some Official Correspondence of George Canning* (2 vols., London, 1887).

CASTLEREAGH

Alison, Sir A.: *Lives of Lord Castlereagh and Sir Charles Stewart, the Second and Third Marquesses of Londonderry* (3 vols., London, 1861).

CHALMERS

Hanna, Rev. W.: *Memoirs of the Life and Writings of Thomas Chalmers* (4 vols., Edinburgh, 1849–52).

CLONCURRY

Cloncurry, Lord: *Personal Recollections of his Life and Times* (Dublin, 1849).

Fitzpatrick, W. J.: *The Life, Times and Contemporaries of Lord Cloncurry* (Dublin, 1855).

COBBETT

Melville, L. (ed.): *The Life and Letters of William Cobbett in England and America* (2 vols., London, 1913).

COCKBURN

Cockburn, Henry: *Memorials of his Time* (Edinburgh, 1856; new ed., 1909).

COKE

Stirling, A. M. W.: *Coke of Norfolk and his Friends* (London, 1908; new ed., 1912).

COLCHESTER

Colchester, Second Lord (ed.): *The Diary and Correspondence of Charles Abbott, (First) Lord Colchester* (3 vols., London, 1861).

The third volume (covering the years 1817–29) is important as a record of ultra opinions and activities.

COPLESTON, E., BISHOP OF LLANDAFF

Copleston, Rev. W. J.: *Memoir of Edward Copleston . . . with selections from his Diary and Correspondence* (London, 1851).

Whately, Richard (ed.): *Remains of the late Edward Copleston* (London, 1854).

CREEVEY

Maxwell, Sir H. (ed.): *The Creevey Papers* (2 vols., London, 1903).

CROKER

Jennings, L. J. (ed.): *The Croker Papers* (3 vols., London, 1884).

The transcripts in this useful work are sometimes inaccurate.

CUMBERLAND

van Thal, H.: *Ernest Augustus, Duke of Cumberland and King of Hanover* (London, 1936).

Willis, G. M.: *Ernest Augustus, Duke of Cumberland and King of Hanover* (London, 1954).

The chapter on Catholic emancipation is taken from Cumberland's memoir, in the Prince of Hanover's archives.

DOYLE, J., BISHOP OF KILDARE AND LEIGHLIN

Fitzpatrick, W. J. (ed.): *The Life, Times and Correspondence of the Rt. Rev. Dr. Doyle* (2 vols., new ed., Dublin, 1880).

DUDLEY

Copleston, Edward (ed.): *Letters of the Earl of Dudley to the Bishop of Llandaff* (London, 1840).

Romilly, S. H. (ed.): *Letters to 'Ivy' from the First Earl of Dudley* (London, 1905).

DUNCOMBE, T. S.

Duncombe, T. H. (ed.): *The Life and Correspondence of Thomas Slingsby Duncombe* (2 vols., London, 1868).

DURHAM

Reid, Stuart J.: *Life and Letters of the First Earl of Durham* (2 vols., London, 1906).

ELDON

Twiss, H.: *The Public and Private Life of Lord Chancellor Eldon* (3 vols., London, 1844).

ELLENBOROUGH

Ellenborough, Earl of: *Political Diary, 1828–30* (ed. Third Lord Colchester: 2 vols., London, 1881).

An important source for the final crisis of Catholic emancipation.

FOX. *SEE* HOLLAND

GEORGE III

Letters from his late Majesty to the late Lord Kenyon, on the Coronation Oath . . . and Letters of the Rt. Hon. William Pitt to his late Majesty; with an introduction by Rev. Dr. Henry Phillpotts (London, 1827).

GEORGE IV

Aspinall, A. (ed.): *The Letters of George IV* (3 vols., Cambridge, 1938).

GLADSTONE

Morley, J.: *The Life of W. E. Gladstone* (3 vols., London, 1903).

The first volume contains extracts from Gladstone's diary, showing popular anti-catholic feeling at Oxford.

GRAHAM, SIR JAS.

Torrens, W. M. (previously W. T. MacCullagh): *The Life and Times of . . . Sir J. R. G. Graham* (2 vols., London, 1863).

Parker, C. S.: *Life and Letters of Sir James Graham, Bt.* (2 vols., London, 1907).

GRANVILLE

Leveson Gower, Hon. F. (ed.): *Letters of Harriet, Countess Granville, 1810–45* (2 vols., London, 1894).

GREGORY

Gregory, Lady (ed.): *Mr. Gregory's Letter Box* (London, 1898).

GREVILLE

Strachey, L., and R. Fulford (eds.): *The Greville Memoirs, 1814–60* (8 vols., London, 1938).

GREY

Trevelyan, G. M.: *Lord Grey of the Reform Bill* (London, 1929).

HERON

Heron, Sir Robert: *Notes* (Grantham, 1851).

HERRIES

Herries, E.: *Memoir of the Public Life of the Rt. Hon. John Charles Herries* (London, 1880).

HOBHOUSE, HENRY

Aspinall, A. (ed.): *The Diary of Henry Hobhouse, 1820–27* (London, 1947).

HOBHOUSE, J. C. (LORD BROUGHTON)

Broughton, Lord: *Recollections of a Long Life* (ed. Lady Dorchester; 6 vols., London, 1910–11).

 This autobiography of John Cam Hobhouse has much useful material on Catholic emancipation.

HOLLAND

Holland, Third Lord: *Further Memoirs of the Whig Party, 1807–21* (ed. Lord Stavordale, later Sixth Earl of Ilchester; London, 1905).

Ilchester, Sixth Earl of (ed.): *Journal of Henry Edward Fox, 1818–30* (London, 1923).

———: *Chronicles of Holland House, 1820–1900* (London, 1937).

———: *Lady Holland to her Son, 1821–45* (London, 1946).

HUSKISSON

Melville, L. (ed.): *The Huskisson Papers* (London, 1931).

JEBB, J., BISHOP OF LIMERICK

Forster, Rev. Charles (ed.): *Thirty Years' Correspondence between Bishop John Jebb and Alexander Knox* (2 vols., London, 1934).

JEFFREY

Cockburn, Lord: *Life of Lord Jeffrey* (2 vols., Edinburgh, 1852).

KNATCHBULL

Knatchbull-Hugessen, Sir Hughe: *Kentish Family* (London, 1960).

Contains Sir Edward Knatchbull's correspondence with Sir Richard Vyvyan on the project of an ultra government in 1829–30, and other letters on this subject from the Vyvyan Papers.

LIEVEN, PRINCESS

Robinson, L. G. (ed.): *Letters of Dorothea, Princess Lieven, during her residence in London, 1812–34* (London, 1902).
le Strange, G. (ed.): *Correspondence of the Princess Lieven and Earl Grey* (2 vols., London, 1890).
Sudley, Lord (ed.): *Correspondence of Princess Lieven and Lord Palmerston, 1828–56* (London, 1943).
Temperley, H. W. V.: *The Unpublished Diary of the Princess Lieven* (London, 1925).

LIVERPOOL

Yonge, C. D.: *The Life and Administration of the Second Earl of Liverpool* (3 vols., London, 1868).

LONDONDERRY. SEE CASTLEREAGH

MACAULAY, Z.

Knutsford, Viscountess: *The Life and Letters of Zachary Macaulay* (London, 1900).

MELBOURNE

Sanders, L. C. (ed.): *Melbourne Papers* (London, 1889).
Torrens, W. M. (previously W. T. MacCullagh): *Memoirs of Viscount Melbourne* (2 vols., London, 1878).

MOORE, THOS.

Russell, Lord John (ed.): *Memoirs, Journal and Correspondence of Thomas Moore* (8 vols., London, 1853–6).

NEWMAN, J. H.

Mozley, Anne (ed.): *Letters and Correspondence of John Henry Newman during his Life in the English Church* (2 vols., London, 1891).

Letters showing Newman's anti-catholic views and commenting on the Oxford University by-election of 1829.

NORFOLK

Norfolk MSS. (*Report of the Historical Manuscripts Commission*, various collections, vol. ii, London, 1903).

O'CONNELL

Fitzpatrick, W. J. (ed.): *Correspondence of Daniel O'Connell* (2 vols., London, 1888).

PALMERSTON

Bell, H. C. F.: *Lord Palmerston* (2 vols., London, 1936).
Bulwer, H. W.: *The Life of Viscount Palmerston* (2 vols., London, 1870).
Lorne, Marquess of: *Viscount Palmerston* (London, 1892).

PEEL

Mahon, Lord, and E. Cardwell (eds.): *Memoirs by the Rt. Hon. Sir Robert Peel* (2 vols., London, 1856–7).

Vol. 1, *The Catholic Question*, publishes many, though by no means all, of the important letters from the Peel Papers covering the 1828–9 crisis.

Parker, C. S. (ed.): *Sir Robert Peel . . . from his Private Correspondence* (3 vols., London, 1891–9).

Many useful letters taken from the Peel Papers, but often given in an abbreviated and inaccurate form.

Peel, George (ed.): *The Private Letters of Sir Robert Peel* (London, 1920).

PLUNKET

Plunket, Hon. David: *The Life, Letters and Speeches of Lord Plunket* (2 vols., London, 1867).

PUSEY

Liddon, H. P.: *Life of Edward Bouverie Pusey* (4 vols., London, 1893).

ROBINSON, H. C.

Sadler, T. (ed.): *The Diary, Reminiscences and Correspondence of Henry Crabb Robinson* (3 vols., London, 1869).

RUSSELL, LD. JOHN

Russell, R. (ed.): *Early Correspondence of Lord John Russell, 1805–40* (2 vols., London, 1913).
Walpole, S.: *The Life of Lord John Russell* (2 vols., London, 1889).

SCOTT, SIR WALTER

Grierson, H. J. C. (ed.): *The Letters of Sir Walter Scott, 1787–1832* (12 vols., London, 1932).
Partington, W. (ed.): *The Private Letter-Books of Sir Walter Scott* (London, 1930).
Tait, J. G. (ed.): *The Journal of Sir Walter Scott, 1825–32* (3 vols., Edinburgh, 1939).

SHAFTESBURY

Hodder, E.: *The Life and Work of the Seventh Earl of Shaftesbury* (3 vols., London, 1886).

SHEIL, R. L.

MacCullagh, W. Torrens (afterwards W. M. Torrens): *Memoirs of R. L. Sheil* (2 vols., London, 1855).
Sheil R. L.: *Sketches Legal and Political* (ed. M. W. Savage; 2 vols., London, 1855).
    Includes impressions of the Clare election and the Penenden Heath meeting.

SHELLEY, LADY

Edgecumbe, R. (ed.): *The Diary of Frances, Lady Shelley* (2 vols., London, 1912–13).
    Includes some useful correspondence of Lady Shelley with the Duke of Rutland and Mrs. Arbuthnot.

SIDMOUTH

Pellew, Hon. George: *The Life and Correspondence of the Rt.*

Hon. Henry Addington, First Viscount Sidmouth (3 vols., London, 1847).

SUMNER, C. R.

Sumner, G. H.: *Life of C. R. Sumner, Bishop of Winchester* (London, 1876).

THORNTON

Forster, E. M.: *Marianne Thornton* (London, 1956).
Contains some interesting correspondence between members of the Clapham Sect.

WELLESLEY

The Wellesley Papers (ed. anon., London, 1914).
Pearce, R. R. (ed.): *Memoirs and Correspondence of Richard, Marquess of Wellesley* (3 vols., London, 1846).

WELLINGTON

Wellington, Second Duke of (ed.): *Despatches, Correspondence and Memoranda of the Duke of Wellington . . . in continuation of the former series* (1818–32). (8 vols., London, 1867–80.)
Maxwell, Sir H.: *Life of the Duke of Wellington* (2 vols., London, 1899).

WHATELY, R.

Whately, E. J.: *Life of Richard Whately, Archbishop of Dublin* (2 vols., London, 1866).

WHISHAW, J.

Seymour, Lady (ed.): *The 'Pope' of Holland House. Selections from the Correspondence of John Whishaw and his Friends, 1813–40* (London, 1906).

WHITE, BLANCO

Thom, J. H. (ed.): *The Life and Correspondence of Joseph Blanco White* (3 vols., London, 1845).

WILBERFORCE

Wilberforce, A. M. (ed.): *The Private Papers of William Wilberforce* (London, 1897).

WILLIAMS WYNN

Evans, Gwyneth: 'Charles Watkins Williams Wynn, 1775–1850' (unpublished M.A. thesis, University of Wales).

WORDSWORTH

de Selincourt, E. (ed.): *Letters of William and Dorothy Words- worth—The Later Years*, vol. i, 1812–30 (Oxford, 1939).

Useful contemporary letters are also published in some of the articles and books listed below, and in A. Aspinall and E. A. Smith (eds.): *English Historical Documents*, vol. xi (1783–1832) (London, 1959.)

(ii) Secondary Sources

A. ARTICLES

Aspinall, A.: 'The Coalition Ministries of 1827', *EHR*, xlii (1927).
——: 'The Canningite Party', *Trans. Royal Hist. Soc.*, fourth series, xvii (1934).
——: 'The Last of the Canningites', *EHR*, l (1935).
——: 'Canning's Return to Office in September 1822', *EHR*, lxxviii (1963).
Best, G. F. A.: 'The Protestant Constitution and its Supporters', *Trans. Royal Hist. Soc.*, fifth series, viii (1958).
——: 'The Constitutional Revolution, 1828–32', *Theology*, 1959.
——: 'The Whigs and the Church Establishment in the Age of Grey and Holland', *History*, xlv (1960).
Briggs, A.: 'Press and Public in Early Nineteenth Century Birmingham'; *Dugdale Society Occasional Papers*, No. 8 (Oxford, 1949).
Greaves, R. W.: 'Roman Catholic Relief and the Leicester Election of 1826', *Trans. Royal Hist. Soc.*, xxiii (1940).
Hexter, J. H.: 'The Protestant Revival and the Catholic Question in England, 1778–1829', *Journal of Modern History*, viii (1936).
Machin, G. I. T.: 'Catholic Emancipation as an Issue in North Welsh Politics, 1825–9', *Transactions of the Cymmrodorion Society* (1962).
——: 'The Catholic Emancipation Crisis of 1825', *EHR*, lxxviii (1963).
——: 'The No-Popery Movement in Britain, 1828–9', *The His- torical Journal*, vi (1963).

Machin, G. I. T.: 'The Duke of Wellington and Catholic Emancipation', *Journal of Ecclesiastical History*, xiv (1963).

B. VARIOUS SECONDARY WORKS

Anon.: *Memoirs of the Life and Writings of Michael Thomas Sadler* (London, 1842).

Aspinall, A.: *Politics and the Press, 1780–1850* (London, 1949).

Bagehot, W.: *Biographical Studies*; ed. R. H. Hutton (London, 1881).

Bain, A.: *James Mill: A Biography* (London, 1882).

Baines, E. (jun.): *Life of Edward Baines* (London, 1851).

Briggs, A.: *The Age of Improvement* (London, 1959).

Brock, W. R.: *Lord Liverpool and Liberal Toryism, 1820–27* (Cambridge, 1941).

Campbell, Lord: *Life of Lord Chancellor Lyndhurst* (Lives of the Lord Chancellors, vol. viii, London, 1869).

Cole, G. D. H.: *The Life of William Cobbett* (London, 1924).

Coupland, R.: *Wilberforce* (Oxford, 1923).

Davies, G. C. B.: *Henry Phillpotts, Bishop of Exeter* (London, 1954).

Davies, H. W. C.: 'Catholic Emancipation'; chapter xix of the *Cambridge Modern History*, vol. x (Cambridge, 1934).

Elvins, W. B.: 'The Reform Movement and County Politics in Cornwall, 1809–52' (unpublished M.A. thesis, Birmingham University).

Feiling, K. G.: *The Second Tory Party, 1714–1832* (London, 1938).

Forester, E. G.: *Northamptonshire County Elections and Electioneering, 1695–1832* (Oxford, 1941).

Gash, N.: *Mr. Secretary Peel* (London, 1961).

Gwynn, D. R.: *The Struggle for Catholic Emancipation, 1750–1829* (London, 1928).

Halévy, E.: *History of the English People in the Nineteenth Century*: vol. i: *England in 1815* (second ed., London, 1949); vol. ii: *The Liberal Awakening, 1815–30* (second ed., London, 1949).

Henriques, U.: *Religious Toleration in England, 1787–1833* (London, 1961).

Hoskins, W. G., and H. P. R. Finberg: *Devonshire Studies* (London, 1952).

Hughes, P.: *The Catholic Question, 1688–1829* (London, 1929).
Husenbeth, F. C.: *The Life of the Rt. Rev. John Milner* (Dublin, 1862).
Jenkins, R. T: *Hanes Cymru yn y bedwaredd ganrif ar bymtheg* (History of Wales in the Nineteenth Century; Cardiff, 1933).
McDowell, R. B.: *Public Opinion and Government Policy in Ireland, 1801–1846* (London, 1952).
Mackintosh, R. J.: *Memoirs of the Life of Sir James Mackintosh* (2 vols., London, 1835).
Martin, Sir T.: *A Life of Lord Lyndhurst* (London, 1883).
Martineau, H.: *The History of England during the Thirty Years Peace, 1861–46* (2 vols., London, 1849–50).
New, C. W.: *Life of Lord Brougham to 1830* (Oxford, 1961).
Olphin, H. K.: *George Tierney* (London, 1934).
Packe, M. St. J.: *The Life of John Stuart Mill* (London, 1954).
Pares, R.: *George III and the Politicians* (Oxford, 1953).
Patterson, A. T.: *Radical Leicester: A History of Leicester, 1780–1850* (Leicester, 1954).
Ramsay, Very Rev. E. B.: *Biographical Notice of Dr. Chalmers* (Edinburgh, 1850).
Reynolds, J. A.: *The Catholic Emancipation Crisis in Ireland, 1823–29* (New Haven, 1954).
Roberts, M.: *The Whig Party, 1807–12* (London, 1939).
Turberville, A. S.: *The House of Lords in the Age of Reform, 1784–1837* (London, 1958).
Ward, B.: *The Eve of Catholic Emancipation* (3 vols., London, 1911).
Watson, J. Steven: *The Reign of George III, 1760–1815* (Oxford, 1960).
Wedgwood, J. C.: *Staffordshire Parliamentary History*, vol. iii; William Salt Archaeological Society, new series, vol. 34 (Kendal, 1934).
Woodward, E. L.: *The Age of Reform, 1815–70* (new ed., Oxford, 1962).

C. WORKS OF REFERENCE

Burke's *Peerage* (1956 ed.).
Dictionary of National Biography.
Foster, J.: *Alumni Oxonienses, 1715–1886* (4 vols., Oxford, 1887–8).

Gibbs, Hon. V., and others: *The Complete Peerage, by G. E. C.* (13 vols., London, 1910–59).

Judd, Geritt P. (IV): *Members of Parliament, 1734–1832* (New Haven, 1955).

Members of Parliament, 1705–1875; vol. ii of the Official Return of the House of Commons (London, 1878).

New Parliament, 1826 (London, 1826).

Smith, H. S.: *Register of Parliamentary Contested Elections* (second ed., London, 1842).

——: *The Parliaments of England* (London, 1844–50).

Venn, J. A.: *Alumni Cantabrigienses:* Part ii, 1752–1900 (6 vols., Cambridge, 1940–54).

INDEX

MAIN ABBREVIATIONS

Anti-cath.	Anti-catholic	El.	Earl
Archbp.	Archbishop	Ld.	Lord
Bn.	Baron	Ld. Lieut.	Lord Lieutenant
Bp.	Bishop	Marq.	Marquess
Bt.	Baronet	Pro-cath.	Pro-catholic
C.E.	Catholic Emancipation	R.C.	Roman Catholic
D.	Duke	Visct.	Viscount